797,885 Books
are available to read at

Forgotten Books

www.ForgottenBooks.com

Forgotten Books' App
Available for mobile, tablet & eReader

ISBN 978-1-334-28997-2
PIBN 10757714

This book is a reproduction of an important historical work. Forgotten Books uses
state-of-the-art technology to digitally reconstruct the work, preserving the original format
whilst repairing imperfections present in the aged copy. In rare cases, an imperfection in
the original, such as a blemish or missing page, may be replicated in our edition. We do,
however, repair the vast majority of imperfections successfully; any imperfections that
remain are intentionally left to preserve the state of such historical works.

Forgotten Books is a registered trademark of FB &c Ltd.
Copyright © 2015 FB &c Ltd.
FB &c Ltd, Dalton House, 60 Windsor Avenue, London, SW19 2RR.
Company number 08720141. Registered in England and Wales.

For support please visit www.forgottenbooks.com

1 MONTH OF FREE READING

at

www.ForgottenBooks.com

By purchasing this book you are eligible for one month membership to ForgottenBooks.com, giving you unlimited access to our entire collection of over 700,000 titles via our web site and mobile apps.

To claim your free month visit: www.forgottenbooks.com/free757714

* Offer is valid for 45 days from date of purchase. Terms and conditions apply.

English
Français
Deutsche
Italiano
Español
Português

www.forgottenbooks.com

Mythology Photography **Fiction** Fishing Christianity **Art** Cooking Essays Buddhism Freemasonry Medicine **Biology** Music **Ancient Egypt** Evolution Carpentry Physics Dance Geology **Mathematics** Fitness Shakespeare **Folklore** Yoga Marketing **Confidence** Immortality Biographies Poetry **Psychology** Witchcraft Electronics Chemistry History **Law** Accounting **Philosophy** Anthropology Alchemy Drama Quantum Mechanics Atheism Sexual Health **Ancient History Entrepreneurship** Languages Sport Paleontology Needlework Islam **Metaphysics** Investment Archaeology Parenting Statistics Criminology **Motivational**

SUNDERLAND:

HISTORY OF THE TOWN, PORT,

TRADE AND COMMERCE.

BY

TAYLOR POTTS.

SUNDERLAND:
B. WILLIAMS & Co., LTD., PUBLISHERS, 129, HIGH STREET.
1892.

GRAD
DA
690
.S95
P68
1892
BUHR

IN the present work the intention of the writer is principally to relate what has come under his own knowledge and experience, whilst, at the same time, drawing information from such sources as may be necessary to compare *then* and *now*.

The earlier History of Sunderland has been told by our own local historians, whose works are out of print and rarely to be bought. Garbutt's History of Sunderland was published in 1819, and Burnett's in 1830; but of the latter there was only a limited issue, consisting of 200 or 300 copies. Summers' History was published in serial form in 1858, but the work was never completed; one volume has been published, but owing to the unfortunate circumstance of being overtaken by blindness Mr. Summers was unable to continue his researches. All these authors treat the History of Sunderland in different ways and from different points of view. The object of the work now put before the reader is to treat more fully of the trade and commerce of the town, and of the rise, progress, and decay of its varied industries.

TAYLOR POTTS.

Sunderland, June, 1890.

CONTENTS.

CHAPTER	PAGE
1—Sunderland in 1820, and the Low Street	1-24
2—The High Street and Coronation Street—Customs of the Inhabitants	25-52
3—Our River, known to the Romans—remains found of their possession	53-64
4—Our River in 1820-25	65-71
5—The Monks and Monastery of Monkwearmouth, and Bede	72-77
6—Salmon Fisheries	78-86
7—Ship-building and Shipbuilders during the last century	87-111
8— Do. do. up to 1860	112-126
9—Trade and Commerce	127-174
10—Colliers	175-204
11—Custom Houses and Timber Duties	205-216
12—Primage Dues—Pilotage	217-233
13—Sunderland Town Moor	234-253
14—The Piers	254-275
15—The Bridge—Wearmouth Colliery	276-282
16—The Docks	283-306
17—Parliamentary Representation and our First Election	307-318
18—Banks	319-324

APPENDIX.

| Grant de Novo | 325-326 |

CHAPTER I.

SUNDERLAND, in the year 1820, was composed of five different Townships or Parishes, viz. :—Sunderland, Bishopwearmouth, Bishopwearmouth-Panns, Monkwearmouth, and Monkwearmouth-Shore. Each Parish had its own Overseers, and each was separately rated to the poor. At that period it was said to be a very compact town, and contained 30,887 inhabitants.

It was rather under one mile in length from East to West, and under half-a-mile in its then extreme breadth from North to South. There were three principal streets, viz. :—High Street, Low Street, and Coronation Street, (called the "Back Lonnin"). The communications or roads between the High Street and Low Street were called by the names of lanes, stairs, passages and banks; and between the High Street and Coronation Street and the Moor, by the names of streets, lanes and alleys.

The High Street ran the full length of the town, starting from the Low Row, then up a steep bank between the Church and the Rectory, and after passing a sharp narrow turning at the west of Crowtree Road, ran almost straight from west to east, till you came to a steep bank at the east end of the Fishermen's Cottages, where, at the left, two flights of stone steps led down to the Pier, whilst the road, turning sharp to the right, led down to the sands.

The Low Street really began at the Hailing House, at the west end of the Pier, crossing the bridge at the high coble slipway over Thornhill's Wharf, and from Hardcastle Quay ran up to the foot of Beggars' Bank or Russell Street;

entering Panns it then ran up to the public house known as the "Green Dragon," and, turning sharp to the southeast, joined what is now called West Wear Street; there was also a continuation of the road by the side of the bank up to the Bridge, crossing the Bridge Road to Pan Lane, which was the old road to the Panns.

Coronation Street went west from Sunderland Church to the back of Norfolk Street, which formed almost the southern boundary of the town. There were also Zion Street, and a few houses in Nicholson's Square, the west side of Sans Street, Villiers Street, and Nile Street crossing it towards the south. Sunderland Town Moor and the Church Walk, up to Church Street, formed the southern boundary at the east end.

Coxon's Fields stretched from Hendon Road to Sans Street; they were enclosed by a thorn hedge on the north, running from the foundry in Coronation Street to Sans Street, on the west by Sans Street, on the south by "Cutty Throat Lonnin," and on the east by Nicholson Street School and the farm buildings adjoining Hendon Road.

From Norfolk Street to Waterloo Place was all gardens and fields, and from Sunniside a row of houses faced the High Street up to Union Street; from Waterloo Place and Union Street another stretch of green fields extended up to Crowtree Road, the whole being bounded on the south by what is now called the Borough Road. At the south-east corner of Crowtree Road were the high trees on which the crows used to build their nests, and to the north three or four two-storied houses, looking as though they were nestling under their shade. From Maritime Place to South Street ran a thorn hedge. South Street, as its name denotes, was the most southern street in Bishopwearmouth, and Middle Street is between it and High Street. West of Crowtree Road were

Mr. Robert Fenwick's house and Mr. Nicholson's house, with a high stone wall running nearly the full length of the road, turning up in Vine Place, almost to what was said to be the oldest house in Bishopwearmouth. It was a "tee-fall" house, with the stairs inside going from one story to another, or from one room to the next; the gardens and vineries were enclosed by the wall as well as a clump of trees at the side of Vine Place—both houses faced the Green. Then there were the Green, Green Terrace, Low Row, and, at the east of the Church—Church Lane, Gibson's Alms Houses, and Littlegate.

On the north side of the High Street, from Lambton Street westward, the Panns Fields stretched up to Bridge Street. The three-storied houses at the east side of Lambton Street looked upon green fields. There was no West Wear Street, Pratt's Buildings, nor Bedford Street. Bridge Street was not then built; there were two or three three-storied houses next the High Street, and a two-storied house on each side next the Bridge. The Register Buildings at the north side of the High Street occupy the site where Chapman's gardens and vineries used to be. Hutchinson's Buildings now occupy the site of Dr. Clanny's gardens; the house where the Doctor lived still stands facing Bridge Street. Pemberton's Buildings in Matlock Street were not then built, being erected as houses for the pitmen when the colliery was opened.

There was also the open garth running between Cumberland Street and Queen Street from the back of the High Street to the north end of the streets. Messrs. Mounsey afterwards built their new furrier's factory at the south end, now occupied by E. C. Robson & Sons as a flour mill. West of Castle Street or Hopper Street were green fields, which ran further north than the street itself. A wall separated these fields from the Rector's park, which ran west up to the gill, and stretched from the road at the north end up to the rectory gardens on the south ; a wall separating the gill from the park and gardens. West of the rectory and garden wall was a long strip of ground, rather narrow, sloping from the wall towards the open burn on the west. This parcel of ground was cultivated as a garden by the late Henry Gibson, who lived in a house or cottage facing the garden—the shop faced the High Street.

On the rectory wall the small fern Wall Rue—or *Ruta Muraria*—grew and the Common Bracken grew in the gill. At the west of the burn, the road now called Silksworth Row, went to the Keelmen's Lonnin ; all the ground to the west of this road was fields. The late Barnabas Sharp built a house up the bank to the west, almost facing what is now called Hind's Bridge ; the garden in front ran down to the road.

POPULATION.

PORT OF SUNDERLAND.	1801.	1811.	1821.
Sunderland	12,412		
Bishopwearmouth			
Bishopwearmouth-Panns			
Monkwearmouth			
Monkwearmouth-Shore			
Out-Townships		2,423	3,024
Totals	26,511	27,610	33,911

In the year 1719 Sunderland was made a separate Parish from Bishopwearmouth and covered about 220 acres of ground. The new parish, commencing at the sea beach, went south of the Hendon water course and cart road through the Octagon Cottage up to Hendon Lodge, into the grounds of which it passed; at the north end of this there was a stone wall which ran straight up to Coronation Street. At the south-east of this wall a gate was fixed, sometimes locked and sometimes kept on the latch, and there was also an opening or stile in the wall for foot passengers; the east side of this wall was Sunderland Parish and the west side was Bishopwearmouth Parish. In Coronation Street the boundary ran straight up to Sans Street—the north side was Sunderland Parish and the south side Bishopwearmouth Parish. The boundary then ran down Sans Street North, across the High Street, down Beggar's Bank, across the Low Street to the river, then, turning east, went to the sea. The east of Sans Street was Sunderland Parish and the west Bishopwearmouth Parish.

After the cutting off of Sunderland Parish from Bishopwearmouth there still remained to the latter all the distance south to the boundaries of Seaham Parish, and west to the boundaries of Houghton-le-Spring.

On the formation of the Parish—with its 6,000 inhabitants—in 1719, there does not appear to be any record of how far west the inhabitants were located, the supposition is that Pewterer's Lane would then be to the west of the habitable portion of the ground. In Pewterer's Lane the houses are freehold. The ground west would be garths and gardens, the names being handed down to our day as Spring Garden Lane and Covent Garden Lane. The ground deed of the three-storied house facing Flag Lane and Coronation Street is of the Bishop's Manor of Houghton, and recites that the ground was taken from, and was part of, the mill garden; therefore there must have been a mill there at that period.

The promoters of the Act of 1719, no doubt, thought that by extending the boundaries of the township west, even to Sans Street, they would provide ample space for the increase of buildings and the multiplication of the population.

In 1719 the population of the parish was stated to be about 6,000. In 1821, when the census was taken, the population was 14,725; shewing the increase in the population in 100 years to be 8,725, or an increase in the century of 145 per cent. in the population of the parish.

Since 1820 several large open spaces, both east and west of Pewterer's Lane, have been built over, as Moorgate Street, Thomas Street, south-east part of Silver Street, Nesham Square, The Minorca, New Grey Street, and East Sans Street. In 1851 the population of the parish was nearly 19,000.

"In the year 1809 an Act of Parliament was obtained for paving, lighting, cleansing, and otherwise improving the town of Sunderland; for removing the market; building a market house and a town hall, and for establishing a river watch. By this Act Commissioners were appointed, who were vested with powers to levy an assessment for carrying the purposes of the said Act into execution; for removing nuisances, paving, lighting, and otherwise improving the town. After the Act was obtained its beneficial results soon became apparent—many nuisances were removed; a watch was established in the town and upon the river; a more regular police established; the town was lighted, and its general appearance visibly improved.

"In 1826 another Act was obtained, wherein the powers of the Commissioners were more fully explained and enlarged, and wherein the Commissioners were authorised to levy a higher contribution to carry the purposes of this Act into execution. The Commissioners are following up the powers granted them by this Act—they have flagged the footpaths from one end of the town to the other; they have lighted the town brilliantly with gas; they have arranged to build a new market; they have established a cattle market, held once-a-fortnight; a half-yearly hiring for servants is appointed, and many other useful regulations are adopted which had not existed previous to the passing of the Sunderland Improvement Acts."—Burnett, *page 45*.

Unfortunately, Burnett does not inform us as to the appearance of the town in his younger days, before the passing of the Act of 1809. What the state of the town was before these considerable improvements as to lighting, watching, &c., had been made by the Town Commissioners, we are left to conjecture.

We write as we found the state of the town under the Act of 1809 (in our early days). As to

LIGHTING,

The streets were lighted by oil lamps hung on an iron crane fastened to the wall or the corner of the house at the end of the street or lane. The lamp was hung in a socket at the end of the crane; the glass was round, hanging deep, also round or saucer-shaped at the bottom; the lamp within hung from a cross-bar at the top to nearly the bottom of the glass casing, so that it could be taken out and trimmed, and easily lighted; a perforated top on an hinge covered the whole.

Each of these lamps had to be trimmed every morning— a fresh supply of oil, the wicks put in order, and the glass cleaned when required; the supply of oil was so arranged that the lamps generally died out before daylight the next morning. When lighting the lamps, the man carried his lighted torch—with the handle containing the oil—grasped in his hand, the torch being carried upside down, lighting the road as he ran along; after climbing the ladder and removing the lid of the lamp, the flaming torch being put therein lit the two wicks. On a windy night it was no uncommon thing to be without the lamp lights altogether, the gusts of wind often blowing out his torch, and if he succeeded in getting to the lamp the lights were sometimes blown out before the lid could be replaced, and, in despair, the lamp left unlit. The lighting of the houses was by candles, there were three sorts—the common tallow candles, mould candles and rush lights, the latter were only used as night lights. The butchers' shops and the stalls in the market were lighted with oil lamps and cotton wicks, and, if a very windy night, lanterns and candles had to suffice.

The churches and chapels were all lighted with candles, the large chandeliers hanging by a rope or chain from the ceiling, whilst brackets with two or more candles, and sometimes small chandeliers, were lit under the galleries. During the service, generally whilst singing a hymn, also during a long sermon (the sermon often lasting an hour or longer) the chapel-keeper or some other person would stand up on the seat of the pew, and, taking the snuffers from the chandelier where they used to hang, snuff the candles. Twirling the chandelier round in a hurry it often happened, much to the amusement of us youngsters, that a lot of the candles were snuffed out, then a candle had to be taken to re-light those which had been extinguished.

The pulpit had two candles on each side which also had to be attended to, the chapel-keeper going up to the pulpit while the minister was delivering his sermon, and often in his trepidation would snuff them out.

The Precentor or Clerk had a candle on each side of his desk to enable him to read the hymns or psalms, as they were given out two lines at a times.

In 1820, at the coronation of George IV., the whole of the windows in the town were illuminated. Each pane had a candle behind it, and many were the devices employed to get them fixed, especially amongst the middle and lower classes, who fixed them in pipe clay, or pieces of tin fastened to the sash.

In my early days few females were found bold or hardy enough to venture out of the house on a dark night without having a lantern in her hand to light the path. The dim lights from the street lamps—which were placed at long distances from each other—and the candles and the oil lamps in the shop windows, only seemed to make the darkness more complete.*

There were no lucifer matches in those days, every housewife had to see to her tinder box, flint and steel. Tinder had to be made before the flint and steel could be of any use. Thus—mother would take a piece of linen or linen rag, hold it with the tongs before the fire until it was perfectly dry and scorched; the tinder box being ready, the rag was lighted at the bottom, and, before the flames had altogether died away, was dropped into the tinder box, after which the lid was put on and held tight down until the flame was extinguished and the embers put out. The matches had to be made or bought, they were tipped with brimstone and called brimstone matches. To get your light the tinder box must be opened, and the flint struck by the steel just over it to produce a spark of fire, which, falling on the tinder, set it on fire, then you applied the match, together with a gentle blowing on the tinder to keep the fire alive till you succeeded in lighting it.

WATCHING.

The town at nights was patrolled by watchmen, generally staid or oldish men, nick-named " Old Charlies."

In winter the watch boxes used to be brought out and set up in certain places, generally close to or under one of the oil lamps; if the night was wet or cold they used to take shelter in the watch box during the interval of their rounds. It was no uncommon thing to see the watchman and box upset in a street row or for a lark. The watchmen went their rounds every half-hour, and their voices could be

---

* Very often the paving stones on the footpath were loose or holes were left, into which the ladies' pattens often stuck. There were no flagged footpaths then.

heard calling the time night and morning, and telling whether it was fine, rainy, cloudy, or frosty, thus:—he would call "past one o'clock, fine morning, all's well;" the last hour called was five in the morning. They used to call running fitters, keelmen, or any other person that needed to be called for the tides or any other purpose. As the watchman had to make his rounds twice in the hour you could always sleep sound, depending on the call.

There were only two Constables for Sunderland. The cages or lock-ups then were, and now are, in Coronation Street, close to the side entrance to the Assembly Rooms, opposite the present Market and west of the Church; the old iron doors are still there, an iron shutter to the window of one and an iron grating to the other. I have seen the friends of the prisoners passing spirits to them through a tube from the outside through the grating.

Although there were only two Constables, yet, upon any emergency, the Magistrates swore in a batch of Special Constables to assist in keeping the peace. They were each supplied with a staff from 10 to 12 inches long, with a crown painted on, and "G.R." underneath it. The staff was retained by the Special to be ready when called for.

Taking the town in its transitional state, before and after the passing of the Act of 1826, and beginning with the

LOW STREET,

we find it to be a busy hive of industry from end to end.

WATER SUPPLY.

The principal water supply for the town and for all the shipping frequenting the port was from the Low Street.

Close to the foot of Water Lane, in the Low Street, there were three wells and three pumps; the principal pump was next to Water Lane, and was kept by Barbara

Salmon, which is now boarded up, yet the pump is there. There was another pump in a small opening a little to the west of Mrs. Salmon's; the third was at the other side of the Low Street, down a narrow passage which led to the river, now called Chisman's Entry.* These pumps supplied nearly all the lower part of the town with water. The last named pump was principally used for supplying water to the colliers, a long hose pipe leading from the pump to the water boat in the river.

In my early days nearly all the water had to be carried home from the pumps, principally on the head in skeels or pans, three items being necessary, viz. :—the skeel, the wease to fit on the head on which to rest the skeel, and a small bowl or float, which floated on the water and acted as a steadiment from a shake or unsteadiness, when the water might splash over. When the household work was over, the females, tidying themselves, would go to the pump for water. All had to pay for it—some were customers and paid monthly or quarterly, others had to pay as they got it.

In the evenings Mrs. Salmon's yard was sometimes crowded with women and girls waiting for their turn at the pump. Many a skeel have I seen gently tipped from behind by a friend, thus compelling her to go back again to the pump.

It was noted that the girls in Sunderland walked the most erect of any girls in the north, and this was attributed partly to the upright steady walk with such an unstable article on the head. There was also Bodlewell pump, known all over the town, but not quite so famed as Mrs. Salmon's, that is if the number of customers be any criterion of popularity. The customers at Bodlewell were supplied as they stood in the street. The nosel of the pump still shews through the wall.

---

*A Metal Pump still stands over the Well.

There were also supplies of water in other parts of the town, viz. :—George Street, 1 pump; Horn's Lane, 1; Queen Street, 2; Zion Street, 1; Butchers' Slaughter-houses, 1; Church Street, 4 or 5; Workhouse, 1; Barracks, 3; Pottery, 2, as well as some others. Afterwards carts came round and supplied water at a half-penny per skeelful. A few years later, when the first Water Company got into full operation, they erected pants in different localities amongst the poor population and charged a farthing per skeel. There were several pumps and springs in Bishopwearmouth, viz. :—in the Rectory grounds, on the Green, and elsewhere.

BREWERIES.

The principal breweries in the town were located in the Low Street, and close to the river. Each brewery had its own well, from which they drew their supplies for the purposes of their trade; they had also to supply their collier customers with water. The brewers had their large boats to seek up the ale and beer barrels from the colliers, and take them back again when filled; they also had their water boats with two or three large casks open at the top, which were filled from the brewery pump, and the water was hoisted on board the ships with buckets to fill up the water casks.* Horn & Scott's brewery (afterwards Scurfield & Co.) faced Noble's Quay, with an entrance from the High Street; the place is now occupied by Mr. Lamb and others. The Mark Quay brewery, for many years in the occupation of the late Alderman Thomas Reed, still carries on the trade. Fenwick's brewery has been in the occupation of the family for at least three generations, if not four; it has been all re-built and extensively enlarged. The Subscription

---

*At that period neither tea nor coffee were supplied to sailors, the provisions of the ordinary collier not extending beyond beef, biscuits, and beer.

Brewery, which paid all the shareholders their dividends in ale and beer, was closed, and Wylams wharf now occupies the site. The Panns brewery, standing on the Panns Quay next to the river, was pulled down many years ago in order to give place to W. & A. Adamson's slipway, now occupied by S. P. Austin & Son as an iron shipyard. Hindmarch the brewer afterwards built a new brewery at the east end of the town, in High Street and Bank Street. In other parts of the town there were Horn's Lane brewery, once in the occupation of Mr. Taylor, father of the late Tom Tayor, novelist and humorist, and Queen Street brewery, since pulled down and enlarged, now occupied by St. John and Annison; these last two breweries had their own wells.

Out of the five breweries at one time in full operation in the Low Street only two of them at the present time remain and carry on their business.

It must not be thought that since the water supply has gone into the hands of the Water Company the quality of the water which they supply is superior or even equal to to the quality we received from our local wells. The water in former days was soft, sparkling, clear, and did not leave that thick deposit of lime in the kettles that we find in our present supply. As a proof of this, the two breweries in the Low Street prefer and use the old supply. The then owner of the Mark Quay brewery told the writer some time ago that they had tried the water supplied by the Company, but they preferred their old well water, which was clear and softer, and that they got far better returns in their brewings.

Some years ago, when Messrs. Fenwick re-built and enlarged their premises, they found that the old well required extensive repairs. On inspection, the shaft was found to be so defective and difficult to repair, and likely to be expensive, that they determined to sink a new shaft or well, which they did, sinking it deeper than the old one; this would, I believe, drain the old Bodlewell dry. This soft, sparkling, clear, pure water, they continue to use up to the present time.

Following the Brewers, we come to the Licensed Victuallers or

PUBLIC HOUSES.

In the Low Street, from Thornhill's wharf on the east, to the Green Dragon at Panns Ferry on the west, there were *41 public houses; 20 were situate between the Low Street and the river, and 21 on the south side of the street—several of these were night or tidal houses, as noticed hereafter. Such a number of houses seem to be large for one street, especially when we consider that on the north side, next to the river, where not more than one-third of the street was occupied as dwelling houses, and the number of public houses seems out of all due proportion to the number of residential inhabitants. Thus, in Bishopwearmouth Panns—according to the census—the residential inhabitants, in 1821, were 483; whilst of public houses there were six, making the average number of inhabitants to the number of public houses 80·5, including women and children. The remaining portion of the street in Sunderland Parish, as to the number of residential inhabitants, would be nearly in the same proportion, viz.: 80½. The custom or trade of these houses depended only in a degree to the residential inhabitants. The principal thoroughfare for the trade on the river was the Low Street, and these houses were first-of-call for sailors, keelmen, and castors, and the last-of-call in going off to ships or keels. Out of these the separate wharves had their own public houses for labourers, corn porters, and others. Wylam's wharf has its public house at the present time. Holmes' wharf and Thornhill's wharf public houses are closed.

---

* The Public House kept by Mr. Thurlbeck, in the row of houses between the hailing house and Joe Humble's shop, is not counted in.

At the gates of the shipyards the carpenters were accommodated, a foreman in the yard being sometimes landlord, the wife attending to the business.

The Glassmen were also specially provided for; the different landlords of these houses, as licensed victuallers, catered for the necessities of their customers. These classes are not now to be provided for, and the whole volume of trade has been lost to the locality.

In September, 1888, there were only 12 public houses and 2 beer houses open to the trade, instead of 41 public houses as in 1821, a reduction of 29, or two-thirds.

Some of the licensed victuallers in the Low Street were very respectable people; taking the trade as a whole they were respectable, we will name a few of them:—Mrs. Scott kept the "Lynn Arms,"* in front of Hardcastle's quay, at the foot of the Long Bank, she was an old lady indeed in all things; Robert Gowland and Roger Watson, both fitters, married daughters of Mrs. Scott; the late William Briggs married Miss Hedley, a grand-daughter of Mrs. Scott; Robert Scott Briggs bears his grandmother's name. "Joe" Parkin, who was a little dapper body, kept a public house on the Low Quay, next to the narrow passage from the Quay to the Low Street, he was running-fitter to the late Robert Scurfield; "Bob" Nesbitt married his daughter, who was the mother of Mrs. St. John. Martin Douglass was running-fitter, shipowner, and publican, or rather his wife kept the public house up a blind alley between Canny's Place and Akenhead's Square; Robert Holmes' shop in the square backed the premises; his son Martin married a Miss

---

* The "Lynn Arms" public house afterwards came into possession of the late Rev. James Everitt, together with John Christy's public house, which was in the same row, through his wife, who was a Miss Hutchinson; the reverend gentleman, remembering his principles, would not even sell the licenses, but allowed them to drop, and closed the public houses. It is only fair to relate that they had no family, and that Mr. Everitt was a teetotaler.

Mordey and was father of the late Mordey Douglass. Mrs. Kidd kept a public house just west of the Mark Quay, on the north side of the street, in the corner ; the late William Sheraton, the tinner, married one of her daughters, and John Frost, the cooper, married another.

GAS WORKS.

The original gas works were erected by the Company in the Low Street, on the east side, and at the bottom of, Beggar's Bank.

On March 9th, 1824, the town was first lighted with gas; Mr. Coates was Secretary and Manager, commonly called "Coates, the gas man."

Burnett, in relating the improvements that had been made by the Town Commissioners, amongst others, says, that the town was brillantly lighted with gas, which was supplied from these works.

"In a Raft Yard at the other side of the Low Street, Green's balloon was inflated with gas, and John Vipond, painter and glazier, took his place in the car along with Mr. Green. When the balloon was freed it rose with the two in the car, and was driven by the wind towards the river, where it got entangled in the rigging of a collier lying in the tier, when Vipond embraced the opportunity of getting out of the car on to one of the collier's yards, thus ending his ballooning experiments, whilst the balloon, getting freed from its entanglements, rose and floated away towards Souter Point."

The original works of the Monkwearmouth Gas Company were situate in the Strand, now called Strand Street; Lumsdon's chain and anchor works afterwards occupied the site.

In January, 1856, the Sunderland Gas Company was formed. The ostensible reason set forth before the public was to cheapen the price of gas by competing with the older companies. Instead of carrying out the principle of competition to cheapen, they came to terms with the old companies, bought up their works and plant, and thus got the monopoly in their own hands, and have been paying 10 per cent. per annum on the original shares ever since.

COOPERS.

The Coopers' trade was principally located in the Low Street between Bodlewell Lane and the Mark Quay. Hodgson the cooper had his cooperage to the east of Water Lane. Drysdale had his cooperage between the Low Street and the river, the passage is called Drysdale's Entry, it is nearly opposite Water Lane. Mr. Robson and the two Browns had their cooperages between Spenceley Lane and Bodlewell Lane, and the passage leading from the Low Street into the High Street, up a few steps, which shortened the distance for the coopers, was called Coopers' Entry; the principal part of their trade was in connection with shipping. For dairy purposes or for skeels, bowls, dishes, and other articles for household use, Burdon the cooper, in the High Street, was the principal, his cooperage was at the back and in the lower story of the house, and in connection with the Low Street and Stob Lane. Hetherington, and one or two more, had their cooperages in Monkwearmouth and the Shore.

MAST AND BLOCKMAKERS.

Several of them had their workshops and places of business in the Low Street, viz. :—Mr. Richardson, at the foot of the Pottery Bank, facing Thornhill's wharf. John Barry, at the east side of Hardcastle's slipway. George Iley, on the Low Quay, also Harkess the blockmaker. Stephen Huntley, down the dark entry off the Low Street on the Black Bull Quay; he afterwards took into partnership two of his sons—Daniel and Jeptha, and the firm became S. Huntley and Sons; they afterwards removed to the

South Dock. Thomas Byers had his place of business in the Strand, and Thomas Russell at the North Quay Ferry Landing.

The masts and yards for new ships were generally made on or near the shipbuilders' yards, so that the smiths could put on the iron work, whilst the blocks and dead eyes were made in the shop, and sent to the blacksmith's as might be required.

BLACKSMITHS AND JOBBING SMITHS.

Many of them were located in the Low Street, or in close proximity thereto, as also were anchorsmiths and chain makers. The elder William Nicholson had his blacksmith's shop in the West House on the Low Quay, next to Noble's Quay; the family lived in the house above the shop. Afterwards he took another shop, at the other side of the street. Some years after he took Tommy Carr's yard in Bank Street, Farrer's, the pipe makers shop and kilns, in High Street, and the yard next to Wellington Lane, occupied by pig styes, the whole making a large plot of ground, on which he erected the chain, anchor, and general smiths' shops. The foundry and shops in Warren Street and the Hat Case were afterwards built. The same William Nicholson built Nicholson House, with grounds bordered by Grey Road on the south, Mowbray Road on the north, and Stockton or Ryhope Road on the West.—What a rise, yet only for one life.

The elder Mr. Penman had his blacksmith's shop in Bank Street, the dwelling house facing the High Street; the hardware shops were next door; there was a garden at the back of these which stretched down to Bank Street, the smiths' shops were in the garden; there was an open view on to the river. In these shops the late David Holsgrove served part of his apprenticeship.

In the Long Bank, Willy Crass hammered on the anvil during a long life. He lived in the passage or entry in the High Street opposite the top of the bank, the entry bearing his name—"Crass's Entry." In the Long Bank Baglee, the nail maker had his shop, he died a few years ago, aged 95 years.

In the Long Bank, also, old Mr. Clark (grandfather of the present Messrs. Clark, engine builders), engineer, had his first engine shop or works, the shop stands in the corner at the turn or elbow of the bank. I remember talking to John Clark, his son, about it, he said—"Yes, my father had that shop before he went to Farrington Row, afterwards to Wellington Lane, Deptford."

In Panns, Young and Thompson had their anchor and chain shops, situate at the foot of the stone steps leading from Number's Garth to the Low Street. There were also several other small jobbing smiths' shops in the Low Street.

In Monkwearmouth-Shore there were a great many jobbing smiths, also chain and anchor manufacturers, viz.: the Lumsdens, in the Strand; Moor, on the Quay end, and several others on the North Quay and in Wear Street.

BOAT BUILDERS.

Three of the principal boat builders were located in or near to the Low Street. Humble had his shops below the high coble slipway. The Brothers Wake had their shops in the large yard of the Old Custom House, using Hardcastle's slipway for launching the boats. One of the brothers built a new house on the bank, facing Bank Street, at the west of the Old Custom House, the back door leading down to the Quay.

Hardcastle's shops were on the Quay. He built a new residence over part of the boat-building shops, in which he lived, the entrance being down the bank by the wall of his boat-building yard. Mosey Hodgson was his foreman. After Mr. Hardcastle's death Mosey carried on the business on his own account.*

Dodds & Shotton's shops were on the side of the road leading down to the beach, almost opposite Tulip's lime kilns. The only boat builders that the pilots would trust to build their cobles were Dodds & Shotton, Humble, and Hardcastle. I think the latter, through Mosey Hodgson's ability, carried off the palm.

A great deal of boat building was carried on in Monkwearmouth-Shore, by Huddleston, Wake (the father of the late W. Morgan Wake), afterwards C. Potts & Brothers, Michael Robson, and others.

SAILMAKERS.

Sail Lofts, as a rule, occupied the top flat of a large house, extending sometimes over two or three houses. Sailmakers liked to have their lofts in the Low Street or on the North Quay, close to or facing the river, where it was handy to get the sails ashore for repairing, or sending them off. When the colliers were laid up for the winter, it was a common practice to send the sails ashore to get them overhauled for the next year's work. Wood and Parker had their loft a little above the Ferry-boat Landing, Low Street; the end of the loft faced the river, where the sails were hauled up from, or lowered down to, the boat. After the dissolution of partnership, Mr. Thomas Wood and his son carried on the business for years. The loft occupied by him, before he retired from business, was on Thornhill's wharf.

---

* Mr. Hardcastle married a Miss Mordey, aunt to the late Dr. Mordey. The name is registered with the Ettricks and Bowes as Hardcastle's Quay. An old Lady, named Mitcheson, a daughter of Mr. Hardcastle, is still living at the time we write.

Allison Whitfield's Sail Loft was at the top of a four-storied house on the Mark Quay. At one time he lived in rooms beneath the loft. Hardy, the clothier, lived next door; the two houses are still standing.

Bracy Robson had his loft in the Low Street, he was a little dapper body, under medium height, wearing a swallow-tailed coat, knee-breeches with buckles, and buckles on his shoes.

Brown Young had his loft facing Noble's Quay, he emigrated to Melbourne in 1852. Several of the ship-owners and shipbuilders had their own lofts, having a practical man as foreman, viz. :—Mr. William Potts in the Low Street, and Messrs. Gales at Hylton. Mr. Norman was foreman for John Gales and Mr. Lewis for William Gales. These two men had to walk to Hylton and back nearly the year round. *Nicholas Smirk often worked as a journeyman in William Gales' loft; he used to lodge for the week at Hylton. Smirk afterwards had his own loft, and his son helped him in the business, in which, for some time, they were successful, when he bought a new ship and called her the "Nicholas Smirk."

WHARVES.

The principal wharves in the town, indeed we may say the only wharves, were in the Low Street.

"Thomas Huntley's key is now known as Holmes' wharf, having been, previous to the year 1827, called 'Neddy Wright's key'; about which time John Holmes, wharfinger, bought it, and considerably extended its eastern and western boundraies by the purchase of adjoining properties; at the same time he called it Holmes' wharf. It is the oldest established wharf in Sunderland for general merchandise, as appears by the return in 1676."—Summers, *pages 323 and 324.*

---

* Smirk was a man of strong leanings or passions; and the lads used at times to shout: "Nichol spoilt the jib," when poor Nichol, with his knock-knees, would try in vain to run after them. If a religious mania was upon him he was all religion. He has been known to chop the head off a cock on the Monday because he thought the fowl had desecrated the Sabbath the day before. When he saved a little money, with barter and credit, he purchased the ship, which, after some time, became unfortunate, and the losses ruined poor Nichol.

The successor to Mr. Holmes was a Mr. Walker, who, previously, had been the captain of a vessel belonging to the father of the late Thomas Ovington Harrison, of Sunderland, and who died in London. Mr. Harrison's father lived in Bridge Street (on the west side), two doors from High Street. The wharf is now called Smurthwaite's wharf.

Thornhill's wharf will go back to a date prior to 1750; it derives its name from John Thornhill, named elsewhere as defender of the copyholders' rights as to quarrying and leading stones from Building Hill. Old Thomas Robinson and his son John were tenants in my early days. It was the principal emporium for imported tar, pitch and hemp. I have seen several ships discharging hemp at this wharf at the same time—a busy place then. The wharf was afterwards purchased by David Johnassohn, Thomas Wood, and others, principally for the discharging of ballast by steam power on a high gantry; this business only succeeded for a short time. The whole of the property was afterwards purchased by the River Wear Commissioners.

Wylam's wharf, often called French's wharf, having been occupied by the late William French as wharfinger for many years. These were the licensed Custom House Wharves, where bonded goods, or goods chargeable with duty, could be landed or shipped.

BALLAST KEYS OR QUAYS.

From the fish market to Hardcastle's slipway, in the Low Street, where ballast was landed and carted over the town, were Ettrick's, Bowes' and Hardcastle's Keys. The latter was the Key which the late John Gordon Black first occupied when he came to the town. It was afterwards occupied by Mr. John Ray, of Ray and Hopper at Hendon Landsale, and Ray's coal wharf in London.

From Mark Quay, and by the Dark Entry, nearly all the poor inhabitants were supplied with coals from the keels.

PERAMBULATING THE BOUNDARIES OF THE PARISH OF SUNDERLAND.

"The first perambulation of the Parish of Sunderland was made on the 3rd September, 1811, by the Rev. John Hampton, M.A., Rector; the Rev. John Hayton, Curate; Mr. William Mounsey, Churchwarden; Mr. George Wheatly and Mr. William Bulman, Overseers; Mr. George Wood, Assistant Overseer, and others.

"Previous to setting out on the perambulation, a resolution, usual on such occasions, was unanimously passed in the vestry—that in case any action or actions for trespass were brought by any person or persons concerned in perambulating the boundaries, such action or actions should be defended by the parish at large.

"The perambulators, under a merry peal of the old five bells of the Parish Church, headed by the Rector and the Parish Officers, with their official wands, proceeded up Coronation Street, then called "The Back Lonnin," at different parts of which, and upon the boundary line adjoining Bishopwearmouth, "S.P.," for Sunderland Parish, was for the first time painted up, and a plentiful supply of gingerbread nuts thrown away among the youngsters. They then passed down Sans Street and Beggars' Bank (Russell Street), at the foot of which several cobles were in waiting (steam boats at that time being unknown). Here the party embarked and proceeded down the river to sea, where they took a good offing to claim the boundaries of the parish down to low water mark. The perambulators landed from the cobles on the beach at the "way foot" in the dene at the south end of the town moor, led on by Mr. Paxton, joiner, an aged man, who well knew that part of the southern boundary of the parish from his father, having been for many years the the herd of the cattle stinted upon the town moor. They then passed up middle of the small stream on the south side of the Octagon Cottage— then the land in dispute. In order that no part of the parish might be lost, here some boys "plodged" or waded under the arch that carries the carriage road to Hendon house over the stream, which was diverted between the arch and the sea in 1821, by George Robinson, Esq., of Hendon lodge, allowing some thousands of tons of ballast to be deposited upon his land on the south side of the stream, for which he received twopence per ton from the wharfingers. This proceeding diverted the stream (the natural boundary between Sunderland and Bishopwearmouth) about seven feet northwards into the Sunderland boundary. On entering the plantation of Hendon lodge, now the site of Moor Terrace, &c., John Mailing, Esq., once an inmate of the lodge—grandfather of C. M. Webster, of Pallion hall,—joined the perambulators, and assisted Mr. Paxton in pointing out the Sunderland part of the Bishop of Durham's Waste, upon which parts of the north and south ends, including a portion of the drawing room and kitchen, of Hendon lodge are built, and through these rooms some of the perambulators passed.

"The second perambulation of the boundaries was made on August 7th, 1828, by the Rev. Robert Gray, M.A., Rector ; the Rev. Ebenezer Leach, Curate ; Mr. Thomas Hodge and Mr. Henry Preston, Churchwardens ; Mr. W. Boyes Walker, and Mr. George Lord, Parish Clerk, &c. A steam boat and cobles were engaged for this perambulation. The procession having returned to the vestry-room, it was resolved— 'That this meeting having been prevented, from motives of courtesy, from passing through Mr. George Robinson's kitchen at Hendon lodge, part of which, it is understood, is included in this parish, that an entry be made in the vestry book to that effect.'

"On the 12th May, 1845, a third perambulation of the parish was made by the Rev. William Webb, M.A., Rector ; Mr. Martin Moore and Mr. Robert Holmes, Churchwardens ; Mr. James Douthwaite and Mr. John Samuel Barron, Overseers ; Mr. Henry Burdon Taylor, Assistant Overseer ; and Mr. George Lord, Parish Clerk, &c. At this perambulation, in addition to the usual liberal distribution of gingerbread nuts, a large quantity of half-farthings, brought from London expressly for the occasion, were thrown amongst the youngsters.

"On the 3rd May, 1853, the fourth perambulation of the parish was made by the Rev. Henry Peters, Rector ; Mr. Thomas Bradley and Mr. Joseph Humphery, Churchwardens ; Messrs. William Thompson, David Palin Huntley, and John Potts, Overseers ; Mr. Thomas Fenwick Hedley, Assistant Overseer ; and Mr. George Lord, Parish Clerk, &c.

On the 3rd June, 1856, the boundaries of the parish were perambulated for the fifth time, by the Rev. Henry Peters, Rector ; the Rev. John Thomas Smith, B.A., Curate ; Mr. George Lord, Parish Clerk ; Mr. R. B. Porrett, Churchwarden ; Mr. John Bruce, Overseer ; Thomas Fenwick Hedley, Assistant Overseer.—Summers, *pages 54 to 65.*

CHAPTER II.

THE HIGH STREET.

Among a few of the Rolls of the Court Barron and Frank Pledge of the Borough of Sunderland, which have been preserved, occurs the following:—

"In the presentment of 1681, Adamson's Lane, leading from the High Street to the Low Street; Bear's Lane, leading from the High Street to the River; and Ludgate Lane, leading from the High Street to the Town Moor, are mentioned."

Adamson's Lane, leading from the High Street to the Low Street, in all probability would be what is now called Water Lane, at the foot of which the inhabitants had to draw their supply of water after the public well in the High Street was closed.

Bear's Lane, leading from the High Street to the river, would be the lane now called Moss Lane. This is the only lane leading direct from the High Street to the river; crossing the Low Street it went down by a passage at the east of the two four-storied houses still standing, ending in a flight of stone steps at the river. The place where the steps were is now boarded over, and a wall built in front of the river. The lane further east is called Bull Lane, leading from the High Street to Akenhead's Square and the Low Street, thus we have the Bear's Lane and Bull Lane following.

Ludgate Lane, leading from the High Street to the Town Moor, would be the lane directly opposite Bear's Lane, and the two lanes would form a straight road from the Town Moor to the river, crossing the High Street.

Ludgate Lane, as its name implies, would probably have a gate to prevent cattle straying from the Moor, or there might have been a check gate at that period; it had evidently been the road from the Moor to the High Street and the lower parts of the town.

Thirty-eight years after the presentment to the Court Barron (1681) Sunderland became a parish, *i.e.* in 1719; and in 1740, twenty-one years after, the Poor-house was built in the Church Walk by subscription, and the workshops for the employment of the poor were afterwards added; these were built directly opposite the head of Ludgate Lane, where probably the gate had already been done away with, and, dropping the terminal gate, would be called Love Lane instead of Lud Lane. It was called Love Lane as far back as 1770, and was so called in 1820, and for years after, until it was changed into Mill Street; and Mill Street has also been swept away under the Corporation Improvement Scheme. Thus, out of the five streets and lanes mentioned in 1681, only the High Street and Low Street retain the names they had 200 years ago.

Continuing the presentment :—

"Also, that the common well in the High Street, opposite the house of John Babington, be repaired and covered by the adjoining neighbours within 14 days, under the penalty of 39s. 11d."—

Garbutt, *appendix 40*.

It would be interesting to know which was the house where John Babington lived, and the spot and locality where the common well was which the adjoining neighbours had to cover and repair within 14 days; after the lapse of 200 years it can only be conjectured. The probability is that the well would be in the slack or hollow in the High Street, near to where, in after days, the public were amply supplied with water; in which case it would not be far from Water Lane, and not far from the foot of Church Street.

In course of time, as trade increased, the well in the High Street would become an obstruction to traffic, and be filled up and closed.

"In 1682 (quoting from the Court Rolls), Mrs. Ginewell, for setting a cobbler's shop to fare into the street, was fined 6s. 8d. ; showing that they would not even allow a cobbler's shop to encroach on the public road.

"Thomas Lambton, for being drunk and assaulting Mr. Thomas Huntley in his own house, 13s. 4d."—Garbutt, *appendix 41*.

We quote the last because he was the same Thomas Huntley who was owner of the oldest Key or Wharf, as noticed in the previous article dealing with the Low Street.

Burnett, writing in 1830, says :—

"Fifty years ago—that would be about 1780, or 100 years later than 1681,—at the entrance of Sunderland Parish, on the south side of the street, there was a high and rising ground, beginning at Sans Street and ending at George Street. The houses that were situated there had a terrace before them, which extended a considerable way into the street. At the north side of this terrace there was a wall, and by several steps you descended to the horse road, which was considerably lower than the terrace ; this part was then called the High Justice Trees. A gentleman informed me he recollected when the stumps of some of these trees were to be traced upon this terrace. Proceeding eastwards from George Street to Maud's Lane, on the south side of the street, the ground was high forming—a sloping bank, but not terraced. From Maud's Lane to the foot of Grey Street a high and rising ground commenced, which was terraced, and a wall built at the north side of it. This terrace extended a great way into the street, and was considerably higher than the horse road ; this part was called the Low Justice Trees.* These high grounds were afterwards lowered, which considerably improved the appearance of the town—where cellars formerly had been there arose shops.

---

* This terrace, or Low Justice Trees, was the end of a high spur of ground running from Coronation Street, between Maud's Lane and New Grey Street, to the back of the houses in the High Street. On the brow of this spur tall old trees grew, and standing on the steps of the Exchange, or walking down that side of the street, to look and see far above the tops of the houses opposite, the old trees, with their branches waving to the wind, was indeed a beautiful sight, not soon to be forgotten.

Previous to the opening out of the ground at Bishopwearmouth as building sites, the most respectable inhabitants resided at the east end of Sunderland, but as the new streets in Bishopwearmouth were erected they regularly removed thither."--Burnett, *pages 41, 42, and 43.*

I have often heard my grandfather talk about these terraces when I was a boy, some years before Burnett published his history.

Burdon the cooper's house and shops were directly opposite this terrace on the north side of the High Street; it was a double two-storied house, and stood a short distance from the retaining wall of the High Street, having sufficient ground in olden times for a flower garden in the front. The roof of the house was a little above the then level of the High Street. At the edge of the footpath there was an iron railing to prevent the public from falling over, and alongside of the retaining wall was a flight of stone steps, with an iron railing at the outer edge, which led down to the house and shops of an old respectable and well-to-do tradesman. His shop had been on a level with the footpath on the north side of the High Street in former days, whilst at the opposite side of the street was the high terrace with 20 steps down to the horse road.

The houses and shops at the north side of the High Street had a retaining wall to hold up the footpath, and there were iron gratings in front to let light into the kitchens below. Between Stob Lane and Water Lane there are several blind alleys or courts running up to the backs of the houses and shops in the High Street, the back doors of which opened out into the alleys, whilst on either side were houses inhabited by the poorer people. East of Water Lane the High Street rises, and at the Mark Quay Brewery there is a steep perpendicular drop; at Noble's Quay Brewery the drop is deeper, and Chancery Lane ended in a deep supporting wall down to the level of the Low Street;

besides these retaining walls, the lanes and stairs down to Bull Lane act as so many buttresses, holding up the High Street. There is not a cart road leading from the High Street to the Low Street between Bodlewell Lane and the Long Bank.

MARKETS.

The Markets were held in the High Street, Friday being the market day. The Town Commissioners, under the Sunderland Improvement Act, 1809, on the 18th day of November, 1820, changed the day from Friday to Saturday, which has continued to be the market day. The market, in its different parts, extended nearly the whole length of the parish.

The Seed and Corn Market was always held in front of the Exchange ; the farmers' long carts, laden with produce, side by side, would very often extend from above George Street down to below Maud's Lane. The farmers stood on the edge of the footpaths or flags with their boles of corn or other produce in front of them; the buyers were always numerous. At that period there were from 16 to 20 windmills* around the town and in the neighbourhood, and the owners or tenants required corn to supply their customers. Besides these millers there were the dealers in hay and straw, together with the dealers in seeds, and, in the season, a market for pigs was also held—it was a busy hive while the market lasted. There was also the Weighing Machine, and—if I remember rightly—Mr. Renney, the Clerk at Bishopwearmouth Church and Librarian of the Subscription Librarian, was the recorder of the averages, and he held the office for years. Each of the farmers had his particular hostelry where the horse was stabled during the market.

---

* It was at one or other of these wind-mills to which the poor gleaner would carry her corn to be ground into meal for the winter's use of the household.

The Poultry, Butter and Egg Market extended from the foot of Queen Street to Barron's, the old "Bull and Dog" public house, below Arras' Lane; this market was only held at the south side of the High Street.

The Butchers' Market extended from Beehive Lane to Water Lane on the north side, and from the Poultry Market to Church Street on the south side. Several of the large butchers had their shops on the south side of the street in the market, viz. :—Hunter, Holmes, Nattrass, Blackett, and Reed. The last two were purchased by the Town Commissioners for an entrance to the present market—the arcade occupies their sites.

A small market was held at the west of Beehive Lane for the sale of boots, shoes and clogs.

*The Green, Fruit, and Potato Market extended from Water Lane to Moss Lane on both sides, but principally on the north side of the street.

The Earthenware Market was east of Moss Lane on the north side of the street. Stalls for the sale of old clothes were set up in this market, but the market for old clothes was really held in Old Grey Street.

The Hawker's Vans, with their goods of cutlery, hardware, &c., which were sold at night by "dutch auction," under the glare of large tallow lamps, were at the top of Neil's Passage and Bull Lane.

---

* The late Thomas Gibson told the writer that he always, on the Saturday night at ten o'clock, went down to the market and remained until its close to help his father to pack up and get the horse and cart home, and regularly about half-past ten or eleven o'clock, just before the close, Mrs. Hudson would come into the market to see what bargains she could pick up, and one of her sons with her carrying the basket; she came from the low end of the town, he could not tell what street. The lad that carried the basket, we suppose, would never forget the lesson of thrift inculcated by his mother.

The Market for Crabs, Lobsters, Oysters, Cockels and Whelks was held between Spencely Lane and Water Lane. The butchers used to set out their stalls for the morning market and removed them in the afternoon, except on Saturdays, when they were pushed into the middle of the street, and the space vacated was occupied by the sellers of shell fish. There are sometimes a few to be seen in the same market when these fish are in season, but the fish shops have spoiled the market. *Joe Addey was the principal oyster vendor in the town. The oyster pits were on the Low Quay, and the tide flowed in through the quay wall. The Scotch boats lay alongside the quay to discharge the oysters.

The Fish Market was on the Quay, commonly called the Fish Market Quay, now named Ettrick's Quay.

THE STOCKS.

In the Market Place, near the foot of Church Street, the Stocks were placed; they were kept in the church porch, and had to be brought down to the Market Place for those to whom the Magistrates had ordered the punishment of sitting for so many hours with their feet fastened in them. I have seen both men and women undergoing the punishment of having their feet fastened in the Stocks. The Stocks on Bishopwearmouth Green were fixtures in the Ground.

THE CATTLE MARKET.

Prior to 1826, the Cattle Market for supplying the district was held at Morpeth, and the Sunderland butchers had to go to Morpeth market for their stock. They generally travelled by coach to Newcastle and then walked to Morpeth, and they very often had to walk back to Sunderland. After

---

* Joe's Wife was called Nelly, she had the shrillest and loudest voice ever heard in the town; wherever you might be you could hear Nelly calling fresh oysters. The Keelmen said that on a calm night Nelly's voice could be heard on Glower-ower-em.

the passing of the Act in 1826, the Town Commissioners formed a Cattle Market in Sunderland, which was held once a fortnight, in Barrack Street. The penns or stalls were erected close to the Barrack wall. It was only in existence for a few years, when it died a lingering death. Its place was afterwards occupied by the Durham and Sunderland Railway Company, which was opened on the 7th day of August, 1836.

HIRINGS.

The Town Commissioners, under their Act, established half-yearly Hirings; these were held in the Corn Market, High Street, in front of the Justices' Room in the Exchange. There were rows of Farm Servants, both male and female, to be seen standing in the Market-place, and farmers and their wives going up and down the rows striving to suit themselves with men or women servants waiting to be hired.

THE FAIRS.

The Fairs were held in May and October, and they occupied the whole of the High Street from Sans Street to the end of the town; the shows and caravans were located in Barrack Street. I have sometimes seen so many crowding the space that some of them had to be taken on to the ropery or town moor. Billy Purvis was a regular frequenter of the fairs, in fact some people did not think it was a fair if Billy's show was absent. At nights, during the fair, nearly all the public houses at the lower end of the town had fiddling and dancing.

From the Pier up to Sans Street there were at that time about 42 public houses, 21 of them being on the east side of the High Street. I think now—at the time of writing— the number is about the same. I would not like to pass an opinion as to their characters *then* and *now*.

A great number of the tradesmen were located in the High Street, principally below the Methodist Chapel on the south side and the Friends' or Quakers' meeting house on the north side. The shops were congregated together in groups; from Sans Street to George Street there were Ritson, the chemist; Richardson, the grocer; Milburn and Teesdale, woollen and cloth merchants; Thomas Robson, draper (father of E. C. Robson, miller); and Gowlands, jewellers and clock and watch makers, at the corner of George Street. All these houses had a long strip of ground or garden behind, running back to Cross Street, and trees grew behind Mr. Ritson's shop. Below George Street there were Diston, boot and shoe maker; B. Bray, chemist; and at the corner of Spring Garden Lane, Robert Tate, (a) the draper, had his shop; and behind, in Spring Garden Lane, there was a small piece of ground where flowers used to be cultivated. Satchel, the draper's shop, below Spring Garden Lane, was up a flight of stone steps, just above the Saddle Inn; the garden at the back went almost up to the theatre, by the side of Drury Lane, and beyond the theatre was an open space where tall trees grew. This ground was afterwards occupied by the late William Tate, on which he erected his saw mills.

Service, the hair dresser, had his shop above Flag Lane, and Calvert, the stay maker, at the foot. Kirk, the draper's shop, was at the north-east corner of Maud's Lane, up some stone steps, and inside the shop there was a rise of three or four steps to the back part of the shop, and up the lane, behind the shop, a lot of trees grew. At the foot of Grey Street was the George Hotel or Inn. It was in connection with the stable yard of the Inn, up Grey Street, and to the west, where grew the tall trees named

---

(a) The late John Candlish, M.P., the late J. H. Wake, and the present Mr. Service served their apprenticeships with Robert Tate.

elsewhere. Below Golden Alley was the shop of Cawood, the tobacconist, and at the other side of Walton Lane, (*b*) Walton, the grocer; the old shop was pulled down and a new one built on its site. The lane at the side is called after him. At the east of Pewterer's Lane was Watty Cockburn, the hatter's. Watty was hunchbacked. There were also Stephen Watson, the draper; and Hodge, the stationer. All the backs of these houses communicated with Pewterer's Lane, and in the lane at the back there was a space of ground, with a small grass plot and a few trees growing. At the foot of Queen Street, and facing the High Street was the (*c*) Golden Lion Hotel; the premises extended a long way back, between Pewterer's Lane and Queen Street, and included the stable yard and coach houses. There was a splendid well of water also in connection, and a pump in Queen Street, and on the bank in the yard some very fine tall trees grew, whilst at the back of the hotel, facing south, beautiful flowers were grown. On the other side of Queen Street, was (*d*) Spoors, the grocer's, it was accounted a large establishment in the trade. At the east of Arras Lane was old Nesbitt's spirit shop, next door to the Old Bull and Dog; the further distance to Church Street was almost solely occupied by publicans and butchers.

(*b*) Walton, being in difficulties, went to a Friend to seek advice. "Does anybody know?" asked his friend. "No," said he. "Then thou wants no assistance. Capital situation, friend Walton, pull the shop down and build a new one." Walton did so, and kept his business. Walton Lane is called after him.

(*c*) The Golden Lion used to be the hotel of the Tempest family, when in town, and afterwards of the Vanes and Londonderrys. It was at the door or the front part of the hotel in High Street, where the mob attacked the Marquis in his carriage, pelting him with mud and rotten eggs, when the Marquis in his passion said he would make the grass to grow in Sunderland streets. My father was on the carriage helping to protect him.

(*d*) Richard Spoor, one of the sons, was afterwards Mayor of Sunderland, and was the duellist with Joseph John Wright at Marsden, when the seconds loaded the pistols with cotton balls—so sang Peter Flint, of local fame, at that time.

At the foot of Church Street was the large battlemented house and shop facing north and west, kept by John Robson, the grocer, and many years after occupied by the late Alderman Barnes as a butcher's shop.

At the foot of Love Lane Mr. Parker had his grocer's shop, which is now occupied by Mr. Brantingham. At the foot of Ropery Lane, Mr. Preston, (e) chemist and druggist, had his shop. At the foot of John Street, old Mr. Palin had his chemist's shop, and young Benjamin was afterwards associated with his father in the business; the shop is now almost a ruin; the passage next to it on the west was called Palin's Passage.

At the east side of Vine Street there was a large stone building, said to have been inhabited by the Lilburn family. Broad stone steps, in the centre of a walled terrace, led up to the front door, and on each side of the steps the terrace was cultivated as a flower garden; at the back of the mansion there was a large garden where apple and pear trees grew and blossomed.

On the north side of the High Street, west of the Long Bank and at the corner of Dean's Yard, was the shop of John Hopps, grocer, celebrated in his day. Next door was Lilburn, (f) the baker, noted as one of the best bakers in the town; the bakehouse was at the back, in Dean's Yard; the entry to it was spanned by the jaw bones of a whale, and in the north-west corner of the yard two or three large trees grew. Next door, on the west, was Chalk's, the newspaper agent, a kind of poor stationer's shop. Then Brabant, the butcher, opposite Silver Street, who sold the cheapest mutton in the town, and killed scores of sheep weekly; on Saturday nights his shop was always crowded

---

(e) Preston committed suicide by poison; he had poverty on the brain, though he left a good sum behind him.

(f) Lilburn, the father of the late Charles Lilburn, J.P.

with customers. Next door was Mrs. Lightfoot's public house, then Willie Dunn's, (*g*) the pawnbroker. Dunn's house was a double one, with a flight of stone steps in the centre; the pawn shop was entered by a side passage, down which was a common bakehouse; about 50 stone steps led down from this passage to the Low Street, and were formerly called the Custom House Stairs, but the whole is now called Dunn's Passage. Neal, the boot and shoe maker, had his shop adjoining the steps and passage bearing his name. (*h*) Mrs. Anderson, a widow, kept an orange and apple shop, which was entered by a side door down the steps; she used to set out her stall in the market, directly opposite her house. The passage bears her name —"Anderson's Passage."

The only name I remember now living in this locality is Pearson's, the haberdasher, their old shop was next door to Cranston's, the confectioner; these two lowly old shops were pulled down and new ones built. Pearsons have been in the locality upwards of 65 years, and Cranston is still alive, upwards of 90 years of age. At the head of Water Lane stood the celebrated shop of Ogden, the chemist and druggist, afterwards Jeremiah Sowerby's (*i*). At the south-west corner of Spencely Lane (*k*) Barker, the chemist and druggist, kept his shop; he was a comely looking young man. Further west, we find Dobbing, the hatter; in former days this shop had been in the occupation of the forefathers of the present Mounseys, as hatters, prior to and after they had established the furrier factory in Dunning Street, locally called the coney cutting factory.

(*g*) Thomas Longstaff, the butcher, married one of Mr. Dunn's daughters, who helped him in his shop, which was at the foot of Church Street, in the High Street.

(*h*) Mrs. Anderson's was almost the only place at that time where oranges, apples, and nuts could be purchased on a Sunday.

(*i*) In this shop Reginald Peacock, John Forster, and others served their apprenticeships.

(*k*) Barker, the chemist, committed suicide by poison.

Then followed Miss Atkinson's china shop, the largest and best in the town; next door was (*l*) Stafford, the baker, the bakehouse was entered up one of the blind alleys from the Low Street. Then came (*m*) Caleb Wilson, grocer, chandler and general merchant; the house being occupied by the merchant and his family prior to the house in Tavistock Place being built. Then followed Alderson, the currier and leather seller, who married one of Willie Dunn's daughters. Next came Binns' drapery shop, which was generally full of "bairns." No Quaker in the town had so many quivers in his sheath, Henry Binns being one of them. (*n*) Joseph Andrews' grocery shop was at the head of Beehive Lane. Andrews was also a shipowner. Passing a shop or two west of Beehive lane, we come to Haddock the ironmonger's, afterwards Haddock & Clay; then Bradley, the draper's shop, where a great many of the respectable families dealt, driving down in their carriages. Bradley was rather lame or short in one of his legs. The shop next to, and adjoining Cooper's Entry, was occupied by (*o*) Mr. Brass, boot and shoe maker. This shop was for many years afterwards occupied by Mr. H. Thompson, surgeon and chemist. Then there was old (*p*) Mr. Reed, the printer, stationer, chart seller and shipowner, whose shop was directly opposite the foot of Grey Street. Reed's

---

(*l*) Stafford, the baker, was for many years clerk to the Independents at Bethel Chapel, Villiers Street, and read the hymns from the desk.

(*m*) On the occasion of a celebrated victory Caleb would not illuminate with the rest of the inhabitants, whereupon the people assembled, smashed his windows, and nearly wrecked his premises; he afterwards had shutters put on the outside of every window to protect them from mob violence. Caleb Wilson originally came from Cotherstone, in Yorkshire—his son, the late Joshua Wilson, being my informant.

(*n*) Joseph Andrews was a Quaker, but not of the strict type; he would go across to the Golden Lion and have his pipe and grog.

(*o*) Brass was, at one time, Superintendent of Bethel Sunday School.

(*p*) Grandfather of the present Col. Reed; the business must have been established for upwards of a century.

is the oldest and most continuous business in the High Street, though now removed from the old shop. Next door was (*q*) Mr. Hodgson, the grocer.

Above Bodlewell Lane were Young, the woollen draper, and Edward Smith, printer and shipowner. Above Stob Lane were Spoor, the woollen draper; Burdon, the cooper, already mentioned; and Mrs. Dunning, the tinner. Above the Exchange there was old Bowron the Quaker, grocer, and spirit merchant; above Half Moon Lane, Booth, the gunsmith; above Fighting Cock Lane, the Brothers Joseph, watchmakers and jewellers; above Russell Street, Turner Thompson had his draper's shop, and over the shop (*r*) Mr. Booth had his insurance office, with the entrance in Russell Street. Above this shop, in front of the office window, was a sign with a sea piece painted on it. Passing up the High Street, just above Number's Garth, there was Mesnard's, the draper; and just below the Friends' meeting house was the hosier's shop occupied by Barnabas Sharp. Above the meeting house, up a flight of steps, was Jackson the hatter's shop; the entrance to the house was up the Curtain. At the high end of the Curtain stood a noted public house, under the sign of the "Oak Tree." Above the Curtain, and at the corner of Sunderland Street, was the (*s*) Bridge Hotel, standing within some railings a few feet from the footpath; some years after, the front of the hotel was brought out on a line with the houses in the High Street, partly to give more room in the hotel and partly for

(*q*) Father of Mr. S. S. Hodgson, Clerk to the Guardians.

(*r*) Father of the present Mr. G. R. Booth, J.P. The sign was painted by Stansfield, the great marine artist, who was a native of Sunderland. I have often wondered what became of that sign board—it would be worth a gold frame now.

(*s*) The Bridge Hotel was not only a large coaching establishment, but it was also the hotel where the Lambton Family made their head quarters when in town, and from the windows of which John George Lambton addressed the freeholders of the county on electioneering occasions.

the convenience of the public. We refrain from going further west, as what we have written will suffice for our purpose.

One good and notable feature of the tradesmen of the town in the olden times was that they stuck to their business, and were not above occupying as their dwellings the rooms above and the kitchens underneath their shops ; besides, they were all within easy touch of their churches or chapels, as the case might be, when the solemn stillness of the morning of rest gave rest to them.

There were some peculiarities amongst most of these tradesmen, and that was the costumes they wore, viz. :— the Quakers were always dressed in drab, wearing white neckcloths, knee breeches, and low crowned broad brimmed hats ; some of the others were dressed as if going to an evening party, almost always in black, with white cravats, frills on their shirt fronts, high starched collars, swallow-tailed coats, and many of them with knee-breeches and silk stockings, with buckles on their breeches and shoes ; and if it was a cold day a spencer would be worn, and woollen mittens instead of kid gloves.

There was nothing *in fra dig* in those days about an attorney or solicitor setting rooms apart in the house in which he lived for offices, or having the offices at the back. A little above Sunderland Street, little Bobby Wilson had his offices at the back, and (*t*) John Peck Kidson lived next door, and Stephenson at the corner of East Cross Street, Robert Smart at the corner of Nile Street, Anty Snowball in Nile Street, Thompson at Parchment Hall, corner of Fawcett Street and High Street, Nichol Reed in Fawcett Street, and R. B. Cay, who lived at

---

(*t*) Father of the present John Kidson, J.P.

the corner of King Street and High Street. Indeed nearly all the lawyers had their offices in or contiguous to their dwelling houses. There was one lawyer living out of the town, so to call it; he lived in Green Terrace, and the old house is now occupied as a school.

(*u*) The Walk, or Bishopwearmouth Walk, was on the north side of the High Street. It extended from Bedford Street to East Cross Street, paraded principally from Lambton Street down to William Street. It was a beautiful walk. The three storied houses at the north side had gardens, with flowers, and pear trees were trained and grew up the fronts, and at the south side there were the Sunnisides with their three and four storied houses, with pear trees trained up to the tops of them; and between these was Mr. Maude's large stone built house of three stories, standing back from the High Street, with an enclosure in front, and behind the mansion, the large garden running down almost to the Back garrs, now Borough Road. And in the early morn or quiet evening the song of the lark could be heard on the Walk. Some of our then noted townsmen lived in these houses facing the Walk. There was Nathan Horn, of the firm of Horn and Scott, shipowners, fitters, and bottle manufacturers; (*v*) Shaftoe, the lawyer, afterwards of Bavington Hall, North Tyne; Fred Horn, lawyer and shipowner; Doctor Dobson, both doctor and coal fitter; (*w*) Robert Scurfield, shipowner, coal fitter and brewer. Scurfield was one of the trustees

---

(*u*) As an old lady told the writer, it was beautiful to go along the Walk in the spring time and early summer, to see the blossoms on the trees and the flowers in the gardens. We lived in Bishopwearmouth, and my mother used to take me down to Maling's Rig Chapel on the Sunday mornings.

(*v*) Shaftoe was at one time closely connected with the Bethel Chapel, Villiers Street, and was also a teacher in the Sunday School carried on in the Long Bank.

(*w*) Hill Parker was his clerk and Watson Wayman his running fitter. Dr. Dobson built Cresswell Hall or house, and died shortly after its completion.

pointed for the Marquis of Londonderry when the whole of the estates were put in trust to liquidate the debts.

Henry Tanner was a large shipowner and coal-fitter in partnership with a (x) Mr. Beckwith, under the firm of Tanner and Beckwith. (y) Dr. Brown lived on the Walk. In Sunniside lived Mr. Ferguson, surgeon, Mr. Maling, surgeon, and old Dr. Atkinson; Dr. Burn lived in Norfolk Street.

On October 4th, 1827, the great Duke of Wellington visited Sunderland, in company with the Marquis of Londonderry, when the town kept holiday on the occasion. A Grand Triumphal Arch crossed the High Street (at the Walk), directly opposite Mr. Maude's house, and amidst the evergreens and flowers above, six girls were ensconced, waving white flags as the Duke was passing underneath.

At the high end of the town the carriage was stopped and the horses taken out, it having been determined to draw the hero through the town. The keelmen, under the orders of the running-fitters, fastened two ropes (z) to the front, i.e. one on each side of the carriage; a rope was also fastened to the back of the carriage to regulate its speed. As the procession came to the triumphal arch—the bands playing "See, the Conquering Hero comes!"—the girls on the arch waved their flags, and the ladies and gentlemen at the windows and in the streets waved their handkerchiefs, while the people in the procession were shouting "hurrah!"

(x) Henry Tanner was the father of Mr. James Laing's first wife. Mr. Beckwith lived in Norfolk Street.

(v) As a physician, Dr. Brown gave advice gratis to the poor, and his anti-room was often full of patients waiting for their turns.

(z) Being within the ropes drawing the carriage, the above is written from personal observation.

F

at the top of their voices, and the tall beavers waving round the heads of their owners. The Walk only once witnessed such a sight—it was then. The procession moved down to the Exchange buildings, where the banquet had to be held, which was in the large room, referred to elsewhere. In the evening the whole of the lower and then interior part of the Exchange, together with the front of the building, was hung with hundreds of variegated lamps, and the High Street was illuminated with fireworks and tar barrels; it was indeed a beautiful and grand sight, such as our High Street has not seen since. How short lived is popular applause—scarcely twelve months had elapsed when the Marquis was pelted with mud and rotten eggs in the same High Street, and Apsley House, the then London residence of the Iron Duke, was attacked by the mob and almost wrecked.

Then and Now.—Any old inhabitant returning to the town after a long absence might look in vain for the Walk, or make enquiries, but few of the young or middle aged people would be able to tell where it was situated. Mr. Maude's house has been pulled down to make room for shops, which after being occupied for some years, were in their turn pulled down to make room for J. Backhouse & Co.'s bank. You can look and examine the stately building, but you look in vain for the bye-gone beauties of the Walk, where the pear and apple trees grew and blossomed, and the flowers from the gardens scented the air; even the grass has almost ceased to grow and the weeds to flourish, the shrubs and trees in the shrubbery, after struggling for a brief existence, wither and die, and even the fronts of the houses, where the gardens were kept trim, are cemented over to keep them decent and clean. In walking along Norfolk Street, in the summer of 1888, the remnants of a pear tree was observed still striving to grow from the depths of the area below.

Now, what a change, shops here, shops there, shops everywhere. The business of the High Street has moved west, with the increase of population. Where the gardens were in front of the houses on the Walk, is now covered over with shops, and the tops of the residences now are only visible above the shops. Even the Sunnisides are offices and shops. Every private dwelling from Bishopwearmouth Church to Sans Street, or the little garden enclosure in front have been turned into shops. You can now walk in front of shops for miles, shops beyond the Willow pond, ay, shops up to the Mile lonnin.

Now, what of the old business parts down the High Street ? The shops are occupied by a different class of tradesmen, the business and population have changed, many of the shops are empty, not a few in a dilapidated state, some in ruins.

One exception may be taken as to the decay of business, and only one ; that is the case of the licensed victuallers. In 1821, the population of the parish of Sunderland was 14,725, at the present time, 1889, the population is about the same. In 1821, the public houses in the High Street in Sunderland parish numbered about 42, at the present time the number is about the same. The amount of capital invested in the trade, must, at the lowest estimate, be four to five-fold more than it was in the same number of houses. What were neat old-fashioned public houses we now see transformed into long bars and gin or whisky palaces ; I merely mention these facts, over which moralists can moralize. But there are no gin or whisky palaces that can compensate for the disappearance of the quaint old public houses which remind us of the past. There was the old "Bull and Dog," with Barron's butcher shop in front, over and behind which were the licensed victuallers' rooms, and the county carriers' waggons standing at the front ; or, the "General Wolfe," in the market-place, where you had to descend a flight of stairs from the High Street to get down into the public room. Now there is nothing left of the old place except the General in his uniform; the *sign is there still—the only remnant of former days.

The three or four two-storied houses and shops below the Exchange, occupied by Mrs. Dunning, the tinner, and others, together with Mr. Burdon's house and shops, were pulled down to make room for what was then considered a grand hotel, and was called Horner's hotel. Five or six years was longer than it prospered—the hotel did not pay; and now the building is let off into shops, and for other purposes in the higher stories, though still retaining the long bar.

All the hotels and Coaching-houses in the Parish of Sunderland have been converted into gin or whisky palaces, and travellers have to find accommodation in the new hotels, all of which are within about three minutes' walk of the railway station.

The Exchange Buildings still stand, but no merchants there do congregate, their voices are not heard, nor the step of the lounger ascending the stairs to the news room; the seat of justice has been removed westward; nearly the whole of the building is at present unoccupied. What a change in the prospects that were anticipated! What a contrast since its opening, or in our memories.

Garbutt says of the Exchange, "In this elegant structure, we behold united ornament and utility." The foundation stone was laid in grand Masonic procession, by Sir Henry Vane Tempest, on the 10th August, 1812, and the building opened to the public on the 20th May, 1814.

---

* The original sign was painted by the late John Turner, about the year 1833.

The news room, 68 feet in length and 28 feet in breadth, with the exception of those of Liverpool and Manchester, is superior in size and accommodation to any other in England. The erection of this building furnishes a happy illustration of the good effects of unanimity in a public cause. There is no commercial jealousy, no political prejudice or religious bigotry shewed its baneful influence. The sum required, nearly £8,000, was raised without difficulty; and to the credit of many, we can declare from our own knowledge, that in several instances shares were taken to promote so useful an object without any solicitude as to the return which may be expected. We are happy, however, to find that a fair interest may be looked for at no distant period.—Garbutt, *pages 329 and 330*.

Change and decay—no comment is needed on the facts, and yet in the trade and commence of our town, even greater changes have occurred than the vicissitudes that have befallen the Exchange Buildings.

COACHES.

The coaches used to start from the different hotels or coaching houses in the High Street. The Golden Lion was the one furthest east. The guard of the mail coach wore his red coat, and always had his long trumpet in its socket, to blow his blast when the coach was coming to a corner round which it had to turn. The Stockton coach used to be driven four-in-hand, and the Newcastle and Durham coaches with a leader or three horses. The Shields coaches afterwards dwindled into a one horse small bus, running from the Wheat Sheaf, Monkwearmouth, several times in a day. By the Stockton coach you could book to Thirsk, Leeds, the West, South-West, and Midland Districts, as well as to York and London. You could also go to Durham, and run the chance of getting a seat on the Newcastle coach passing through. Many people preferred going to Newcastle, whence several of the coaches commenced their journeys, and where they stood a better chance of booking their seats. In February, 1836, the Highflyer was advertised, Newcastle to London in 36 hours, only one night out.

Leaving Newcastle about 12 o'clock we arrived at York between 10 and 11 p.m., then went to bed, and were called up next morning by boots; after partaking of a cup of coffee, &c., we started for London at 5 o'clock, travelling all that day and all the next night, and arriving in London about 7 a.m. on February 29th, 1836. This was a journey from Sunderland to Newcastle and London *via* York on the coach top.

A few years later, and the coaches were all knocked off the road, at least so far as Sunderland was concerned. A great effort was made to continue running the 'bus to South Shields at a fare of 6d., but nothing could withstand the iron horse.

Shortly after the Stockton and Darlington Railway was opened, the writer travelled from Stockton to Darlington on the top of the coach, or the coach top; the original railway coach on the Quaker line carried both inside and outside passengers, it was simply the old stage coach put upon wheels running on the iron way, and drawn by the iron horse or locomotive at the satisfactory speed of 12 miles an hour. When the Company preserved their old locomotive, what a pity it is that they did not also preserve a specimen of the first coaches.

In the early days of which we write, it was quite a common occurrence for young ladies to travel from Barnard Castle, Staindrop and Auckland to Sunderland during the bathing season and back by the common carrier; and the young folks from Hexham used to come down by similar conveyances to enjoy the sea bathing.

Now, travelling by coaches and carriers are things of the past, and our High Street neither echoes the trumpet blast of the one nor the whip crack of the other.

POST OFFICES

Were generally located near to the places of starting and arrival of the stage coach, and for the convenience of the general public. The oldest post office which I remember was in Church Street, in an open leading from Church Street to Little Flag Lane, up a few stone steps. I remember seeing the paper in the window notifying the same to the public. At that period the postage of a letter was 1s. 1d., or thirteen pence as it was termed; there were no postage stamps, and the postman received payment when he delivered the letter. The coach started from the Golden Lion, foot of Queen Street. As the population increased westward, the post office was removed from Church Street up to George Street, close to the pump, and opposite Cross Street, for greater convenience to the public and also to the office. It was again removed to the high end of Russell Street.

I think it was whilst in Russell Street the postages on letters were reduced to 8d. Mrs. Robinson was postmistress. The business still further increasing, and the opening out of the Railway, caused the office to be removed to the west side of Bridge Street, when the money order office was added thereto, and the postage reduced to 4d. Mrs. Robinson was still nominally post-mistress. On the introduction of the penny postage, larger accommodation had to be provided, and the office was removed to premises opposite, occupying the area underneath the Unitarian Chapel. As the population and business increased, these offices in their turn had to be abandoned as too small and confined, when the offices were removed to John Street, and although new offices have been built, and the place enlarged at great cost, now, on account of so many departmental offices being added thereto, under the same supervision, the present premises in their turn are found to be too cramped for space and inconvenient for the large amount of business conducted therein, and a larger place is required.

CORONATION STREET, OR THE BACK LONNIN.

Here there were but a few names that we need notice. At the very top, or high end of the street, at the corner in Nile Street, lived the Rev. J. Hayton, who kept a school at the opposite side of the street, commonly called Hayton's school. He was the translator of the Charter of Bishop Morton from the Latin, dated March 31st, 1634—(Garbutt, appendix, *page 9*). When the chapel was built at Ryhope, he was appointed to the living. The School of Industry occupied the south side of Coronation Street, and facing Sans Street. It was in this school room that the ministers preached whilst Bethel Chapel was building, and in which the Sunday school in connection with the chapel was carried on for years after.

Mr. Butterfint, the miller, had his flour shop between Spring Garden Lane and Walton Place, at that time facing Coxon's fields. At the north end of Walton Place, Joseph and John Doxford had their raff yard and saw pits, at which they worked. Joseph was the grandfather of the present Messrs. Doxford, iron shipbuilders and engineers; he was at one time teacher of the first class in Bethel Sunday school. Nixon, the whitesmith and bellhanger's shop was between Walton Place and Flag Lane, facing the fields. Lee's foundry (lately Glaholm's) stood in the fields at the south side of the street; the west portion of New Grey Street was then being built. Rodney Taylor, the watch and clock maker, had his shop at the head of Walton Lane. Rodney was considered the best and most skilful of his craft in the town.

Between Walton Lane and the back of the houses in Pewterer's Lane was an open garth, afterwards built over by Caleb Wilson, for bonded stores, warehouses, &c.

Between Pewterer's Lane and Queen Street there were three little shops, which still exist. The corner shop at Pewterer's Lane was occupied by Betty Summers and Mrs. Chapman as a small grocer's shop, in which they also sold songs. Betty was the mother of Jeremiah Summers (commonly called "Jerry"), the author of a history of Sunderland—very scarce, but never completed; he lost his sight latterly, and had to be led through the streets, this loss completely preventing him from continuing his work. The middle shop was occupied by *Mr. Browell, joiner and funeral furnisher; Mrs. Browell made and sold candy cushions, "only three for a half-penny." The corner shop at the head of Queen Street was a penny-pie shop, kept by Mrs. Thompson, mother of the late William Thompson, many years foreman for G. W. & W. J. Hall, ship builders and repairers. Some years after the shop was occupied by Mrs. Branfoot, as a grocery shop; I believe she was the widow of a Primitive Methodist minister, and mother of the present Mr. W. Branfoot, of the firm of Tyzack and Branfoot.

At the corner of Moor Street and Coronation Street, was Mr. Robinson, the barber, father of the late W. S. Robinson, solicitor. The second shop above was occupied by Vipond, the painter—this property ran through to Zion Street; and in the south-west corner was an entrance to a common bake-house. The front of Mr. Vipond's shop was most beautifully paved with small stones, and "Vipond" was printed thereon in large letters with light coloured stones; he would never allow the lads to play in front of the shop. The footpath in Coronation Street, opposite the

---

* Father and Mother of the late David Browell, lessee of the ferry boats, Sheriff's officer, and auctioneer.

corner, was somewhat higher than the pavement in front of the shop—this is the same Vipond mentioned as going up in a balloon with Mr. Green. In this block of buildings (which ran from Coronation Street to Zion Street by Moor Street), in the north-west corner of Moor Street and Zion Street, stood the celebrated school conducted by William Robinson, known as Robinson's school; he was left handed, his right arm being short and withered. Samuel Storey, commonly called Sam Storey, who had only one leg, was his usher. At that time Sam wore a wooden leg, but he afterwards got a cork one. It was in this school that Robinson made his money. I remember him giving us a holiday to go and see the "Triumph" launched; she was built by the Brothers Liddle, and Joe Parkin was the managing owner, Robinson having a large share in her. It was while he had this school that he became one of the Superintendents of Bethel Sunday School; he was a regular attendant at Bethel Chapel. I don't think he did so well after he built his new house and school in Nicholson Square.

Below Moor Street stood the shop of Nichol Dale, the hunch-backed jeweller; the back premises ran down to Zion Street, and the apple trees blossomed in his garden. Between Butchers' Lane and the back of Church Street was an open garth used as a bleaching ground for yarns; the market now covers the space. Opposite to this garth, in Coronation Street, was the side or private entrance to the Assembly Rooms, the principal entrance was up a flight of steps facing the Assembly Garth, separated from Church Street by a wall with iron railings on the top. The north and south sides of the garth were houses occupied by old or disabled seamen. The building is now called the Seamen's Hall, Church Street.

The Assembly Hall, at the period of which we write, was the only place in the town suitable for balls and dancing parties. On occasions of large balls, the carriages would drive down the High Street to the side entrance, and return up Coronation Street. There were no cabs in those days; the hackney carriages would be in requisition, so few were they and the expense so great. Then there were the chairs or Sedan chairs,* a kind of high box with a door in front, in which a window was inserted; there was a seat inside on which the occupant sat. At the outside two strong staples were securely fastened on each side of the chair, through which two long poles were inserted; and when the lady had got into the chair, the front closed and the top let down, the bearers—one in front and one behind—would lift the chair, moving gently into the street, and if they had more to wait upon, would move off in a fast walk or gentle trot, whilst a man in front, carrying a link or flambo, lit them on their way (this man was also used as a spare hand ready for a change of bearer) until they set the chair and its occupant down in the passage or ante-room for

---

*From the *Newcastle Daily Chronicle* of February 13th, 1890 :—

"An interesting letter has been sent me from Mr. Henry Elgey, of Bell's Court, whose mother, the last of the Sedan Chair proprietors, died recently.

"He states that his mother's address was, for nearly all her life, in Bell's Court, Pilgrim Street. His father, Mr. Michael Elgey, succeeded his grandfather in the Sedan Chair business, and he estimates that the family carried on the profession of proprietors of that class of vehicle for upwards of a hundred years. The five Sedan Chairs which his father kept were most liberally patronised, and he can recollect in his youth as many as from forty to fifty orders being in for one ball night at the Assembly Rooms in Westgate Road. The chairs were frequently let to Vicar Moody, of the Vicarage, Westgate Road. All the members of the late Richard Grainger's family were, at one time or another, carried to church in them to be christened; and many of the leading families in Newcastle patronised them on baptismal and marriage occasions. When the old Mansion House, in the Close, was in its glory, the Sedan Chair was in its glory too, and the chair-bearers were so well known that they were frequently employed as pall-bearers at the funerals of gentle folks belonging to the district. The men who carried the chairs were generally steady fellows; they wore blue coats with red facing and horn buttons, a tippet or large collar, and a tall hat. From the ends of the poles which ran through the sides of the chair there were generally large horn lanterns suspended, and the whole turn out was about as picturesque as it could well be.

the guests. I have stood—on the occasion of a ball—in Coronation Street watching the company arriving, both in carriages and in chairs, and some with lanterns in their hands. Chairmen were often engaged to convey ladies to and from evening parties. Sedan chairmen and chairs are now considered as things of the past.

FIRE ENGINES.

Sunderland Church stands at the east end, and partially faces Coronation Street. In the large or central porch of the Church the two Manual Fire Engines belonging to the parish were kept, and on the walls numerous leather buckets hung, ready for use.

CHAPTER III.

OUR RIVER.

Of old, our river's mouth at low water spring ebbs extended from the rocks on the north, called the "Beacon Rocks," to the rock ends on the south, or nearly a mile in width.

The high limestone cliffs, running inwards in a south-westerly direction from the holey rocks, formed the river's mouth on the north, whilst the high clay promontory formed the southern boundary. At high spring-tides the waves of the north sea washed up to the basement of both, shewing a broad estuary.

A bar of sand or shingle stretched across the mouth of the river at a distance east of the promontory, and at low tide the widening stream found its way to the sea by different branches or channels over low lying rocks and shingley beds, which appeared as diminutive islands shewing themselves among the running streams until the rising tide again hid them from view.

Inside the bar the haven widened into a broad expanse for nearly a mile up, where it contracted and was confined in a rocky gorge, the entrance to which was about 220 to 240 feet in width, narrowing towards the upper end, and overhung by high limestone cliffs, which terminated at the Wear.

The high clay promontory on the south, standing out towards the sea, was underset by the marl rock and intermixed with the clay; trending westward, it had a sudden depression from Silver Street to Maling's Rig, continuing westward to Bodlewell Lane. At the Exchange this topping of clay is replaced by the limestone ridge which runs through or down by Panns, and the rock from which the the arch of the bridge is sprung, past the jackdaw rock—which overhung the river—and other high rocks up to the Rector's Gill. Passing the ravine it then runs up to Hetton Staiths, where it ends in a bold bluff, turning sideways in a south-westerly direction. The burn emptied itself by the ravine into the river over a shelving rock which jutted a considerable way into the stream and was dry at low water.

On the north the high limestone cliffs, from the holey rock at Roker, trended in a south and south-westerly direction—now hidden from sight by the deposits taken from the North Dock—still shewing itself at Dame Dorothy's Rock on the north side of the dock, and trending westwards again shews itself at Wilson's yard below the bridge—the foundation of the bridge at the north end resting upon it. It then runs up and ends abruptly in a bold rocky cliff at the Sheepfolds, where it checks or snecks the river, turning the outflow of the stream towards the south side (of old, into the Wear), now into a channel of little more than half its previous width over a shelving rock.

The rocks on either side of the river were left dry by the receding tide, and at low spring ebbs the contracted stream ran through a deep rocky gorge 40 feet or more in depth. Seventy years ago the keelmen had to wait till the tide made before they could pass upwards with their keels; they said the gorge was very deep and the long set could not reach the bottom. This was literally a natural run for the fish to pass up towards the higher reaches of the river; there was deep water both above and below the gorge or Wear, wherein the fish could rest.

When the river was in flood it covered all the low lying ground below Hylton, washing the base of Claxheugh Rock, then down to Pallion, Hylton Dene, and over the Salt Grass at Southwick, also covering the Salt Grass at Deptford and Ayre's Quay, shewing a broad and long expanse of water about three miles in length, whilst the fresh water from the upper reaches of the river was still waxing and over-topping the rising tide, which seemed to hold it in check for a time, yet on the return ebb the accumulated waters had to find their way through this narrow contracted part of the river. During the period of great freshes the tide recedes faster than the fresh falls, then the rush of water through this narrow part became greater, so that vessels lying at the Lambton spouts, just below the outlet, have been known to break loose from their moorings, and, drifting down the harbour, coming across other tiers of vessels, dragging them from their moorings and drifting together in a block towards the flat—then a noted shallow part of the river opposite Hardcastle's quay—upon which some vessels grounded, some sank, and were condemned as a total loss, whilst others received more or less damage. At one of these freshes, as noticed elsewhere, the amount of damage done, and the call made upon the capital under-written in the mutual associations was upwards of 8 per cent.; the vessels drifted from the Lambton spouts.

The high rocks on either side of the river had of old evidently extended to the brink of the gorge, and the passage of the waters had been through the rift in the rocks formed by the natural stank or great dam causing the wear, which gives the name to the river or stream. The wear was the only connecting link between the upper and lower parts of the stream, the upper part being called the river, the lower part the haven or harbour.

"In 1358, under the survey of Bishop Hatfield, the said Bishop leased the fisheries in the Wear, and for the right of drawing a net in the Harbour of the said borough, to Thomas Menvill."

In former days the river had been widened above the low water mark at the gill dock by removing a portion of the rocks, so as to enable keels or small vessels to use the higher reaches of the river.*

In recent times the rocks at the gill have been partially removed, the quay line set back, the river widened, its bed deepened; and over the rocks that used to be dry at low water large steamers now load afloat, both above and below the gill dock.†

On the north side, the rocks ‡ at the Sheepfolds were excavated on the lower level to make the shipbuilding yard. The vessels were launched almost straight up the river.

The cliff is hidden from the west view by the ballast hills directly opposite; a road to the river separates the hills from the cliff. The slack of the ground to the north of the cliff has been levelled and filled up to its present state by ashes and other deposits.

The little public house by the side of the road still nestles under, and claims the protection of the cliff, as we remember of old.

---

* After the Hetton Spouts had been erected, and the Company had purchased the "Neptune" tug boat in 1826, they generally had to wait the slack of tide before starting, such was the volume of water rushing through this narrow part, and after they had got one vessel through the tug had to back for the others.

† These later improvements were made when Mr. Murray was engineer.

‡ The caves under the cliffs, formerly used by the shipbuilders as store houses for the workmen's tools, &c. had gates with an open space at the upper part to let in the light; these have been filled up some years ago. A road-way was cut to the lime kilns, and also to the dock above the bridge. The lime kilns, which are now pulled down, were built against the side of the rock.

The quay line here has been altered. The indent in the corner and the ruggedness of the shore is hidden, though there is yet a portion of the rock to be seen in front of the Quay. A substantial corner has been built at the *now* south end of the sneck, at the corner of the Lime Kiln Quay.

In the formation of these limestone cliffs large and deep fissures are here and there to be found; in some of them the antlers of the stag and remains of other wild animals have been fished up.

Just above the wear or stank, between the Sheepfolds and the Wreath Quay, there is a deep pocket; and the quay on which the Wearmouth drops are erected has several times fallen into the river after the dredger has been deepening the loading berths. The rock on which the Wreath Quay is built ends at the corner.

At the Hetton drops the piles and quay walls have also fallen into the river from the same cause; the same has been experienced with some pockets at the Lambton drops.

When the Railway Bridge* had to be erected the same difficulty arose. There was rock both to the east, west and south, but at the place for erection no foundation could be obtained, and cylinders, filled with concrete, had to be sunk to a great depth. Rock was got at about 44 feet below low water.

Close to the entrance of the Graving Dock above the bridge, in Monkwearmouth, a quicksand existed, and the dock always leaked at the entrance. It was only after considerable expense by putting in concrete that the leak was stopped.

---

* Upon searching for foundations for the present Bridge none were to be found within the limits of the space covered by the tide which flowed between rocky shores, distant from each other in the narrowest part about 240 feet.—Garbutt, *page 304.*

The Romans had a station on the river at Chester-le-Street, about eleven or twelve miles from the sea. There can be no doubt that they also occupied the town or village situate on the promontory at the mouth of the river, thus guarding against an attack in the rear of the legions protecting the Roman Wall.

At that period the promontory would stand well out towards the sea and would be a place of some importance, which could be defended by a few soldiers. It would be quite a natural fortress, and unlikely to be over-looked by them; its height would be about 90 or 100 feet. Washed by the waves of the North Sea on the east and south, by the river on the north, and protected by a high cliff on the west, it could only be approached from the south-west. On this promontory the ancient inhabitants found refuge, built their dwellings, and were ready to defend them.

About the year 1810, as some workmen were digging the foundations of a house near the south end of Villiers Street, Dr. R. G. A. Collingwood found a Roman copper coin of the reign of Constantine the Great—upwards of 1,500 years old.

In the month of January, 1849, a most interesting discovery was made in the north-east corner of that portion of the Town Moor formerly known as the Coney Warren. Whilst making the river entrance to the Sunderland Dock it became necessary to remove the workshops of the River Wear Commissioners, and in order to make way for the latter, some old houses, occupying the Pier or Commissioners' Quay, were pulled down,* and under them were found the

---

* This row of two-storied houses was built at the foot and in front of a high bank at or on the north-east corner of the then promontory, facing the river. An old resident of the row describes it thus :—We lived between the hailing house and Joe Humble's boat-building shop; my father kept the public house in the row. At the back of the row was a marl rock, which was a good height, with a clay bank and soil on

remains of what was supposed to have been the site of a Roman Pottery. About eight feet below the surface there appeared a circle, twenty or twenty-five feet in diameter, hewn out of the limestone rock. In the interior of this was a circle of small rubble stones, in arrangement resembling a gin or horse mill, which had apparently been erected for the purpose of grinding clay. Near this place was found a quantity of red and yellow ochre and some broken earthenware, with four perfect specimens of Roman bottles of common unglazed red ware, one of which was presented by Mr. Meik to the Newcastle Antiquarian Society; and another one, very perfect in all respects, was presented by the same gentleman to the Sunderland Museum. The latter specimen is nearly fourteen inches in height; its neck, which is about two inches in diameter at the mouth, is nearly six inches long; and its under part or body, which is round, about eight inches high and seven inches in diameter at the broadest part.

In 1885, while the Commissioners' dredger was deepening the bed of the river in the higher reaches, between Hylton Dene and Park's Nook, the bucket of the dredger brought up, from a depth of eighteen feet below the bed of the river, a Roman sword in a perfect state of preservation. It was found lying on a bed of gravel. In composition it seems to be a kind of bronze.*

---

the top; between the back of the row and the marl rock was a passage the length of the row, entered from the quay by a common way or road through one of the houses; in this passage was a wooden gallery for the tenants occupying the upper parts of the houses. At the east end of this passage was the door to the engineer's garden and back premises of the house, in which was a well and a pump. The garden had a high wall round it; to the west of this wall there was a flight of stone steps which led up to the top of the bank, just a little to the east of Billy Burton's cottage, and west of the stone steps leading down to the pier, and facing the road to the sands.

There is also another row of houses facing the river, from the Long Bank upwards, with their backs to Dean's Yard, where the gallery is used by the occupiers of the upper stories as the only entrance to their rooms; this gallery is entered from the Long Bank.

* Now in the possession of H. H. Wake, Esq., C.E.

Some years ago, as the Commissioners' workmen were removing the rock and other impediments to the navigation at Hylton, they recovered from the bed of the river some finished stone work, amongst which was the key-stone to the arch of a bridge supposed to have been erected at that spot by the Romans during their occupation of the country; the foundation of the bridge on the north side could be distinctly traced. A number of the stones were taken to the shipbuilding yard of J. G. Lister, at Hylton.

It is very remarkable that above the *Wear* this is the only place where a bridge could be conveniently carried across the river; it is narrow here, and flows over a rocky bed. On either side were rocky foundations, with high ground at each end, and a quarry on the spot for the stones.

The road at the south end of the bridge would run up the bank and cross the road from the station at Chester-le-Street, which ran almost in a straight line from that station to the Minor Watch Station on the promontory at the mouth of the river. At the north end the road, after climbing the high ground from the bridge, separated into two roads, one leading to the north-west or north, the other leading north-east to the station at the south-east point on the banks of the Tyne, called the Law, where the remains of a Roman Station were a few years ago laid open to view.

The bridge would either be destroyed by the Romans on their retreat or probably fall by decay, or be destroyed by the natives to prevent the crossing of the river by their enemies—the Scots and Picts. The Monkish historian, who flourished about 200 years after the departure of the Romans, makes no mention of it.

"Constantine the Great was saluted by the legions as Augustus and Emperor, on the 25th July, A.D. 306, at York, which is only about 80 miles south of the river."—Gibbon, *vol. i., chap. 13, page 432.*

61

The Romans retired from their conquests after being occupants for nearly 400 years. The Saxons, who followed them, came as settlers, and made the country their permanent abode.

It was not till a century later—about the year 547 that Ida, the Saxon, conquered Northumberland and the Bishopric of Durham, and peopled the northern counties with his followers. It was during their occupation of the country that they gave the name to our river and called it the Wear, on account of the natural obstacle of rocks forming a dam or stank which caused the *Wear** at the higher part of the Harbour. They also called the ancient town on the promontory—which was high and steep, almost surrounded by water, and unassailable by any petty rover,—Sonderland or Sunderland.

Had Ida, after his conquests, stationed himself at Southwick and looked upon the river towards the setting sun, he would have seen what we have already attempted to describe—a long and broad expanse of water from Claxheugh rock down to the rock upon which the glass-houses at Southwick were built. At low water, the bed of the river for this long and wide stretch would then be 16 or 18 feet below the present bed, *i.e.* before the Com-

---

"The Romans retired from their conquest and bade a final adieu to Britain about the year 448, after being masters of it during the course of nearly four centuries."—Hume, *vol. I., page 11.*

"On the retirement of the Romans, the Britons—being hard pressed by the incursions of the Picts and Scots—invited the Saxons over to assist them. They came over about the year 449 or 450, landed on the island of Thanet with about 1,600 men, and immediately marched to the defence of the Britons against their northern invaders."-

Hume, *vol. I., page 16.*

* Wear or Warr is a Saxon word, which means Stank or Dam in a river fitted for taking Fish or conveying the stream to a mill, pronounced Weer in Durham and Northumberland.

missioners' dredger began to deepen the channel of the river in the higher reaches. As already noticed, between Hylton Dene and Park's Nook the dredger brought up, from the depth of 18 feet below the level, a Roman Sword.

At Park's Nook a ridge of rocks stretches partly across the river (the Commissioners had to blast this rock, which was very hard, in order to get the present depth of water in the channel), and the water would fall over the rocks down upon the gravel bed below; this depth of water would be continued from below Hylton Dene·to the rock at Southwick. At a depth of 20 feet or upwards, the dredger came upon large oak trees which had to be fished up out of the bed of the river, and whose ages told of years long before the Romans held their sway or the Saxons conquered Britain.

Had the conqueror retraced his steps a little and stood on the head of the rock at Cornhill when the river was in flood, he would have looked upon a broad expanse of water, rising up on the south side to the foot of the banks leading up to Hylton Road; and downwards, to the high rock at Hetton Staiths,* from which it rebounded with a sweep to the north, where it was intercepted by the high rocks at the Sheepfolds† that stretched across the river and seemed almost to block the stream, which could only find an outlet by a narrow channel or wear towards the south, where it had been carving its way towards the ocean for ages.

One of these trees was photographed by the late William Morgan Wake where it was landed and then lay—in the yard of the Commissioners, at the South Dock (a copy of

---

* There was no Ayre's Quay, no Deptford, no Ballast Hills, and the floods would then cover the whole space now occupied by these encroachments.

† On the north side there were no Ballast Hills then to hide the rocks at the Sheepfolds from view.

the photograph has been kindly presented to the writer by his son, Mr. H. H. Wake, engineer to the River Wear Commissioners). The dimensions are as follows: 32 feet in length, 5 feet in diameter, and would have contained 485 cubic feet of English oak timber, or rather more than 12 tons in weight. It had not been cut down by the axe or saw, as the long roots of the tree were charred or burnt through as well as part of the trunk. In all probability it had grown on the banks of the river and when it fell had rolled into the stream, which, when in flood, carried it to the place from whence the dredger dislodged it.* It may be called the Druids' Oak.

About the year 1866 or 1867, when Peverall and Harford were erecting the cement works at Hylton, they came upon a paved road underneath the salt grass, then supposed to be of Roman origin, but with the stone bridge which the Romans had built, only half a mile higher up the river, there would be no necessity for a paved road to the ford. I am inclined to think that this road would be of more modern date, some 500 or 600 years after the departure of the Romans—somewhere about the period of the first Barons of Hylton.‡ The road led to the Ford, crossing the river to the landing place directly opposite, commonly called Baron's Quay or the Baron's Quay and landing place. The landing was by the beach at the west of the Quay. The road led from the Ford to the back of Hylton Castle, and the passage of the Ford could only be used at low water; the paved road at the edge of the bank, as found on the south side, would be laid there to make a sure footing for horses and cattle after crossing the stream or

---

*According to its condition when examined it must have lain in the bed of the river some hundreds or thousands of years.

‡ At that time it would be called a Quay. The word "Quay," according to Bailey, means a broad space of ground upon the shore of a River or Harbour, paved for the loading and discharging of goods.

river. The lane from the river side or the Ford leads right up to the Keelmen's Lonnin, passing the farm houses and through the farm yards on its way.

Nearly the whole estate on the south side of the river is called Ford or Ford Hall, &c.

In my early days I have seen cattle and horses and carts crossing the river by the Ford.

On the south side there was a cottage with a garden on the bank side (a little up the lane, not far from the river), in which lived Tommy Minican. Tommy was an old man when I was a boy; he was celebrated for having the largest nose in the county.

The Caunch, which was a little lower down the river, was an island at low water, and was called Minican's Caunch.

The Carcashes on the south side were placed there to train the water into the north channel.

CHAPTER IV.

OUR RIVER IN 1820–1825.

In my time, *i.e.* about 65 or 70 years ago, a loaded collier had many obstacles with which to contend in going to sea, after waiting for a sea tide perhaps some weeks or months—the last obstacle was the bar. The bar was a ridge of sand or gravel washed up by the sea, which the scour of the ebb tides and freshes were not strong enough to wash away, as the sea used to wash the sand round the end of the North Pier, which was dry at low water. From the west end of the North Pier the Potato Garth curved up to the Sand Point. The west part of the Pier was open woodwork, with stones at the bottom to break the seas as they rolled up the harbour.

At some distance above the lighthouse a flight of stone steps adjoined, which led up to the top of the Pier; up these steps the coble men took the line or warp's end, either to make fast to a post or for a hail out to sea. The lower part of the Potato Garth reached down to these steps.

At the north side of the Pier, a short distance west of the lighthouse keeper's cottages, a broad flight of stone steps led down to the Potato Garth.

On the south side of the river, below the Low Coble Slipway, a caunch ran down by the South Pier, almost to the end of it, sweeping round to the north and narrowing the channel, so that vessels, after clearing all obstacles above, would sometimes come to grief here by grounding on the end of the Potato Garth. The channel generally ran close to the Pier from below the stone steps half-way down to the lighthouse, but the washing up of the sand round the end of the Pier formed a curve, which caused the tide to sweep or set towards the South Pier, and ships had to cross from the north to the south in order to get into or keep in the channel, but this depended more or less on the wash-up of the sand or the back scour of the ebb tides and freshes.

From the South Pier a wooden breakwater ran out on this low caunch, filled at the bottom with large stones. Along the top was a narrow width of planking, along which the hailers had often to walk or creep to push the hailing rope over the end of it; the outer end of this breakwater was often damaged by vessels running against it when sailing up the harbour.

Above the Low Coble Slipway, up to the Commissioners' steps in the corner, with a curve towards the hailing house, was a hard rocky bottom, dry at low water. In summer time some of the pilots would moor their cobles here to be in readiness for any vessel that might be expected.

At low spring ebbs the Potato Garth was seen stretching a great distance across the river, leaving only a narrow channel close to the south shore, across which you could wade. I have often seen two or more colliers lying aground on this hard bottom, and almost dry at low water. Under the top layer of gravel and stones the marl and limestone rock stretched right across the river. Through this rock the Commissioners caused a channel to be cut—500 feet in length, 180 feet in width, and $5\frac{1}{2}$ feet in depth; this was in or about the year 1774. Since then the rock has been excavated to a greater depth, the diving-bell having been used for the purpose.

At a short distance above the Commissioners' stone steps, and at the end of the curve almost opposite the hailing house, was piled a high ridge of large stones, running from the Quay to low water mark, to break the force of the waves as they rolled up the harbour; between this ridge of stones and the bottom of Pottery Bank, or Thornhill's wharf, was the Caunch proper; and about half-way up, or the middle of the Caunch, was the High Coble Slipway.

Above the Low Coble Slipway a wooden breakwater was afterwards erected to protect the keels whilst discharging their cargoes—which consisted generally of stones—at the Commissioners' cranes.

The lifting power of the lower crane was by steam, the engine house being erected some distance to the south of the crane; the drum on which the chain wound was fixed outside the engine house; the moving round of the crane was assisted by hand power.

A few yards to the east of the engine house stood Rochester's house; it was a substantial stone building, specially built for the foreman of the pier works and his subordinate. The entrance to the upper story, in which Rochester lived, was up a flight of stone steps.

Rochester's house was the most easterly house in the Parish of Sunderland; it stood south of, and directly opposite to, the Low Coble Slipway. A quay wall was built to the east of the house in order to protect it and the coble slipway from the sea.

Further out, seaward, at the south side of the pier, opposite the low shed, a ridge of stones was deposited at right angles with the pier for the purpose of breaking the waves. Carcashes were afterwards erected opposite Rochester's house, on the east side, for the same purpose.

After the erection of the breakwater for the crane at the Low Coble Slipway, as already named, on the occasion of a heavy sea or high tide all the cobles had to be hauled from the slipway on to the pier, or removed elsewhere, because the rebound of the waves from the breakwater, meeting the advancing waves, rushed up the coble slipway, whilst the rushing wave from the sea, breaking over the breakwater and meeting the wave from the river, completely surrounded the house and washed into the lower apartments; at such times even an entrance to the upper storey could not be effected. The house was at last abandoned as uninhabitable, left to ruins, and ultimately pulled down.

Opposite Hardcastle's Quay and Slipway was the Flat. The deep water channel lay close to the Sand Point, and was really very narrow although the river was broad; if one vessel got aground very few could pass her. It was a common occurrence to see as many as six or eight vessels aground on the Flat. When a pilot saw that the channel was blocked he would generally moor his vessel in a tier. It was usually considered that when a ship got clear of the Flat all danger of her taking the ground was over, but sometimes they were stopped lower down, as previously stated.

From the Folly End on the north side, and opposite the Low Quay, ran a ledge of rock; at spring ebbs it was almost dry to the edge. Over the ledge was deep water, where the revenue cutter used to lie with her pendant streaming to the breeze; one of her guns was fired every evening at sunset. The ledge had a very sharp turn, and vessels going to sea with a fair wind would send the coble with a warp to make fast to the post* on the North Quay Point. If the warp happened to break the vessel ran the chance of doing damage to the tiers; and if sufficient rope was not

---

* For every warp made fast to the post on the North Quay, Sir Hedworth Williamson charged one shilling. No sooner was the warp made fast to the post than his man was alongside of the ship demanding his shilling; pulling his boat from vessel to vessel, demanding and receiving it.

payed out, or the check was too sudden, she stood a chance of grounding on the ledge, and very likely the result would be a broken back to the ship.

The Pann Sands were partially dry at low water, and stretched from Robson's Saw Mills up to the Panns Ferry; it was on these sands where the keelmen generally moored their keels. At the Panns Quay there used to be a man and his boat stationed for the purpose of putting them off and bringing them ashore after mooring their keels, for which the keelmen paid him a certain amount. Sailors and others, who wanted to get on board their ships, had to pay him their half-penny or penny. Loaded vessels coming down the river had often to wait, after warping down so far, until the tide flowed to enable them to proceed over the Panns Sands. These caunches, &c, were some of the obstacles with which loaded vessels had to encounter in proceeding to sea.

Proceeding up the river, we come to the deep water in stotton, which began below the bridge and reached up as far as Wreath Quay. Above stotton was the rack, where the sand at the higher part, opposite the bottle houses, ran down to the Hetton drops and almost crossed the river. On this sand the light vessels used to lie when waiting their turns at the drops; there were also tiers of light colliers laid up here for the winter. At the head of the rack was the wheel, or raven's wheel, from which a low shelving rock* jutted into the river, against and over which the ebb tide swept, making it dangerous for both ships and and keels; the depth of water in front of this shelving rock was about thirty feet. The wheel jutted so far into the river as to cause an eddy tide, which ran up on the north

---

*A portion of this rock or shelf has since been removed by the Commissioners or their engineer, of about forty-five feet in length, and to about nine feet below low water.

shore whilst the ebb tide was running down. Above the wheel, the sand on the salt grass, on the south side, curved almost to the mussel beds under the rocks on the north.

Then there was the sand above the pottery, opposite the lime kilns, and on this sand tiers of colliers were laid up in winter. Above Webster's ropery, up to Featherstonhaugh's bottle-works, was another sand, dry at spring ebbs, and over which the ferry boat could hardly cross at low water; on this sand there were also tiers of colliers laid up during the winter months.

At Featherstonhaugh's Quay there was a hard caunch, and at the west a shelving rock jutted out a long way into the river. Up to and beyond Fatfield were sands and caunches. At the lower part and west end of Pallion Quay an extensive caunch* ran up almost to Minican's, covering a large space in the bed of the river at low water; then came Minican's, caunch, Low Hylton, High Hylton, Head of the Haugh, Coxgreen, Dog-hole and others, with which the keelmen had to contend in going up. On a fine tide they had to wait till the tide flowed before the keel could pass over them.

Now, in the higher reaches of the river trade has almost ceased, consequently the same care and attention has not been given to it. Then, from the Ford at Biddick, downwards, there were "karkishes" or stream conductors placed where necessary, to regulate the ebb current and freshes in order that deeper water might be obtained alongside the staiths where the keels loaded, and also to cause a deeper channel in the curves of the river, so that the keels, when loaded, might pass down; these erections have been allowed to decay, the purpose for their erection having ceased.

---

* This Caunch was used for storing floating timber, and was so secure that it was called "Abraham's bosom."

But, coming to the lower reaches of the river, you see the very great improvements that have been made. Then the Commissioners had two or three keels by which they used to deepen the berths with spoons; the sand and dredge was lifted with a spoon, then put into the keel, and afterwards taken to sea. Afterwards came the first small dredger. The hoppers to receive the dredge were five or six small sailing schooners manned by old seamen, each hopper carrying from sixty to eighty tons. These vessels could only get to sea in fine or moderate weather; if it was a leading wind they sailed out on one tack and back on the other—sometimes the wind failed them and they had to do the best they could.

Now, in the first half-yearly report of the River Wear Commissioners for 1885, there had been 428,590 tons of dredge taken from the river and dock and sent to sea.

Ask an old keelman, and he will tell you there is no "puying" with the set now (puying is a local term, and means pushing with the set); no waiting for the rising tide to get over the caunches; the river is too deep for his long set, and he has to tow up to Hylton.

By dredging from the lower to the upper reaches of the river the influx of water has been so great that the out scour of the river over the bar seems to have swept away the sand to a depth unknown before—practically speaking, the bar has almost ceased to be.

Where the vessels used to lie and take in their cargoes you now sometimes see a solitary one lying. They generally tow up west of the Mark Quay, to get as far as possible out of the range of the surf.

It is a question whether the large volume of trade which was carried on by the colliers from the year 1821 to 1825, could with safety be carried on in this part of the river now. For these years, on an average, 7,823 vessels cleared at the Custom House.

CHAPTER V.

THE MONKS AND MONASTERY OF MONKWEARMOUTH.

About a century after Ida had conquered Northumberland and the Bishopric of Durham, that is about the year 634, a monastery was founded in honour of Peter, prince of the Apostles, at the North Bank and at the mouth of the river Wear, by Benedict or Bennett, surnamed Biscop—Burnett, *page 65*.

In the twenty-fifth year of his age, Benedict abandoned all temporal views and possessions to devote himself wholly to religion; for that purpose, in the year 653, he travelled to Rome, where he acquired a knowledge of ecclesiastical discipline, which, upon his return, he endeavoured to establish in Britain.

In the year 665 he took a second journey to Rome, and after some month's stay in that city he received the tonsure in the monastery of Lerines,* where he lived in strict observance of the monastic discipline for about two years. At this period he again determined to undertake a third pilgrimage to Rome,—that would be 667 or 668—nor was it long before the arrival of a trading vessel enabled him to execute his design.

On this visit Pope Vitalian enjoined him to quit the peregrinations which, for the love of Christ, he had undertaken; to return and conduct to his native country a teacher of divine truth named Theodore, whom it would be in his power to serve as a guide in his travels and an interpreter in the discharge of his pastoral functions.

*A small island on the coast of Provence, now called St. Honore, St. Honoratus, who founded a monastery there towards the close of the fourth century.—Garbutt, *page 40*.

On their arrival at Canterbury, Theodore took possession of the see, and Benedict assumed the government of Saint Peter's Monastery.

Two years afterwards—that is about 669 or 670—he resigned this dignity and undertook a fourth journey to Rome. On this journey he collected a number of books on various subjects, partly by purchase and partly by the gratuitous donations of his acquaintances—

Garbutt, *pages 42 and 43*.

On regaining his native shore he turned his steps to the realm and place of his nativity. On his arrival he addressed himself to Egfrid, king of Northumbria, who listened to his discourse about what he had done, how often he had been to Rome, how he had studied the monastic discipline, and what relics of the Apostles and Martyrs he had brought home, together with a valuable collection of books and other things; and, being moved by the holy man's exertions, assigned him seventy hides of the royal domain, with injunctions to found thereon a monastery dedicated to Peter, the chief of the Apostles. The monastery was accordingly built on the North Bank and at the mouth of the river Wear in 674.

After forming the rules and establishing the discipline of his convent, Benedict determined to make a fifth pilgrimage to Rome; the acquisitions obtained on this journey infinitely surpassed, in number and importance, all the collections he had made on former occasions. He now imported an immense library of books on every branch of learning; a copious present of relics of the Apostles and Martyrs of Jesus, not only for the benefit of his own, but for any of the other British churches (which had not yet bowed the knee to such things); and also an extensive and valuable assortment of holy pictures (Garbutt, *pages 46 & 47*) which were plastered round the roof and walls, so that the sacred edifice presented to the eye one continuous scene of pious instruction, accommodated to the capacities of all who entered, even the humble of the unlettered multitude.

So pleased and charmed was King Egfrid with Benedict's pious zeal that he resolved to augment his original grant by a fresh donation of *forty hides of ground, which addition was accordingly made.—Garbutt, *page 48*.

In the year 682 Benedict built another monastery, at Jarrow, dedicated it to St. Paul, and placed therein seventeen monks, and an abbot named Ceolfrid—these were joint institutions. There were no less than six hundred monks in these two monasteries. –Burnett, *page 66*.

About this time he appointed a presbyter named Easterwine to be joint abbot with himself of the monastery at Wearmouth (Garbutt, *page 52*), soon after which he took his sixth and last journey to Rome. But on this occasion he brought home the life of our Lord Jesus Christ described in one series of paintings, with which he beautified the whole interior of the church annexed to the monastery at Wearmouth, whilst for the new abbey and church of St. Paul's he procured another set, in which was displayed the concordance between the Old and New Testaments.
Garbutt, *page 52*.

On Benedict's return from his last journey to Rome and France he imported two cloaks, woven entirely of silk, and most admirably wrought. In exchange for these he obtained from King Alfrid three hides of land near the mouth of the river Wear, on the south side.†

The last three years of Benedict's life were passed under the pressure of continual sickness—his lower limbs being

---

* 46 hides of land.—Burnett *page 66*.
† Probably the present situation of Sunderland—Burnett, *pages 66 & 67*.

paralyzed, so that he died below whilst he lived above ; the portion of animation left him being barely sufficient to protract a sorrowful existence.

The night destined for his exit, namely, the twelfth day of January, in the sixteenth year after the foundation of the monastery, was ushered in with rude and wintry blast. Sleep is banished from every eye ; the monks throng into the church ; many crowd into the cell where the dying saint is laid in humble expectation of a new and better life. The solemn darkness of the night is spent in watching, psalmody, and prayer.

When his end approaches he receives the viaticum of the sacred body and blood of our Lord. Soon after this consoling act of religion his happy soul, purified from all earthly dross by the chastening flames of long and profitable sufferings, quits the confinement of this mortal frame of clay, and securely wings her flight to the etherial realms of endless peace and immortality[*]

Benedict was supposed to be twenty-five years old when he became of a religious turn of mind. We put it at the time the first monastery was built, in 634 ; it was only a temporary building, consequently, when the foundations of the abbey were laid, in 674, he would be sixty-five years old, and at the time of his death, the twelfth day of January, in the sixteenth year after the foundation of the monastery, would be eighty-one years of age.

The monks seem to have shewn great taste in choosing the site ; it was just within the mouth of the haven, with the open sea, on the east, with a gentle rise from the river

---

[*] Wilcock's translation of Bede's Lives of the Abbots. From the two last paragraphs in the translation we are rather inclined to the common prejudice that during the wars of the elements the Monks were afraid of the devil running off with the Abbot's soul.

on the south and east, and within sight of the high rocky gorge on the west, whilst the high grounds on the north and north-west tended to shelter them from the northern blast.

Could the abbot and monks have made choice of the site on account of the abundant supply of salmon and other fish in the river and on the coast? It could not be on account of the abundant supply of fresh water, for they had to sink a well many fathoms deep in order to obtain that necessary of life.

In my early days this well was the only source of supply for the people of Monkwearmouth-Shore.

BEDE VENERABLE.

In the monastery at Wearmouth Bede spent the greatest part of his life. He published his history in the year 731, when, as he informs us, he was forty-nine years of age; he would, therefore, be born in the year 682, that is the same year of the foundation of the monastery at Jarrow. At the age of seven years (*i.e.* 689) he was brought to the monastery of Wearmouth and committed to the care of Benedict, under whom, and his successor Ceolfrid, he was carefully instructed for twelve years. Benedict died in the year 690, that is one year after Bede entered the monastery; during the remaining eleven years he would be instructed by Ceolfrid and others. At the age of nineteen he became a deacon; and at the age of thirty he was ordained a priest by John of Beverley, Bishop of Halgut-Stad or Hexham, who had formerly been one of his tutors or preceptors.

For some time before his death he had taken up his residence at the monastery at Jarrow[*] In 1020 his remains were translated to Durham, and enclosed in a bag and

---

[*] At which place he died, according to some, (the date appears to be contested) on May 25th, 735, at the age of fifty-three, and his body was interred in the church of the Monastery at Jarrow.

wooden trunk, and deposited in the same shrine as St. Cuthbert—Burnett, *page 72*. His acquirements were real, and the extent of his erudition truly wonderful. He wrote an Ecclesiastical History—from the time of Julius Cæsar to his own time, "a copy of which is in the Cathedral of Durham, six hundred years old."—Burnett, *page 71*. And a great many volumes of church history.

And yet, after giving Bede credit for these attainments and labours in this part of literature, there is the lack in his writings of things appertaining to the general public, something wanting in his every day work, something of the world out of the church.

For instance, there was a village or town at the south side of the harbour, known to have been occupied by the Romans long before the Saxons conquered the country.

After the occupation of the country by the Saxons, there can be no doubt that they named the river the Wear; and the village or town situated on the promontory on the south side, Sunderland, or Sonderlande; this would be upwards of one hundred years before the foundation of the monastery, "surely it must have had a name as well as the river." And yet the ancient scribe, whilst recording the doings of the church, evidently thought this village or town not worthy of being noticed in the records of the monastery; though the probabilities are that the ghostly counsel of the monks would often be called into requisition, to administer to the spiritual necessities of these poor people, who in return would supply the temporal necessities of the monastery.

And now the abbots and monks are all gone, the monastery itself has crumbled into dust, but the village or town on the promontory has continued with its name down to the present day.

CHAPTER VI.

SALMON FISHERIES.

The most ancient commerce carried on upon the river Wear was the salmon Fisheries. The Britons, the Romans, and the Saxons all seem to have had the pleasure or sport of either spearing, netting, or otherwise catching the fish.

The many channels through which the upper waters and the flow and ebb of the tides found their way over the bar into the sea seem to have been tempting to the run of the salmon.

At the upper part of the Harbour there was the great dam or stank forming the Wear, from which the river derives its name.

The entrance to the river at that period was literally a place for taking fish. Both above and below the run of the Wear was deep water; and all the way upwards, to the higher reaches of the river, were large deep pools of water. At one stretch—from the rock which stood out in the stream at Southwick, up to Park's Nook, opposite to Claxheugh, was one long and deep pool, being 18 or 20 feet below the present bed of the river and more than a mile in length, in which the fish could sport or rest before taking the leap at Park's Nook.*

The long salt grasses and other vegetation that grew upon the low lying grounds of this large expanse of water served to screen the fish, and also as a feeding ground. The

---

* Park's Nook was a ledge of rock running from the north side nearly half-way across the river; through this the Commissioners have made the channel by blasting the rock. The sand or gravel of the ancient bed of the river was eighteen feet below the level of the rock or nook.

inlet at Hylton dene, running up the foot of the castle, used to be a place for catching trout in my early days. In the higher reaches of the river there was, here and there, deep water; and the overhanging bank served as a hiding place for the fish. Where the ruins of the abbey of Finchale now stand, on the banks of the river, also tells us that the monks who built it had in view the food that could be extracted from the river. The stream at this place, running amidst rocks and boulder stones up to the end of Kepier woods, was a natural run for salmon.

And going upwards and onwards, passing the old shrine of St. Cuthbert, whose prior, as will appear in the sequel, at a more recent date had to pay for the privilege of his yare at Durham, to catch the fish in order to serve the necessities of the monastery over which he presided.

The river almost seems to have had a peculiar sanctity attached to it, as providing food for the necessities of the monks for their fast days, etc.; for there were three abbeys erected on its banks close to the stream. There was the abbey at Wearmouth, the abbey at Durham, and midway between the two, the abbey at Finchale; all within thirteen or fourteen miles from the sea, or from the river's mouth, without taking into account several minor establishments at Bishopwearmouth, the religious house at Offerton,[*] and others, whose names have passed into oblivion.

In those days there can be no doubt that the river was free. The monks caught all the salmon that they required, and the sparse population or inhabitants also helped themselves to the fish; this freedom continued for hundreds of years after the foundation of the abbey at Wearmouth.

---

[*] Some years ago part of the ruins could be traced. On a large stone in the wall "1031" were cut in figures. What of its history?

It was not till the Bishop claimed the river and all the fish that swam therein that this common right was disputed or invaded, and he (Bishop Hatfield) then sold or leased this right for his own private benefit at a sum of twenty pounds a year; and these leases continued to be renewed, or other-otherwise, from time to time for the space of about three hundred years. In this Act the Bishop, under his princely authority, usurped the common right—the right of private individuals, also the right of the monks attached to the monasteries as to fishing; this would be about the year 1358. This was rather hard lines for the monks, as they had a settlement in the monasteries long before the Bishop had place; and rather hard upon the commons, whose forefathers had held the land long before Christianity was established. But it should be remembered that a Bishop was a Bishop, and a prince in the land.

So far back as the year 1358, *i.e.* nearly seven hundred years after the foundation of the monastery at Wearmouth, it is recorded that Bishop Hatfield leased the borough of Sunderland, with the fisheries and wolton-yare, to Richard Hedworth, of Southwick or Suddick, for twenty years, under twenty pounds rent; this Richard Hedworth died in 1376, and was succeeded by Sir John Hedworth, who was knighted by Henry I., in 1434. Under the survey of the same Bishop, Thomas Menvill held the borough with the same rents, worth 32/8, the fisheries in the wear, the borough court, the tolls, and the stallage, with eight yares belonging to the Bishop; and eight shillings rent from the prior of Durham for Ebyare, and eight shillings from John Hedworth for his yare—called Owen's yare, and for the right of drawing a net in the Harbour of the said borough.*

---

* "At the same time Menvill held a place called Hynden for the plying of vessels."—Garbutt, *page 126*.

In 1464 Edward IV. granted the borough, with the passage of the river and the fisheries, to Robert Bartram during the vacancy of the see, and the king engaged to provide his lease with a ferry boat.

In 1507—1508, Sir John Hedworth obtained a license from Bishop Bainbrigg to alien his fisheries to trustees. This Sir John Hedworth died in 1564.

In 1590 Bishop Hutton leased the borough, the ferry boats and the fisheries to Ralph Bowes, of Barnes, esquire, under four pounds rent, in as ample a manner as his grandfather, Sir Ralph Bowes, knight, occupied the same.

In 1606–1617, in Bishop James' time, Richard Hedworth (commonly called John of the deanery) had special livery of the manor of Southwick, which means delivery of lands, etc. to him who has a right to them.

In 1630, April 30th, Richard Hedworth sold to G. Grey his fisheries in the Wear. It is rather singular that two hundred and seventy-two years after Bishop Hatfield's lease, in 1358, a lineal descendant of the same family and of the same name should, in 1630, be possessed of these fisheries in fee.

June, 1647—The fisheries are mentioned in a marriage settlement between Grey and his son, and are called fisheries or yares. In a deed of 1667 they are again mentioned, and also in a deed dated June 18th, 1683. On December 1st, 1809, the fisheries were sold to J. Brunton, and mentioned in a deed of that date. In 1849 they were sold to the late Mr. Thomas Pratt, and are now in the possession of his son, Mr. W. D. Pratt.

One station for the fisheries was at Perilou's haugh, that is opposite to the present Cornhill graving dock and the beach, upwards; the other station was in Pallion reach. Both stations show where the swift tide left a clean stoney bottom.

These leases, as before named, covering centuries, tend to prove that an extensive trade must have been carried on continuously in these fisheries, and that the grants or leases of the monopoly were sought after by men of high standing and repute, even by knights of the shire.

No doubt the fisheries were very productive, and salmon were caught in very large quantities in the river, and became so plentiful and so cheap that the masters used to feed their apprentices on it so as to surfeit them; accordingly a clause was inserted in the indenture of apprenticeship that the apprentice was not to be fed on salmon more than two or three days per week.

Hutchinson, in his history of Northumberland, says salmon was formerly so plentiful in the Tyne that the apprentices covenanted in their indentures not to be fed with it more than twice a week. To show the supply—at Newburn, in 1761, two hundred and sixty salmon were caught at a draught; in 1775, two hundred and sixty-five salmon were caught at a draught at the Low Lights; and in the same year salmon were sold in Newcastle at 1d. and 1½d. per pound.

Brand's history of Newcastle contains the same statement as to salmon takes.

These indentures have become very rare of late, and people have been led to disbelieve in their existence, and to treat the whole as a tale or a myth; amongst these was the late Frank Buckland, who stated that he could not find a copy.

In the *Fish Trades' Gazette*, April 4th, 1885, appears the following:

"In the last number of the *Fish Trades' Gazette* it is stated that the late Frank Buckland was unable to find a copy of an indenture stipulating for the non-provision of salmon more than thrice a week. Had I known that, I could have shown him one in Mr. Taylor Potts' (timber merchant,) office, Sunderland. I have no doubt Mr. T. Potts will know of others on the Tyneside where such stipulations were also entered upon."

The indenture was in my possession, and the writer of the article, no doubt, saw it whilst it was in my custody; the salmon clause was printed or engraved in the body of the indenture, so that every copy taken from the plate must have the clause in it. Indentures at that date could only be had from the government stamp office.* The one referred to in my possession was on parchment, stamped with the government seal and the amount of duty payable on it. The indenture was sent for my perusal by an old person, through my foreman sailmaker, who also intimated that I could keep it if I wished; if not, it had to be returned, and the sender's name kept secret.

I did not, at that time, think it worth much, and returned it with thanks for the perusal. When the foregoing appeared in the *Fish Trades' Gazette* I immediately set about trying to find out the party who had sent me the indenture for perusal; meanwhile my foreman had died, and he had kept the name of the party to whom the document belonged so secret that neither his wife nor any other person could give me the least information on the matter. That the indenture was in my offices and in my possession is as sure as I am writing this. This indenture was one belonging to Sunderland.

The writer of the article also says: "I have no doubt Mr. T. Potts will know of others on the Tyneside where such stipulations were also entered upon." At that time I did not know of any such.

On September 4th, 1885, I was at South Shields, on a visit to my son, in company with Mr. Henry Briggs and others, and having related the foregoing circumstance in conversation, Mr. Briggs said: "That is very singular, I

---

* I expect that there must have been some local Act passed for these districts in reference to this clause, or why should the government issue or sell these indentures through the stamp office containing it.

was looking over some old papers and parchments not long ago, which had belonged to an old lady, and amongst them I found an indenture on parchment duly stamped and sealed, which contained a clause to the effect that the apprentice should not have salmon more than two or three times per week." He was not quite certain whether it was two or three; he referred to Mrs. Briggs, who was in the room, and she said: "he (Mr. Briggs) read it out to me, and I was surprised that they did not like salmon."

I asked him if it was a Sunderland indenture, he said: "No, it was a Newcastle one." Being asked how long it was since he had it, he said it was certainly within twelve months; referring to the date when these papers and documents came into his possession, he also said that several of the pieces of parchment had been cut up for labels on the other side, but neither Mr. nor Mrs. Briggs could tell what had become of the said indenture, they were afraid it had either been cut up or burnt amongst some other papers. They afterwards tried to find it, but were not successful.

Evidently what had been at one period a large and profitable industry, at the present day is almost extinct. It has been said that lately, in the upper reaches of the river, some fine fish have been caught.

Some years ago—from 1854 to 1860—when the stake nets were set up on Roker sands, and the fisherman with his wife and "bairns" were located in a hut close by, some very fine fish were caught. My boys, when down on the sands in the early morning, have bought and carried home a fine salmon just taken out of the nets. At the stake nets on Whitburn sands some fine salmon were often caught.

Some time ago some Tyne salmon fishers were caught fishing in the Wear district and were fined.

One of my keelmen, taking a raft of timber up the river in the early morning, was nearly frightened out of his wits; whilst pulling the boat he received a heavy blow on his face which nearly knocked him off his seat; when he recovered he saw a large salmon trout lying in the bottom of the boat, which he secured and brought down to the office. I bought the fish, which weighed nearly four pounds.

For the decrease of salmon in the river several causes are attributed, viz.:—The outlet of the sewers from the towns on the banks of the river into the stream; the refuse and impurities from the then ever increasing colliery workings; also the discharge of the refuse and impurities from the chemical works erected on the banks of the river or in close proximity thereto were some of the causes, no doubt, tending to drive the fish from the river, and to poison the young after a brief existence in the stream. But the principal cause was commerce. Fish and commerce can hardly be said to occupy the same stream.

At the latter end of the reign of Elizabeth or the early part of the reign of James I., or from about the year 1600, the coal trade found its way into the Wear. The commerce that then began to be carried on was found to be subversive to the salmon fisheries; with the increase of trade on the river the fisheries began to be unproductive, and therefore not of the same value as heretofore. In Bishop James' time, between the years 1606 and 1617, they were sold by special livery to Richard Hedworth. And on April 30th, 1630, were re-sold by Hedworth to G. Grey—the name was there but the trade had ceased to exist.

Account must also be taken of the means by which this increase of commerce was carried on, especially in more recent times. The hundreds of keels and boats plying night and day on the river, the digging and the drawing of the sets and the splash of the oars, besides the large amount of shipping constantly occupying the harbour, and also the quantity of ballast that was constantly, though surreptitiously, deposited or thrown into the deep pools in the upper reaches of the river from the ballast keels, levelling up, so to speak, the bed of the river; by such practices little or no space was left for the fish, they were frightened out of their old haunts and then deserted the stream.

Seventy years ago, when I was a boy sitting at my grandfather's fireside on a Saturday night, where the ballast keelmen used to assemble to share the week's earnings, if the weather had been stormy and ships were waiting for the ballast keels, they used to say that they had been up to Robert Reay's at Hylton, discharging. No doubt they had started with the object of going, but as soon as they were shrouded by the darkness of the night on the broad river the keel was left to drift, and the ballast was quietly dropped over the keel's side into the river, and they never got to Robert Reay's at all.

Last year (1890), I asked an old keelman how it was, about seventy years ago, so many ballast keels used to start, when loaded, with the intention of discharging at Robert Reay's, at Hylton, where there was little or no ballast landed? He laughed, and said: "If all the ballast had been landed at Robert Reay's that was supposed to be, my word, what a ballast hill there would have been! nothing like it about the river."

This was another cause of the fish deserting the stream, namely, levelling up the pools which had been in existence for generations.

CHAPTER VII.

SHIP BUILDING.

Ship building has been the staple trade of the Port of Sunderland for generations.

During the latter half of the last, and the early part of the present century, ship building establishments were not of large proportions. On the river side they were seen, dotted here and there, the builders living in close proximity to their yards.

The following names were amongst the shipbuilders of the last century, viz.:

    Thomas Tiffin the elder, who built in Sunderland.
    Thomas Nicholson, who built in Bishopwearmouth-Panns.
    Mr. Burn, Old Jackdaw Dock, Bishopwearmouth.
    Mr. Heward, at Deptford.
    Harry Rudd, at Pallion.
    William Potts, at South Hylton.
    Mr. Reay, at North Hylton.
    Mr. Havelock, at Southwick.
    Messrs. John and Philip Laing, at Monkwearmouth-Shore.

The vessels they built were generally of small dimensions, though large enough for the then capacity of the port.

In 1786 the average size of the vessels belonging the Port of Sunderland was $134\frac{202}{387}$ tons, or from 134 to 135 tons, and in 1799 the average was $150\frac{9}{100}$ tons.

Vessels of larger tonnage and dimensions were built for other ports.

"On March 2nd, 1798, there was launched from the Southwick Quay the ship "Lord Duncan," admeasuring 925 tons—the largest vessel ever built within the limits of the Port of Sunderland."—*Garbutt.*

THOMAS TIFFIN

Built on the yard at the east of the Pottery Bank and to the east of Thornhill's wharf, launching the ships across the road and over the caunch; he lived in a double three storied house, which had large round pillars on each side of the doorway. The house stood, and still stands, below the Pottery Buildings on the north, and on the east side of the bank; the large gates at the entrance of the yard at the upper end were next to the house. Young Tom said: "I was born in that house in 1800, and my father built in that yard years before I was born."

Old Mr. Tiffin used to boast that he bought the first parcel of American elm (about sixteen loads) ever brought into the port, *i.e.* in 1818, when the low yard was at work.

In 1819 the business was removed to a yard in the Rack, a little to the east of the Ayre's Quay Bottle Company's works, afterwards to the yard at the Sheepfolds. His sons, Tom and Ben, carried on the business after their father retired, in a yard purchased from the Dean and Chapter in 1836, on the north side of the Rack below Raven's Wheel, and to the south-west of the colliery.

In 1819 Mr. Tiffin removed to a house in Queen Street, with its back to Pewterer's Lane; between the house and the lane there was a garden where flowers and apple trees grew and blossomed. He afterwards removed to a new house in Tavistock Place (then considered a grand part of the town), where he died on January 16th, 1855, aged eighty-eight years; his son Tom died May 9th, 1884, aged eighty-four years.

THOMAS NICHOLSON

Had his shipbuilding yard and graving docks in Bishopwearmouth-Panns, they were known as Nicholson's docks. Mr. Nicholson lived in the large double three-storied house in Panns, standing a short distance back from the line of street, with railings in front and stone steps up to the doorway, on each side of which were round pillars; the house almost faced the gates of the shipbuilding yard and docks.

In 1798 Mr. Nicholson bought the large house at the south-east corner of the Green from Teasdale Mowbray, and removed from the Panns to the house on the Green. In the year 1799 Mr. Nicholson obtained permission to enclose the Green under certain specified conditions. See "grant de novo."

MR. BURN

Used to occupy the jackdaw dock, situate above the bridge and east of the jackdaw rock. On part of the quay front, with the rock on the west, were the bottleworks. The dock partly angled between the bottleworks and the high rock on the south. As the trade of the port increased (a larger class of vessels frequenting it) the dock was found to be too small and shallow, and there being no room for deepening and enlarging it, and the whole premises being much out of order, the dock was laid in and filled up. The bottle company then extended their works and built another cone and warehouses on the site.* Mr. Burn had also a shipbuilding yard higher up the river, above the staiths erected and belonging to the Hon. Archibald Cochran and Company, now the Hetton Coal Company, who afterwards required the ground for the erection of coal drops and other purposes; the shipbuilding plant was consequently sold, and Mr. Burn retired from the shipbuilding trade.

MR. HEWARD

Built at Deptford and lived in the house close to the yard; he was the father of old Ben Heward. Mr. Philip Laing afterwards acquired the property, in 1818.

---

* To the east of the dock gates and under the shelter of the overhanging rock to the west of the bridge was a little public house. A long flight of wooden steps led from the yard to the higher ground above.

HARRY RUDD

Built on Goodchild's ground at Pallion, just to the west of the boundary wall separating Deptford from Pallion; a five barred gate crossed the road. Mr. Rudd lived in the house at the head of the yard. Old Luke Crone served his apprenticeship with Mr. Rudd between the years 1790 and 1800.

WILLIAM POTTS,

Of South Hylton, built on the yard just below the Ferryboat Landing; the yard adjoined the landing. He lived in a house going down the bank to the yard and ferry. William Potts the elder died May 2nd, 1798, aged sixty-three years.

He left a will bequeathing the business to his two sons, William and Edward, enjoining them therein to carry on the business in partnership, and not to separate for a certain number of years, so that William and Edward Potts were in business in May, 1798. After the time had elapsed the brothers separated, and Edward laid out the shipbuilding yard below the pottery at the lower part of Hylton. The double two-storied house on the left hand side of the road going down to the ferry was built for Mr. Edward Potts, and was afterwards occupied by Dawson, the potter.

William Potts retained possession of the yard next to the ferry between the years 1807 and 1812; he removed from this yard to the one in the Low Street, which he purchased from the Russell family (it had previously been a raff yard). He also purchased the property opposite the yard in the Low Street, including the large three-storied house in which Colonel John Lilburn was born. There was a pump in the yard at the back of the house. He died on August 18th, 1852, aged seventy-eight years. The late Mr. R. H. Potts was of the third generation of shipbuilders, and was the representative of one of the oldest shipbuilding families on the Wear or Port of Sunderland, having been shipbuilders for over a century.

MR. REAY.

Built at North Hylton on the high end of the quay and south-west of the pottery; he lived in the double house just outside the yard, facing south, and which had a garden in front. The house was afterwards occupied by Mr. Austin the potter, and latterly by the late Mr. Ettrick. Mr. Reay married the sister of William Potts the elder; after Mr. Reay's death the widow carried on the business, her brother William, then a young man, acting as foreman and partly manager. When he left to commence business on his own account, at South Hylton, he recommended Neddie Brown, who had been working in the yard as a carpenter, to be the foreman. The late Robert Reay, who was only a young lad, when his father died, afterwards carried on the yard with Neddie Brown as foreman, and made a good deal of money. Mr. Reay afterwards bought the estate at Hylton and removed the shipbuilding yard down to the flat below the carriage road to Newcastle, which ran north through the estate; he also built the large house or hall on the estate, known as Hylton Grange, afterwards the property of George Hudson. (Squire Reay was never married.)

Neddie Brown, afterwards known as "Old Neddie," occupied the yard vacated by Robert Reay, and lived in the public house in the road north of the pottery, close to the yard.

Mr. Reay's is the oldest firm of shipbuilders we have been able to trace, and goes far back into the last century.

As we have related, William Potts the elder, who died in 1798, aged sixty-three years, went, when a young man, to be foreman for his sister, the widow of Mr. Reay.

MR. HAVELOCK

Built on the yard at Southwick, and lived in the double two-storied house in the yard. Two pear trees grew in front of the house or in the village near by. He afterwards removed to Ford Hall, and on retiring from business went to live in the south of England. The ship "Lord Duncan," the largest vessel ever built in the Port of Sunderland, was launched by Mr. Havelock from the Southwick yard on March 2nd, 1798.

JOHN AND PHILIP LAING.

John Laing built in the north-west corner of the North Sands. The yard is now occupied by the Strand Slipway Company.

In the year 1793 his brother Philip joined him, and the firm became John and Philip Laing.

In 1804 John and Philip Laing opened the bridge graving dock, Monkwearmouth, and carried on business there till 1818, when probably the lease expired. The partnership between the brothers was dissolved.

In the same year (1818) Mr. John Laing* occupied the yard at Southwick, previously tenanted by Mr. Havelock; and Philip Laing† bought the property at Deptford, and lived at Deptford House, the back of which looked on to the shipbuilding yard; the office being on the ground floor at the back and facing the yard. Deptford house was pulled down some years ago by Mr. James Laing‡ to make more space for iron shipbuilding. Previous to pulling it down a drawing was taken of the old house, and I think it now hangs in his office.

---

* John Laing built the house known as the Grange, Monkwearmouth, in which the late George Hudson died.

† Philip Laing married Miss Rudd, of Red House or Redby House, for his first wife, and lived in the large house at the corner of Broad Street and Church Street, Monkwearmouth, not far from the yard.

‡ Should Mr. James Laing live till 1893, then father and son will have carried on shipbuilding for a century.

The late Thomas Ogden served his apprenticeship with John and Philip Laing whilst they occupied the yard above the bridge, from 1804 to 1818. One day when Ogden had received his wages—a one pound note—and was coming along the bridge with the note in his hand, a gust of wind blew it over the bridge, when it fell into the river and was lost. Thomas was sore distressed at his loss, and told his father on his arrival at home; his father said: "never mind, Thomas, never mind," and quoted some lines of poetry from Dryden. (This was told the writer by Mr. J. M. Ogden, June 29th, 1890.)

The late James Allison also served his apprenticeship with John and Philip Laing in this yard. The yard used to be called "the gentlemen carpenter's yard," so many gentlemen carpenters having served their time with them.

At the close of the last, and the commencement of the present century, the shipbuilding trade seems to have been in a flourishing condition, for—irrespective of the annual losses by wreckage, together with the capture of vessels during the war and the sale of vessels to other ports—we find that there was an increase to the registry of the port in three years of fifty-eight vessels, with an aggregate tonnage of 9,181 tons, or an average of 158 tons per vessel. Thus, on September 30th, 1798, there were 460 vessels of 70,614 tons registered, and on September 30th, 1801, there were 518 vessels of 79,795 tons registered, shewing an increase of 58 vessels of 9,181 tons in three years.

From the year 1801 to 1815 shipbuilding establishments had increased from nine to fifteen, or upwards of fifty per cent. in fifteen years.

Burnett writes: "During the war orders were received from all parts of the kingdom for ships, and large profits were made by the builders; the builders then in business generally made their fortunes."

The cost price of a collier during this period was from £14 to £15 per ton.

The "Pomona," a collier of one hundred and ninety-seven tons, was built in 1814, and cost the owners £2,800, or about £14 4s. per ton.

Carpenters' wages at that period were four shillings and sixpence per day; working hours: from six in the morning till six at night, with half-an-hour allowed for breakfast and one hour for dinner.

The blocking up of the north channel, and the building of the North Pier in 1786, caused the formation of a high bank of sand and gravel, stretching from the pier to Roker, and enclosing in the harbour the whole of what previously was the sea beach—from Roker to the Strand. This stretch of ground was immediately utilized and made into ship-building and timber yards by the Williamsons; even the sand bank, formed between the Pier and Roker, was made into shipbuilding yards (one of which was occupied by James Leithead), and the vessels were launched over the Potato Garth into the harbour, or eastward into the sea, behind the North Pier.*

Prior to 1830 the whole of the ground from Roker to the Strand was occupied, and the North Sands became a noted place for shipbuilding, which character it still maintains.

In 1815, after the close of the war, trade fell into a stagnant condition, which continued for several years. The register tonnage of the port kept decreasing, for whereas in 1815 the number of vessels was 613, and the registered tonnage 90,270, in 1822 the number of vessels was 551, and the registered tonnage 80,139, shewing a total of 62

---

* On the occasion of a very high tide and heavy sea I have known the timber and planks to be washed over the yard into the harbour, and the vessel left standing on the stocks.

vessels and 10,131 tons less in 1822 than in 1815. So dull was the trade that shipbuilders left off building on speculation and would only build on contract. A great many carpenters were, consequently, thrown out of employment, the want of work causing great distress; in order to lessen the distress as much as possible, the carpenters' union resolved to commence shipbuilding, so as to give work to as many men as they could employ in their yard, and for this purpose took and entered into possession of the yard then lately vacated by Thomas Tiffin in 1819, managers being appointed to conduct and carry on the business.

With an improved trade in 1822 and 1823, shipowners were induced to come into the market to replenish their stock, As the demand increased the prices of vessels kept rising, and other things required for the shipbuilding trade also kept rising, as will be seen by the prices paid for new vessels from 1823 to 1825, thus—

In 1823—"Windsor Castle," 219 tons, cost £2,542, or £11 12s. per ton.
In 1824—"Osprey,"   224 ,,   ,, £2,685, or £12 0s. ,,
In 1825—"Blackbird,"   194 ,,   ,, £2,581, or £13 6s. ,,
In 1825—"Seaham,"   261 ,,   ,, £3,514, or £13 9s. ,,
*In 1825—A large vessel   349 ,,   ,, £5,050, or £14 9s. 4d ,,

Shewing an increase in the price of a collier of £1 17s. per ton, or sixteen per cent. advance in three years.

An increased demand, with better prices, stimulated shipbuilding; old yards were full of work and new yards were opened.† One set of men commenced building small vessels on the high ground east of the barracks, and launched them over the bank, down the road between the battery and the life-boat house, into the sea. Another set built a vessel

---

* Belonging to Messrs. Horn & Scott.

† The shipbuilding yards, from 1815 to 1830, had more than doubled in number. In the former year there were fifteen, in the latter there were upwards of thirty.

in a yard in Nile Street, and launched her down the High Street and Bodlewell Lane to the ferry-boat landing.*

Burnett says of her:—

"She went to London and was sold to go to the West Indies; her crew consisted of four men; she was to proceed to Jamaica in tow of a West India ship. On their passage a violent storm overtook them, and she was separated from the ship; the sailors were afraid they would not weather-out the storm in so small a vessel. The storm increased; they thought the heavy seas would destroy their little craft; they could not stand upon the deck any longer; they retired below, and made all as right as circumstances would admit; they closed up the hatches, leaving the ship to drive before the wind. In this state they were for five days, unable to make a fire on, living on biscuits and water, and expecting every moment to be engulphed in the mighty ocean. On the sixth day the storm abated; when they came on deck and made an observation they found the ship had been sailing a direct course for the West Indies. They arrived safe. About three weeks after the West Indiaman arrived, and told the merchant that he doubted his little companion had perished. "Nay," says the merchant, "they have been here three weeks." The captain could hardly believe the matter to be true. The master and mate of this little vessel were Sunderland men."

Pages 141 and 142

William Walker was captain, afterwards wharfinger at Holmes' wharf.

The managers of the union yard separated from the union and each commenced shipbuilding on his own account, and a great amount of activity was displayed in the yards, so that the supply soon overtook, and proved to be greater than the demand, thus causing a heavy fall in the prices; and a collier which cost £13 or £13 10s. per ton in 1825 could be bought for £9 or £9 10s. per ton in 1829 and 1830, thus

In 1829—"Jane," 202 tons, cost £1,925, or £9 10s. 7d. per ton.
In 1830—"Neva," 230 ,, ,, £2,225, or £9 13s. 6d. ,,
In 1830—"Castle Eden," 221 ,, ,, £2,025, or £9 3s. 3d. ,,

* This vessel, of fifteen tons, the writer saw building, and also the launching of her down the High Street.

Shewing the reduced price of a collier in the space of five years, *i.e.* from 1825 to 1830, of £4 5s. 9d. per ton, or a fall of twenty-nine per cent. from 1825 to 1829, and of thirty per cent. from 1825 to 1830.

In 1833 a select committee of the House of Commons was appointed to take evidence on manufacturers' commerce and shipping, from which report we quote the evidence of Mr. Henry Tanner, of Sunderland, 10th July, 1833 :—

QUESTION.

6601—How long has there been this great depreciation in the value of shipping property ? *Answer*—It has been going on for a good many years now. There is a very great difference in the price of ships and in the build of them ; there are some ships built and fitted now at a very low sum indeed ; others are built at a very extravagant rate.

6602—What do you pay per ton for a ship in the coal trade ? *A.*—It depends upon the the nature of the ship and the construction of her. For the coasting trade I can now get a ship built and fitted for sea for about £9 per ton, all complete for the coasting trade.

6603—Is not there a great deal of shipbuilding carried on at Sunderland ? *A.*—There is.

6604—Do not people come from other parts to purchase ships at Sunderland ? *A.*—From all parts : from Scotland, from London, from Liverpool, and from Ireland.

6605—In fact, are not ships built at Sunderland cheaper than at most other ports ? *A.*—They are.

6606—Are the ships built at Sunderland generally sold for money ? *A.*—For money or bills, not sold by barter now. There used to be a great deal of the bartering trade ; a man would sell a ship for part rope, part chains, and part canvas, and so forth, but now they are principally sold for money or bills.

6607—Do you know what a vessel would cost fitted for a voyage for the East Indies without copper ? *A.*—I should think from £13 to £14 a ton. A ship was sold a week ago, under bankruptcy, at £9 a ton for the hull complete, and she would cost from £4 to £4 10s. for the outfit.

QUESTION.

6608—Do you include copper? *A.*—No, she was regularly copper-fastened, but not copper bottomed.

6648—Has there been much shipbuilding going on in Sunderland lately? *A.*—A great deal.

6649—Within the last five or six years has shipbuilding in Sunderland increased a good deal? *A.*—It has; there are very few built upon contract; they are mostly built for the market upon speculation.

6650—Are they built entirely for the trade of the port? *A.*—No.

6651—But they find purchasers when they are built? *A.*—They endeavour to do so; many of them lay a good while before they are sold, and many of them are sold under very disadvantageous circumstances from necessity.

6652—But they still go on building them? *A.*—Yes, to a great extent.

6653—And, of course, they are bought at last? *A.*—They are, certainly; we perhaps have vessels lying six months after they are launched before they are sold.

6654—Do you think that people would go on building them if they were constantly losing by them? *A.*—I would not do it myself.

6655—Have you known instances of it? *A.*—I have known many instances of it; it was the occasion of a very heavy failure with us six months ago; a gentleman goes on building and building, till at last he can go on no longer, and he fails, and pays 2/- or 2/6 in the pound.

6656—And somebody else comes in and takes his place? *A.*—Somebody else steps into his shoes.

6657—What number of shipbuilding yards are there at Sunderland? *A.*—Every place where they can build a ship, almost, is a yard.

6749—Is it not a fact that out of thirty-four shipbuilding establishments on both sides of the Wear nineteen have been set up since the peace? *A.*—I should think there are more than thirty-four now, because there are a great number of carpenters' building yards that never had been a building place before; they cannot be called regular building yards, but temporary ones; I do not think there are more than fifteen regular establishments for shipbuilding yards.

QUESTION.

6658—Have many people gone into the shipbuilding trade during the last five or six years in Sunderland? *A.*—I think not many, except some of the ship carpenters who, in order to make more wages, have joined together to build ships, and get a timber merchant to supply them with timber; and when they get the ship sold they pay the timber merchant, if there is sufficient to pay him with, and if not he takes what he can get.

6755—Is the smaller description of shipbuilders, consisting of carpenters that club together, of very recent growth? *A.*—Within the last half-a-dozen years, I should think.

6757—Do they generally build at lower prices? *A.*—They do; they build to make their own wages, if they get a little addition to the wages they would get in the yards; if they can sell the ship they will do so at a low price.

6758—Have men who have embarked in that line generally flourished? *A.*—There are some of them that are still going on, and some of them decline.

6760—But they do, in fact, undersell the large shipbuilders? *A.*—Yes; I do not say that they will build such good ships, but they will sell at a lower price.

6766—When the carpenters commenced building ships on their own account was there a scarcity of work at the time? *A.*—I do not know that there was, but they get into those unions (which have been prevalent all over the kingdom, I believe), and they did not work, probably, to please their masters, and they might discharge them perhaps.

6767—Do you consider that they get better wages by pursuing this business than they did by working for their masters? *A.*—I consider that it was under that expectation that they began to build.

6773—To what do you attribute the advantage which Sunderland seems to enjoy over the other shipbuilding places? *A.*—I can hardly answer that; but it seems to be the only place for shipbuilding at present.

6777—Are you aware that when a ship is contracted for a quarter part of the value is always advanced to the builder? *A.*—Yes, I am aware that it is usual to make payments as the ship advances in her building, consequently the shipbuilder does not require much capital.

QUESTION.

6778—If capital is not necessary in shipbuilding is it anything remarkable that clever men, who have been labouring carpenters themselves, should start in business, to build ships, though not provided with much capital? *A.*—That accounts for the great number of ships built at Sunderland.

6750—Are you acquainted with the rate of wages of shipwrights and carpenters? *A.*—I believe it is four shillings a day.

6751—Do you know whether they have declined since the termination of the war? *A.*—Very little, not exceeding sixpence a day, I think.

6780—What is the usual credit given for the purchase of timber? *A.*—Nine months, latterly

In 1814, *i.e.* during the war, a new collier cost £14 4s. per ton.

In 1825 the cost was £13 to £13 6s. per ton

In 1830 the cost was £9 3s. per ton.

In 1833 could be bought at £9 per ton, or a reduction of thirty-five per cent. from 1814.

If a superior vessel was required to be built the price was regulated according to specification and quality, reaching the amount of £14 per ton and upwards, without copper sheathing, or fifty-one per cent. in price more than the collier.

In 1798 there were nine shipbuilding establishments.

In 1815 (the year of peace) there were fifteen shipbuilding yards; and in 1833 there were thirty-four shipbuilding yards, more or less.

The carpenters' wages, which had been 4/6 per day during the war, in 1833 had been reduced to 4/-, or 6d. per day less—a reduction of eleven per cent.

Though the quantity of coals shipped from the port in 1835, viz. 1,038,829 tons was the lowest since 1822, when the quantity was 1,047,462 tons; yet there was a visible improvement in shipbuilding, the yards being pretty well employed, and the general prospects of the trade looked brighter. On February 17th, 1835, the foundation stone of the North Dock was laid. The Durham and Sunderland Railway was making rapid progress in its construction; the Old Custom House and the houses on the Low Quay had been demolished, and the rubbish cleared away from the places where the drops had to be erected. Where the foundations were good the quay wall was taken down and re-erected in a more substantial manner; in other places long wooden piles had to be driven into the bed of the river in front of the quay on which the drops had to be erected; the wooden gearing above on which the waggons had to be drawn was fast progressing, with the prospect of an early shipment of coal the next year.

In the same year (1835) Sunderland was made a Municipal Borough, and the first Mayor, Andrew White, Esq., was elected to the office January 1st, 1836.

With an increasing trade, Joint Stock Banks, with their head offices in Newcastle, opened branch establishments in the town; the North of England Joint Stock in the High Street, between Number's Garth and Russell Street; and the Union Joint Stock Bank in Sunderland Street, between High Street and the back street.* The Northumberland and Durham District Banking Co. purchased the business of J. Backhouse & Co., and carried on their business in Backhouse's old bank premises. The Sunderland Joint Stock Banking Company bought the shop and premises

---

*They afterwards purchased the business of Chaytors, and removed to their premises in Villiers Street.

occupied by Hugh Panton & Son, and altered them into banking premises. These additions more than doubled the banking facilities for merchants and tradesmen.

In 1835-36 a boom in shipping took place. A number of shipping companies were established along the coast— on the Tyne, Wear, Tees, and elsewhere; through these companies large sums of money were received by the managers from the public at large, to be invested in shipping; consequently, suitable vessels were bought, new vessels contracted for, shipbuilding became brisk, and speculation in shipping rife. Working carpenters, who had been frugal and careful, and had saved a few pounds, found little difficulty in commencing shipbuilding, provided they had a spot of ground in view which could be converted into a shipbuilding yard. Timber merchants were ready to supply all the timber required, and also to supply other goods, and to guarantee payment for other things necessary for the completion of the vessel, and also to find money for wages weekly.† Between the merchant and shipbuilders of this class, it was generally stipulated or understood that the whole of the payments for the vessel, when launched or sold, were to be handed over by the builder to the merchant in payment for the money advanced and for his account. For further security, the ship builder (if so arranged) would hand over to the merchant a blank builder's certificate, to be filled-in after the vessel had been built and the correct dimensions ascertained by the measurements of the Custom House Authorities, which, when handed in and registered by them, gave the legal title to the vessel.

Other carpenters, who had private funds, or who could get some one with capital to join them, also set up on their own account. At Southwick, what had been fields and

---

† On the Saturday these builders appeared regularly at the merchant's office for money to pay their men's wages.

gardens, were converted into shipbuilding yards, and the vessels had to be launched across the public road. The lime kilns on the east were also pulled down and converted into shipbuilding yards, so that the foreshore—from the lime kilns on the east to the glass works on the west—was all converted into shipbuilding yards, making nine or ten new yards.

In 1836, by the sale of land by the Ecclesiastical Commissioners in the Rack, four new yards were made. New yards were also opened out at Hylton, in the Haugh, and at Coxgreen, whilst Mr. Lanchester had his shipbuilding yard at Fatfield, above Biddick Ford, above the jurisdiction of the River Wear Commissioners. We totalise them thus: in 1798 there were nine shipbuilding yards; in 1815 there were fifteen shipbuilding yards; in 1833, *i.e.* eighteen years after, the numbers were thirty-four, more or less; in 1834–35 the number was reduced to twenty-nine or thirty yards, still having doubled in number in eighteen or nineteen years. From 1835 the yards kept increasing year by year, so that in 1840 the shipbuilding yards on the river had increased to upwards of sixty-five, or more than doubled in number during these six years, and four times the number of 1815, *i.e.* in twenty-five years.

Such was the energy displayed by the builders, that the number of vessels built and the amount of tonnage also kept increasing year by year, thus in—

Year		Vessels built			Tons	
1835	there were	98	vessels built, containing		26,134	tons
1836	,,	114	,,	,,	27,134	,,
1837	,,	128	,,	,,	32,343	,,
1838	,,	180	,,	,,	43,512	,,
1839	,,	247	,,	,,	59,441	,,
1840	,,	251	,,	,,	64,446	,,

So that in 1840 the number of vessels built had increased since 1835 from 98 to 251 or 160 per cent., and the amount of tonnage had increased from 26,134 tons in 1835 to 64,446 tons in 1840 or 146 per cent.

The number of vessels built in 1840, viz., 251, has never been exceeded in the shipbuilding industry of the port; the only year approaching near thereto was the previous year, 1839, when 247 vessels were built; and the amount of tonnage has only been exceeded twice, that was in the years 1853 and 1854, when 68,735 and 66,922 respectively were built. The amount of tonnage only refers to wood shipbuilding.

The unprecedented amount of tonnage produced year by year caused a corresponding demand for shipbuilding material, and timber for shipbuilding became in great request, every shipbuilder wanting it. So good were the returns made by the timber agents to their principals, that the falls of English oak in the seasons of 1838-39 and 1840 in the South and West of England and in Yorkshire were eagerly bought up by the merchants at enhanced prices, and forwarded down here for sale; and sometimes the builders had to wait the arrival of the timber vessels for their oak. Such a demand caused a great rise in price, and timber was bought in London and elsewhere, brought down here and sold at more than double the cost to the merchant, and even in such cases the builders were only too glad to get it. American and Baltic timber also rose in price, and other material required for shipbuilding purposes also rose in price, so that when the cost price of the vessel was added up, it was found that it had also risen. Then came the difficulty, amidst the keen competition in the market, how to get cost price for the vessel completed and standing in the yard; ultimately she was sold below cost price, in order to set another on and to keep the yard going, hoping times would change for the better, and thus enable them to recoup the loss on the former sale, but this next one only made matters worse.

Credit was cheap, and a great many vessels had been, and were still being, sold to speculators; some for all bills, three, six, and nine months being the general rule for this class, not a pound sterling in cash being paid, not even for the government stamps on the bills, Others purchased the hulls for part barter and part bills, and fitted them out for the market themselves.

Of the number of those engaged in shipbuilding at that period two old standards still remained at the time of writing (October, 1889), viz.: George Bartram and Benjamin Hodgson; but both have since passed away, the former aged ninety and the latter eighty eight.

Mr. Hodgson says: "It was in 1836 that I commenced business with young Mr. Watson—a son of John Watson, a shipbuilder. Our yard was at the lower part of the Haugh, on the north side, and the first vessel we built, I mind, was all wooden knees, not an iron knee was in her; we afterwards removed down to the flat. When I commenced, there was no shipbuilding between the Ferry Boat and White Heugh; I walked along the road three or four times a day, and used to cross by a boat to our yard. John Todd, Rodham's, Rogerson, Lister, and some more of them commenced about 1838 and 1839. Neddie Brown was building before I began. There were two yards above White Heugh, one occupied by Southern, the other by a man called Stafford. Sykes, Talbot and Sykes built at Coxgreen, on the south side; and Robert Thompson built at Coxgreen, on the north side, for Mr. Elliot, in 1837 to 1840, when the yard was closed."

Amongst others were Cuthbert Potts & Brothers, boat builders, doing a fair business in their own trade; in addition, commenced shipbuilding on the North Sands, close to the boat building shops.*

---

* Some years after, when talking about past times, *i.e.* when they were only boat builders again, Cuthbert said: " Man, my middle drawer used to be chock full of bills, but I could never tell what became of them, they went so fast."

We turn to notice the rapid decline.

In 1841, the number of vessels built was 141, and the registered tonnage 40,396, a decrease from the previous year of 110 vessels, and 24,050 tons, the average size of the vessels being larger by about 30 tons, being 256¾ tons in 1840, and 286¼ in 1841.

In 1842, the number built was 107 vessels, of 26,837 tons, being a decrease of 34 vessels and 13,559 tons from the year 1841, with an average of 250¼ tons, a decrease on the average of 36 tons.

In 1843, the number built was 85 vessels of 21,377 tons, being a decrease of 22 vessels and 5,460 tons from the year 1842, the average tonnage being the same.

Taking 1840 as registering the highest, and 1843 as registering the lowest tonnage, thus—

In 1840 there was 251 vessels built, registering 64,446 tons
,, 1843   ,,   85   ,,   ,,   21,377 ,,
Shews a falling off of 166 vessels, and   43,069 ,,

And comparing the two lowest years, *i.e.* 1835 with 1843, we find that

In 1835 there were 98 vessels built, registering 26,134 tons
,, 1843   ,,   85   ,,   ,,   21,377 ,,
Shewing 13 vessels, of   4,757 ,,

less built in 1843 than in 1835; thus the large increase of shipbuilding from 1835 to 1840, or six years, was more than lost in three years, from 1841 to 1843, on the balance by 13 vessels registering 4,757 tons, so much worse was 1843 than 1835.

In 1842-3-4 several of the yards were kept open and carried on by the foremen and apprentices; and to such a low state had wages fallen that carpenters were glad to get work at 2/6 per day, or 15/- per week; and some were refused 12/- per week, which they offered to accept.

In 1840-1-2-3 things had come to such a pass that buyers were not to be found. The wholesale production of tonnage that had been going on was evidently too much; the market was overstocked; even selling under cost price or at a loss had not the power of tempting buyers. It was in this crisis—"no market," that the speculator found he had to provide cash for the bills he had given for the ship, and often the vessel was mortgaged for this purpose. The tradesman, who had given part barter, was often in the same plight, and had to mortgage the vessel to help him through his difficulties. Others, who thought themselves well to do in the world, and who had speculated largely, kept selling their ships, one after another, for what they could realize, until they found there was nothing left to pay the creditors which remained.

The little shipbuilders who went weekly to the merchant's office for the wages to pay their workmen did not at the time feel the pinch so much, having had constant employment for a long time. They accordingly finished the vessels in hand; and, as there was no sale for them, launched them, and handed them over to the merchant, together with the stock in the yard, to realise it. It was the merchant in these cases who had to bear the loss.*

---

* It was said that, in 1841—1842, Greenwell and Sacker had twenty-nine or thirty hulls of vessels in the North Dock. Meeting Mr. Greenwell some years after, and talking of times gone by, the writer asked him if it was true that they had twenty-nine hulls in the North Dock, or was the number nineteen or twenty; he replied that the latter number was nearer the mark.

It was in the months of July and August, 1840, that the failures began, which continued through the whole of 1841. If I remember right, James Carr, who built at Southwick, was the first to fail; upon enquiry, it was found that old Mitclam, the timber merchant, had security over his ships and yard. (Carr afterwards married Mr. Mitclam's only daughter.)

Amongst the many failures that occurred during this period we will only particularize a few, viz. :—

Samson and Peter Mills, who built at the west of the Saltgrass, Deptford.*

Stothard and Routledge, who built on the yard west of the Panns Ferry Road, north side. A timber merchant sold them a whole cargo of French Oak Logs (about 100 or 120 loads), almost the only transaction he had with them; before the bill became due they had shut up, and the largest part of their assets on the yard was the merchant's French Oak.

We cannot give the number of failures which occurred in 1840 and the early part of 1841. When things seemed to be quieting down, and the hopes of the mercantile community were, that the worst was passed, towards the latter part of the year 1841, much to the surprise of almost everybody, the failure of Mr. Tom Gales, of Hylton, was announced. The assignees appointed to wind up the estate were David Johnassohn, Thomas William Panton, John Clay, and William Hay.

---

* A timber merchant, whom they had patronised largely, made Samson Mills a present of a gold watch worth 25 guineas, which Samson accepted with thanks; within three months the firm failed, indebted to the merchant £1,900 and upwards.

The meetings of the assignees were held in the evenings at the offices of William Hay, in Bridge Street, being conveniently situated for all of them. The estate was realized, and the dividends paid generally on the accounts rendered by the creditors, amongst whom was the late David Holsgrove, for, I think, some six hundred and odd pounds.*

In 1838-39-40, the demand for timber had been so great that the merchants sent out large orders to meet the expected requirements of the trade, a large portion of which was only beginning to arrive when the failures were commencing, and never anticipting such a sudden falling off in sales; consequently, the beaches were covered with floating timber, for which there was little or no market.

The English timber merchants, who had bought heavily in the south and west, kept sending the wood down here to their agents as the only market for which they had bought, with the result that almost all this class of wood had to be landed; and in 1841 thousands of loads of oak were stacked on the yards, as high as the tall long jibs of the cranes would reach.

The winter of 1841-42 was very severe; the higher reaches of the river were frozen over with thick ice for some weeks; when the ice broke away it came down carrying timber and ships with it. So large, thick, and heavy were the blocks that they grounded on the Panns Sand, and all that followed kept piling in one large mass up to and above the bridge, forming a huge dam right across the river, causing the fresh water, then coming heavily down, to rise to a very great height at the back of the ice dam—some six

---

*At the time of the failure Mr. Gales was under a contract for building a vessel for T. O. Harrison, of London, formerly of Sunderland, which was called the "Hyderabad." In looking into the contract the assignees found that for them to finish the vessel would cause a heavy loss on the estate, and they at first objected to do so; Mr. Harrison, however, insisted upon them fulfilling his contract, which they found the law compelled them to do, causing a further loss to the estate.

or eight feet higher than spring tides. At the east side of the bridge was an Arctic scene of ice, with a ship embedded amongst the floes. At the west of the bridge the fresh water was rising higher and higher. When the flood tide made, and the lower portion lifted or floated, the immense pressure of water behind sent the ice and dam crashing down the river; and the back water, which had been accumulating for some hours up the river, fell several feet in a short space of time, snapping the mooring chains, sweeping the timber off the beaches, and carrying it out to sea. Our beach in the rack was clean swept, not a log left. From Coxgreen all floating timber was swept away; and from Hylton Dene, Southwick, Pallion, Deptford, and elsewhere very heavy losses had been sustained, this following all that had been incurred by so many failures.

One of our clerks rode along the beach from Souter Point to Hartlepool to see what had been washed up and could be recovered, but the largest part was a total loss.

So many failures not only threw hundreds of carpenters out of employment but also others depending on the trade, viz.: joiners, blacksmiths, painters, and others usually employed in outfitting. The general trade of the port had also fallen off.

The shipment of coals was less in 1843 by 153,957 tons than in 1841. From the foregoing and other causes so great was the distress in the town that in 1842 and 1843 the poor rate in Sunderland Parish exceeded the gross rental of the property. In Monkwearmouth-Shore (after these years had passed away), in 1845, the poor rate levied was from 15/- to 17/6 in the pound, divided in amount and collected quarterly; the poor rate collector seemed to be continually knocking at your door. The enormous rates, in conjunction with the prevalent distress, caused the ruin of many tradesmen. Carpenters were thankful to have two or three days' employment per week in the stone yards in order to keep body and soul together. The shipwright was considered a lucky fellow if he could get employment at 15/- per week or 2/6 per day, and these men were all selected out of the numerous applicants; others took 12/6 per week, and hundreds could not even find employment at at that rate. 15/- per week was the highest rate of pay in 1843. The working hours were from six in the morning until six in the evening, with half-an-hour for breakfast and one hour for dinner. Shipbuilding, during this period, was almost all carried on by the foremen and lads, in some cases with a few hands to assist.

This dead slackness in shipbuilding enabled those parties holding the hulls of vessels to get them fit out or otherwise disposed of, so that by the end of 1843 the market was almost cleared of this class of vessels.

It was a sad sight, when going up the river, to see so many yards laid idle; the tall cranes* standing, for which no purchaser could be found, whilst others had been taken down and removed to the merchant's premises to save the rent of the yard; saw pits were pulled up, and desolation reigned supreme where a busy hive had been.

---

* The writer, in August, 1844, bought one of these cranes (which had been removed by the merchant) for £25.

CHAPTER VIII.

SHIP BUILDERS AND SHIPBUILDING UP TO 1860.

We have noticed that the lowest depression in shipbuilding was in 1843.

The following ten years bring us to the climax of wood shipbuilding in the Port of Sunderland—

In 1844 shipbuilding shewed a marked improvement. 100 vessels were built of 27,131 tons, being an increase on the previous year of 15 vessels and 5,754 tons, whilst the size of the vessels increased from $250\frac{1}{2}$ to $271\frac{1}{4}$ tons, *i.e.* 21 tons on the average. In 1845 shipbuilding continued to increase—131 vessels of 38,260 tons were built, shewing an increase of 31 vessels and 11,129 tons on 1844; the average tonnage was 292 against $271\frac{1}{2}$, an increased average of 21 tons. These large increases of tonnage caused a corresponding demand for labour, so that during the early part of 1845 carpenters' wages had again risen to 4/- per day.

On the revival of the trade several of the old speculators, who used to be in the market some years before, were quite ready again to patronise young beginners by taking the loan of a vessel for a few months and paying for her in paper at three, six, and nine months' date.*

One feature in the revival of the trade was the larger size of the vessels likely to be required, necessitating larger yards on which to build them. Part of the Rector's lime

---

* In 1845 my firm bought the hull of a vessel from some builders at Hylton, fit her out complete, ready for sea, and sold her for all credit at three, six, and nine months' date.

kilns and quarries facing the river at Pallion were pulled down, the quarries levelled up and made into shipbuilding yards.*

C. M. Webster, Esq., laid out the whole river frontage of his Pallion estate—extending from the corner of the west quay to his eastern boundary—for wood shipbuilding yards, but they were not fully occupied till some years after. Pallion Caunch lay in front of this space, and was dry at low water. Large vessels could not be launched at spring tides until a hole had been made by the dredger, into which the vessel had to dip, and for which the shipbuilder had to pay.‡

The Irish famine, in 1846 and 1847, was a great stimulus to shipbuilding; the high rates of freights obtained by ship-owners, from the Black Sea and American Ports, caused a corresponding rise in freights all round for two years, and stimulated those owners with money to come into the market to purchase ready vessels that they might participate in the high freights going.

In 1846, 133 vessels were built of 41,835 tons, an increase on 1845 of 2 vessels and 3,575 tons; and in 1847 148 vessels were built of 46,901 tons, being an increase on 1846 of 15 vessels and 5,066 tons, and an increase over 1843 of 63 vessels and 25,524 tons. Thus—

In 1847—148 vessels of 46,901 tons were built.
In 1843— 85 vessels of 21,377 tons were built.

An increase of 63 vessels of 25,524 tons in four years.

or more than double the tonnage in four years.

* The "Black Friar" was built for Smith Greenwell, of London, on one of these yards in 1848; the yard was afterwards occupied by John Smith, other builders following, and now only forming a portion of Doxford's yard.

‡ John Smith built a large vessel on his yard at Pallion for Sir George Hodgkisson, and, having neglected to dredge the river in front of the yard, in launching her the stern stuck fast in the bed of the river while the stem remained on the quay, and there she hung for several tides.

This large increase in the output meant more employment for the carpenters, and a desire amongst the men for a rise or a further advance of wages. In 1848 the demand was made, but the masters declined acceding to the men's request. The carpenters' plea was that times had improved, and they thought it only right and fair that they should participate in the improvement by a rise in wages. The masters, on the other hand, said: "it is true we have a better trade, but we have not yet recovered from the bad times, and have certainly not yet felt the benefit of the better or fuller trade." The men still insisted on the advance, or they would strike; the masters were firm in their refusal, and the men came out on strike.

This was the most remarkable strike that ever occurred in the trade; it was the longest—lasting over sixteen or seventeen weeks. It was the only strike in which the masters remained firm and unanimous. The men were also firm, and they declared that they would carry it out to the bitter end; no compromise was thought of on either side; the men stuck to their threats, and the strike continued till the last coppers in their possession were exhausted and their wives and "bairns" literally starving; some of their children were up the roads and streets begging; their homes, in many cases, cleared of everything on which money could be raised to buy bread, and so long as they could get the bit and sup their wives and children might pinch. But this state of things could not go on; the condition to which they had reduced those who were depending upon them was forcibly set before the public in numerous letters published in the *Sunderland News.** In very shame one of their writers asked: "Is there nobody that will write in our favour?"

---

* The *Sunderland News* was at that time printed and published by Mr. Barnes, in George Street, and commonly called "The Penny Whistle." When the letters appeared the whole edition was often sold right off. One of the writers was daily moving about amongst the men and the yards, saw and noted all, and signed himself "a looker on."

There was no response to the appeal; and after struggling on for a short time longer they gave in and went to work on the same terms as when they came out.

This strike was remarkable as being the only strike of any consequence in my recollection, *i.e.* for fifty years and upwards, where the masters succeeded and the men gave in.

The effects of the strike were strongly shewn by the decreased output of tonnage. In the year 1848, 142 vessels were built of 37,878 tons, being 6 vessels and 9,023 tons less than in 1847, and the average tonnage also being 50 tons less than in the former year.

In 1849 the output of tonnage was 44,333 tons, being an increase on 1848, but not equal to the year 1847 by 2,568 tons. The tendency of the trade was for larger vessels, and of a higher class on Lloyd's register; shipowners exchanging their old vessels of small size for new and larger ones of a higher class, as part payment for the latter.

In 1850, 158 vessels of 51,374 tons were built, being an average of $325\frac{1}{4}$ tons per vessel, or an increase of 3 vessels, 7,041 tons, and 33 tons average above 1849.

The year 1851 was noted for another strike by the carpenters. The men gave notice of an advance to five shillings per day; this demand was resisted by the masters for some weeks, and the yards laid idle, so far as the men were concerned. But the masters were not unanimous; some of them could not afford to lay their yards idle—the result was that the men got the advance. This forced idleness of a few weeks told on the output, causing a decrease of vessels built, and a slight increase of the tonnage, viz.: 146 vessels of 51,823 tons, being a decrease of 12 vessels, but an increase of 449 tons and 30 tons on the average of the previous year.

The first iron ship built in the port was launched in 1852. In this year the rush of emigrants to Melbourne took place; the demand, in some cases, was still for larger vessels. 142 vessels of 56,645 tons, or an average of 399 tons being a decrease of 4 vessels, but an increase of 4,822 tons, and 44 tons on the average. This year several failures took place amongst timber merchants who also had carried on shipbuilding.

The breaking out of the Crimea War, in 1853, gave a further spurt to the trade, and large vessels for transports were in request; thus the emigration trade and the transport service, together with the high rate of freights obtained, and other causes, put such activity into the shipbuilding trade that in 1853 there was the largest amount of tonnage built on the Wear that was ever produced in one year by wood shipbuilding; 153 vessels, containing 68,922 tons, or an average of $450\frac{1}{4}$ tons, were built, being an increase of 11 vessels, 12,090 tons, and $50\frac{1}{4}$ tons respectively on the previous year of 1852.*

This seeming prosperity in the trade, and large production of tonnage, stimulated the carpenters to ask for a further advance in their wages; the masters were not then in a position for a strike, and the wages were raised from 5s. to 6s. per day, *i.e.* 20 per cent. advance on the rise of 1851, and double the rate paid in 1843.

---

* The amount of tonnage built in 1853 exceeded the whole registered tonnage of the Port, in any of the years following, viz.:—

In 1807...505 vessels registered, 68,511 tons, $136\frac{1}{3}$ average tons.
„ 1808...480 „ „ 65,543 „ $136\frac{1}{2}$ „
„ 1809.. 509 „ „ 68,551 „ $134\frac{3}{4}$ „
„ 1810...506 „ „ 68,660 „ $135\frac{1}{4}$ „

Whilst in 1853—153 vessels, 68,922 tons, with an average of $450\frac{1}{2}$ tons, were built. And an increase on 1843, as follows:

In 1843, 85 vessels, 21,377 tons, and $250\frac{1}{2}$ tons, average, were built.
„ 1853, 153 „ 68,922 „ „ $450\frac{1}{4}$ „ „ „

68 „ 47,545 „ „ 200 tons more on the average.

This increase of wages, together with the increased prices of all goods used in shipbuilding, quite handicapped the masters, the rates of freights for goods brought in, in this and the following year, being 50 per cent. more in 1853, and 90 per cent. more in 1854 than they were in 1852, before the war commenced. These increases in prices did not show themselves in effect in 1853-54, because existing contracts had to be worked off, and those building on speculation hoped to obtain higher prices to cover the increased cost, hence, in 1854, 151 vessels of 66,922 tons, or an average of 443 tons, were built, viz. : 2 vessels, 1813 tons, and 7 tons less on the average, were built than in 1853.

In 1854 a contract for ten gun and two mortar boats was taken by a Sunderland firm to be built for the government; about half was built in the year, the other half in the year following. The first portion was built at the then current rate of wages—6/- per day, but the carpenters struck for an advance of wages for the remaining portion; their demand was for 8/- per day, which the builder had to pay to enable him to complete his contract in the specified time—an advance of more than 33 per cent., literally filched from the pocket of the contractor. Had more of the shipbuilders accepted contracts from the government, which were offered them at the same time, no doubt the advanced wage of 8/- per day would have had to be paid all round in the same trade.*

In 1855, 151 vessels of 60,778 tons, with an average of 405 tons, were built; being 1 vessel, 6,144 tons, and 38 tons less in the average than 1854.

---

* This incident shews where the patriotism of the carpenters' union lay, and what might or might not have occurred had the occasion arisen.

In 1856, 155 vessels of 63,429 tons, with an average of 409 tons were built; being 5 vessels, 2,651 tons, and 6 tons more on the average than in 1855.

The year 1856 seems to have been the last year wherein 60,000 tons and upwards were produced in wood shipbuilding in the Port of Sunderland.

In 1857, 143 vessels of 54,780 tons, with an average of 383 tons were built, *i.e.* 12 vessels, 8,649 tons, and 26 tons less on the average than in 1856.

In 1856-57 James Laing built the sailing ship "Duncan Dunbar," 1,378 tons, being the largest wooden ship ever built on the Wear. In the same years the "Undaunted," auxiliary screw steamer, 1,244 tons, being also a full-rigged sailing ship, was built of wood by Robert James Brown, Thomas Henderson being manager of the yard.*

The year 1857 was memorable for the largest failure in the trade that had ever taken place in the town or neighbourhood, and which may be said to have been one of the proximate causes of the failure or stoppage of the Northumberland and Durham District Banking Company.†

---

* This vessel was sold to the Australian Auxiliary Screw Clipper Company, London. The auxiliary screw, when the vessel was under canvas, was lifted up the trunkway out of the water so as not to impede the vessel when under sail.

† On the 24th April, 1857, Robert James Brown, of Sunderland, timber merchant, shipbuilder, and shipowner, was adjudicated a bankrupt. The gross liabilities were about £200,000, and after realizing securities, and giving credit for all dividends and moneys received from other persons and estates, there remained 113 proofs and 1 claim, amounting together to the sum of £182,426 0s. 4d. Upon which 2 dividends were paid, viz.: 1s. 9d., and $2\frac{7}{9}$d. in the pound. Amongst the proof of debts was that of the District Banking Co. for the sum of about £83,000, reduced by credits from £4,000 to £5,000 from securities realised, and for moneys received from other persons and estates. Seven months after, viz.: November 25th, 1857, the Northumberland and Durham District Banking Company, stopped payment.

In the bankruptcy of Brown, the two trade assignees, together with the District Banking Company, proved on the estate for upwards of £100,000.

	£	s.	d.
The gross amount realized from the Estate was	22619	13	5
Add 50 per cent., or one half for depreciation on forced sale	11309	16	8
Will leave the value of the Estate as	33929	10	1
Deducting this amount from the gross sum on which dividends were paid, viz.	182426	0	4
Leaves a deficiency unaccounted for of	£148496	10	3

At that time the custom was that the books and papers were swept into the possession of the official assignee; whence the deficiency had arisen was not made known. The creditors' assignees could inspect the books, but only in the office of the official assignees; their part was to do

---

The following is a copy of the Official Assignee's Statement on the gross produce of the estate and of its application :—

Gross proceeds ....£22,619 13s. 5d.

	£	s.	d.	£	s.	d.
Rent, Taxes, Rates, Wages, Salaries, Judgment Debts and Professional Liens	5	8	8	1229	8	5
Solicitors for general business	3	13	3	829	4	9
Solicitors for Chancery proceedings	2	2	10	485	4	4
Messengers' charges	0	17	8	198	10	1
Auctioneers and Accountants	1	18		432	12	2
Court Broker	0	9	5	105	10	9
Fees to Chief Registrar's Account	1	10	10	347	15	6
Bankrupt's allowance	0	11	11	136	0	0
Creditors Assignees' expenses	0	12	10	145	5	4
Official Assignee's remuneration and disbursements	2	3	4	490	19	4
Miscellaneous expenses	0	12	10	145	9	6
	20	1	11	4546	0	2
Dividend of 1s. 11 7-9d. per pound on proofs and claim,£182,426 0s. 4d.	79	18	1	18,073	13	3
	£100	0	0	£22,619	13	5

all the work without pay, whilst the charges of the court and officials were as per account

Messenger's Charges, per cent.	£0	17	8	on	£195	10	1
Court Broker	0	9	5	„	105	10	9
Fees and Chief Registrar's Account	1	10	10	„	347	15	6
Official Assignee's remuneration and disbursements	2	8	4	„	490	19	4
Per Cent	£5	1	3	„	£1139	15	8

Amounting to £1,139 15s. 8d., or £5 1s. 3d. per cent. on the gross realized estate.

The lawyers' accounts amounted to the sum of £1,314 9s. 1d., *i.e.* £5 16s. 1d. per cent., whilst the creditors' assignees, who did all the work in realizing the estate, were paid their expenses out of pocket, viz. :—£145 5s. 4d., *i.e.* 12s. 10d. per cent.

When Brown came up before the court for his discharge, Mr. William Young, of the firm of Young and Harrison, Lambton Street, then quite a young man, pleaded eloquently for him before the court, but there was no getting over the astounding facts, and the bankrupt's discharge was disallowed by the court, and without protection for six months. Against this judgment Brown appealed before the Lords' Justices, who, after hearing cause, etc., confirmed the Judge's decision.*

Brown commenced business in 1846 as a shipbroker and coal exporter.

Greenwell and Sacker dissolved partnership in 1847; shortly afterwards Mr. Sacker was to be found in R. J. Brown's office, supposed to be a silent or sleeping partner, never signing checks or accepting bills; the firm added the

---

* It is a curious fact that the counsel employed by Mr. Young for Brown before the Lords' Justices was Mr. Hugh Cairns, whose brief was endorsed fifty guineas, and being then the highest fee he had ever received up to that time, and this pleading became known. Lord Cairns' advance to the "wool sack" was through his pleading for the bankrupt Brown.

timber trade to their business in 1847-48, and afterwards engaged in shipbuilding, ship dealing, and shipowning, launching out into a large way of business, and were supposed to have been very successful therein. In 1854-55 Mr. Sacker retired with what was supposed to be a comfortable competency, though the amount was never stated.

The retirement of Sacker gave great notoriety to R. J. Brown as being a very successful man in business; and merchants, judging from themselves, did large business with him, giving credit to almost any amount. On the retirement of Sacker, Brown engaged a gentleman of the name of Wilkin as his general manager. On the withdrawal of Sacker some sort of mistrust arose amongst some people, though from what cause was not stated. In general, the credit of the firm was good, indeed stood high, so high that Mr. William Hay, having a large vessel on hand, built by one of the shipbuilders he supported, asked R. J. Brown if he would purchase her, thinking that Brown, having such a good connection, had a better chance of selling her than he (Mr. Hay) possessed; the vessel was eventually sold to Brown for £13,000, and bills at the specified dates drawn for the amounts; no cash was paid, so agreeable was the transaction to both parties.

Shortly afterwards Brown asked Mr. Hay to discount a bill for him for about £3,000, drawn on the Australian Auxiliary Screw Clipper Company, which Mr. Hay did to oblige him. After Brown's getting possession of the vessel he sold her in a very short time for all cash, though the price of sale did not transpire, and he was eulogised as a very lucky fellow in finding a purchaser in so short a time. Before any of the bills became due R. J. Brown was a bankrupt, as already stated; and before the bill discounted on the Australian Auxiliary Screw Clipper Company came to maturity the company were in liquidation or winding-up.

After R. J. Brown's bankruptcy, he went to London and commenced business. On the occasion of one of his visits to Sunderland he called upon Mr. William Hay and expressed his regret that Mr. Hay had lost so much money by him, and promised that if he ever had it in his power he would try to recoup the loss Mr. Hay had sustained, so far as he possibly could; and as an earnest of his intentions (as at that time he was doing very well) he handed over to Mr. Hay a bill of exchange for £140 odd, which was honoured.

In 1868 R. J. Brown was found dabbling in screw steamers; and in February, 1870, we find him arrested and brought before Alderman Gibbons, in London, charged with fraud. When brought before the court on remand no prosecutor appeared against him; the charge was dismissed and the defendant liberated.

A few years later the Rev. A. A. Rees announced from his pulpit, in Tatham Street Chapel, the death of a gentleman in Paris who had, some years before, erected at his own expense, the galleries in the chapel in which they were then worshipping; no name was mentioned, but it was well known to whom the gentleman referred.

JOHN CANDLISH.

Amongst the wood shipbuilders during this period was John Candlish, afterwards M.P. for Sunderland. He first built on the yard at Southwick, now the property of Robert Thompson, junior, and for some time Robert Thompson, senior, managed the yard. John Candlish afterwards carried on business in conjunction with his brother Robert higher up the river, though still at Southwick. Mr. Candlish was the builder of one of the very few vessels that was built in the port to class fourteen years A1 in Lloyd's Register of Shipping.

Whilst building on the first yard Candlish was not satisfied with the way in which the ways for launching the vessels were laid; he considered that they were laid too close to the keel, and that the vessel might capsize in the launching, and insisted upon the ways being laid wider or more out from the keel towards the bilge; the foreman protested, but Mr. Candlish insisted on having his own way; accordingly, the ways were laid as he directed. When the blocks had to be knocked away, the vessel, instead of running into the river, as expected, dropped on to the quay; the ways had slipped out from under her, as Candlish had been told they would do.

It was whilst he was building at Southwick that he bought the bottleworks at Seaham Harbour, and partly paid for them at first out of the proceeds of a new vessel, which monies were to have been paid over to William Hay; when the latter remonstrated with him he said: "You don't want the money, I do; I will pay you all." Some years afterwards, as the writer was going into Mr. Hay's office, he met Candlish coming out. "You met Candlish?" said Mr. Hay, "yes!" was the reply; "well," he said, "he has just paid me the balance of his account honourably."

Mr. Candlish afterwards carried on iron shipbuilding at Middlesbro' as Fox, Candlish & Co., or Candlish, Fox & Co.; neither of them knew anything about the business of iron shipbuilding, and being disappointed in their manager they resolved to wind-up the partnership.

Mr. Candlish was one of those men whose ambition was never satisfied. His fellow townsmen had given him all the honours they had to bestow—they had made him a Poor Law Guardian, elected him a member of the Town Council, afterwards to the dignity of Alderman, and then exalted him to the office of Chief Magistrate; he was also amount of tonnage built in any one year since 1845, as follows :—

In 1845 there was built 131 vessels of 38,260 tons.
„ 1859 „ „ 100 „ 37,184 „

Being.. .... 31 ,, 1,076 tons less than 1845.

And as against 1853 when the largest amount of tonnage was built, thus :

In 1853 were built 153 vessels of 68,735 tons.
„ 1859 „ 100 „ 37,184 „

Being....... 53 31,551 tons less built than in 1853.

There was a partial revival in trade in 1860, when 112 vessels of 40,201 tons were built, but these returns include the iron and composite vessels also built, no specific record of the different classes of wood, iron, and composite being kept.

After 1860 the output of wooden vessels got less and less, although strong efforts were made to keep the trade, until the last wooden vessel, built by William Pickersgill & Sons, was launched in the port on the 22nd April, 1880, a barque called the "Coppenami," of 315·81 tons.

With the introduction of iron shipbuilding and screw steamers Sunderland lost her pre-eminence as a shipbuilding port.

CHAPTER IX.

TRADE AND COMMERCE.

The trade of the river was carried on principally with keels. Keels were not exclusively known or used on the Wear. The trade on the Tyne and the trade on the Humber was also carried on by keels; but the keels of the two latter were of different shape and make, each to suit the locality or river in which they were employed.

The keels used on our river were all built with flat bottoms, so as to draw little water, on account of the shoals and caunches up the river. They had a mast and square sail; otherwise, they were propelled or pushed on by a set or long pole with a forked iron prong at the end.

On going up the river, if there was a strong wind from the west, the keelmen would lash their keels together—thus, the second keel's stem would be against the stern of the first, well secured, and a line or chain from the fore tack pin on each side of the second keel made fast to the after tack pin of the first, and hauled tight, repeating the process to the fifth or sixth keel; by this mode the first keel encountered all the wind, those following being partially sheltered under the stern of the one before; this having been done, and all ready for a start, the keelmen would go into the first or leading keel with their sets. When they commenced "puying" all darted their sets down at the same time, each man keeping step with his neighbour. At the last step, at the stern of the keel, there was a peculiar push at the set, so that the keelman might recover his equilibrium in time to draw the set out of the mud or sand into which it had been forked, and thus they went on the length of the keels, over and over again for miles; one man being appointed to look after the hindermost keel as they turned the sharp curves of the river or angles of the shoals. If the last keel, or any of them caught the ground, the keels following after were all stopped. This method of puying went on till they got to Hylton ferry, when the keelmen were pretty well exhausted. On a cold day or night Corney, who kept the "Gibraltar Rock," (which might be seen on the sign board,) would be in his boat with a small cask of ale, a lamp, and fire with two or three pokers always in it, the keelmen supplying the coals; he would pull alongside the keel and supply ale either cold or warm, as required; it was made warm by putting the red-hot poker into it.

On the quay corner, above the ferry, would be seen a lot of women (sometimes men amongst them,) each with a short stick in her hand; these women were called hailers or haulers*; after a bargain had been made, the keel's line or hailing line was passed ashore, with loops made in it; the loop was passed over the head and rested on the shoulders, and away went the hailers, bent half double, with the stick in the hand assisting the keelmen, redoubling their energies to save tide; thus they hauled and puyed on to the staith at which they were going to load.

There were two methods of loading the keels—if the waggons were running they would be loaded direct from them down a spout. This method was afterwards improved by old Will Paterson, by lowering the waggons down to the keel by the counter-balance and brake, and so great was

* The usual charge of a hailer was from ninepence to a shilling; sometimes they would get as much as eighteen pence each if strong westerly winds prevailed; at other times you could obtain three hailers for a shilling or fourpence each. They were generally beyond the middle age, and lived in the houses at Coxgreen and higher up, on the banks of the river, and used to walk down to Hylton for a hail.

this improvement considered that the late Marquis of Londonderry, in 1827, when the great Duke of Wellington, on the day before visiting Sunderland (he being the guest of the Marquis), was taken specially to Dog Hole to see the operation of the waggons being lowered down to the keels as being a great novelty. The writer was there and saw the great Duke and his friend Charles Stewart, and also the waggons lowered and the coals shipped into the keel.

The other method was the loading off staiths. The staith was a long large covered-in shed where the coals were stored when there were no keels up to load direct from the waggons, and also to keep the collieries at work. The keel was laid against the wall, under a spout, and loaded by women and girls; each woman had a barrow, also a corve or basket, and a shovel to fill it with, and when filled, wheeled it to the spout, capsizing the corve over the top of it, down which the coals slid into the keel. These women were expected to keep an account of every corve or bushel, as each corve was expected to hold a bushel, and so many bushels to the chaldron. It was thought that when the keel was lying aground they could not get wrong, yet they often forgot to chalk for the corve. When loading off staith you always got a larger quantity of coals than when loading from the waggons, in order to make up for the broken, smaller, and more dusty coal, only they were not so large, fresh, nor bright.

It often happened that the keel, when loaded, would not float off, and she might have to lie several days, waiting for the spring tides. So soon as the keel floated, the skipper generally started to puy her against the flood tide, in order to save the water down; and the keel, being deeper in the water on the turn of the tide, used almost to drift down herself, the skipper keeping her in the channel.

When the keel got down, the skipper had to see the running fitter to know what ship he was for, but generally the foreman caster had his orders to look out and tell the skipper. It might happen (if the wind was from the north, and no ships had got down) that he had to look after his keel until the running fitter had a vessel to take his coals. Each keel was supposed to carry eight chaldrons of fifty-three cwts., or twenty-one tons four cwts., which quantity still continues to be a keel of coa's.

One remarkable thing was, how, amidst so many keels, every keelman could tell which was his keel on a dark night, and numerous devices were had recourse to. The stem of one man's keel was partially split, and he used to go to the stem and feel it to be certain. One night his neighbours played a hoax upon him by putting a cap upon the stem, the result being that he lost both his keel and the tide, and went home almost in despair; as soon as he was gone the cap was taken off. At daylight the next morning he went up to seek his keel—she was lying where he had left her, and he could not understand why she had a square head on the stem in the dark and a split one in the daylight.

The gunwales of the keels were only about two feet broad, along which the keelmen had to walk in the dark whilst puying them; to make sure, they would bend low, fingering the gunwale as they went along, and it does seem marvellous how few fell overboard and were drowned. We are writing now of the period when all the coals used to be cast from the keels into the colliers.

But it was not always puying up and drifting down with the keels. Whenever the wind was fair the mast was set, the sail hoisted, the skipper at the tiller, and, with a flowing sheet, the keel flew along the surface; you could see them, one following the other, beating the inflow of the tide, and, consequently, running aground, sticking fast until the tide flowed; then you might see from twenty to forty keels, or more, all jammed together, waiting for the rising flood.

But on the ebb tide, when the wind was fair, all sail was kept set to save water down, and when they came into deep water the sail was lowered; a buoy rope having already been made fast to the flew of the anchor and to a tack pin, the anchor was thrown overboard, and the skipper with his set in hand steadied her down, every now and then giving a tug at the buoy rope to lift the anchor, so that the keel might drift and dredge downwards, till he arrived either at the ship into which he had to discharge the cargo, or the place for mooring his keel.

A PLACE OF REFUGE.

When the keelman arrived, either by tide or overland, at the different staiths, there was always a large room as a place of refuge for him, it was his hotel. On two sides of the room broad seats were ranged alongside of the walls, with a long broad table in front, and loose forms in the middle to draw near to the table. At the far end was a large fire in the grate, at which the skipper could either cook his steak, toast his bacon, or roast his 'tatoes in the ashes. If wet he could sit and dry his clothes, he could also wash the bait down either with cold water or with a gill or pint of ale, as he listed; further than the ale no charge was made. Had he to wait a few hours for the tide, he would lie down on the seat, or, as I have sometimes seen, on the table, to have his sleep, before laying down having asked the girl or the mistress to call him at a certain time.

In short, these long rooms were provided as the keelmen's caravansaries. He could always go in, sit down, or lay his legs up to wait for the tide, or shelter himself from the storm free of charge.

Keelmen as a race were generally strong, thick set, and some of them tall heavy men. A very large proportion of them were unlettered and unlearned, but taken as a whole, men well qualified for the business in which they were employed, and in which their ancestors had toiled, even before the days of Queen Elizabeth.

For upwards of 200 years, they had been the only means of carrying on the principal trade of the port. In the year 1810, it was computed that there were 750 keelmen on the Wear, and 507 casters, trimmers, &c., making a total of 1257. Averaging five persons to one family, 6285 of the population of the whole borough would be dependent on the trade.

In 1811 the population was returned, including

	Females.
Sunderland	7282
Bishopwearmouth	4039
Wearmouth Panns	256
Monkwearmouth	634
Monkwearmouth Shore	2442
Garbutt, page 153	14660

Shewing that in 1810–1811, 25 per cent., or one quarter of the whole population were engaged in, and dependent on the coal trade, as then pursued on the river; the large difference between males and females is accounted for by the non-estimated number of sailors at sea, together with those that had been taken by the press-gang and entered for the Royal Navy.

Taking the foregoing facts into consideration, can it be wondered, when Messrs. Nesham & Co. brought their coals down to the Gill to ship them down the spouts, direct into the colliers, without the use of the keelmen and their keels, that they should resent such a proceeding. The trade had been carried on by them for upwards of 200 years, and this innovation was more than keelmen nature could endure. A combination was formed, and it was resolved that the waggon way across the Gill should be pulled down; accordingly they provided themselves with long cross-cut saws and ropes, and in the year 1815 assembled in a riotous manner, cut the timber and pulled down the waggon way. The magistrates assembled, the military were called out, the Riot Act read; and all for what purpose or for what cause? Simply this, these men had, for generations, had their calling handed down to them from fathers to children, and they could not help resenting such an inroad into their employment, but their mode of stopping it was vain. The ringleaders were sought for, and many methods were employed to send them out of the way. I remember my father saying that they dressed Tom Boys in women's clothes, placed him in the stern of the coble, and rowed him to a collier in the roads as the captain's wife. Boys was afterwards captain of the "Dragon" tug boat for many years.

As already named, in 1810 the estimated number of keelmen employed was seven hundred and fifty, add to this number one lad to three men, and you have one thousand employed. The keelmen estimated that in the best or palmiest days of the craft there were one thousand keels employed on the river, less one, or nine hundred and ninety-nine in all.

Keels with coals have three distinct periods of transition, viz.:—

The first or early period, when all the coals had to be cast from the keel to the collier (which will be hereafter noticed under the loading of the collier).

The second, when tubs were put into the keels, each keel carrying eight tubs; each tub held a chaldron of coals. These tubs were lifted out of the keels at the drops, and run or swung over to the ship's hatchway, when the hasp of the bottom board was unloosed, the coals dropped into the ship, and the tub replaced in the keel.

The third, when the shipping of coals from keels on the Wear entirely ceased, except the supply of coals at the different glass and bottle manufactories and lime works on the banks.

But, besides the coal keels required for the shipment of coals, keels were also required for other purposes—for instance, to the lime kilns, the glass and bottle trade, and the large earthenware or pottery trade. Some keels were required for general purposes, such as the timber and deal trade, and other imports.

Then there was the Crimp keel or keels, which, at that period, say 1820, supplied nearly the whole town with coals. The keelman thus engaged generally owned his keel, bought his cargo of coals at the staith, and retailed them out at certain places; the Mark Quay and the Dark Entry used to be the principal, and the North Quay for Monkwearmouth and the Shore. Women used to go with their baskets into the keels, get their coals, and carry them home. There were always men about, with their pokes under their arms, ready for a crimp job; they were really coal porters, and used to charge so much for every poke of coals carried. The usual poke was a long narrow one, holding a certain quantity of coals; it used to be carried on the top of the back with the mouth above the head, in the same way as the corn porters carried the sacks of corn, only no belt was used to keep the sack on the back.

Except at Nesham's Spouts, all coals, whether for casting into the colliers, or for the lime, glass, pottery, or other trades, had to be cast, either into the collier or on to the separate quays attached to the different works.

The keelmen did not all reside in Sunderland, some took up their abode at Hylton, others at Coxgreen or higher up. The house rent was cheaper, and at any rate they were always between the staith and the collier at the mouth of the river; besides some of them liked and delighted in flowers.

Mr. Hubbard said to his running fitter one fine morning: "Guy, how are the tides? I should like to have a row up the river, get the coble ready, come yourself, no one else." Accordingly the coble was clean washed out, and was made ready for the comely old gentleman, with his white neckcloth, etc. And Guy leisurely pulled the coble, and the fitter kept making his observations as they passed the different places. When they were nearing Coxgreen, he saw a cottage on the south side in a garden, when he asked Guy, "Who lives in that cottage?" "Why, sir, Robin Mushens." "Guy, put me on shore." So the coble was laid alongside the bank, and moored to a stump, and the fitter and his man walked up to the cottage. As it happened, Old Robin was in, he saw them at the garden gate, and hastened to meet them. It was a rare occurrence to have the fitter to call. "Well, Robin?" "Ay, Maister; I'm right glad to see ye." "Guy says I would be pleased to have a look round your garden." "Yes, maister, come along," after supplying his visitors with a bowl of milk each, for Robin had a stint of grass beside his cottage on which he kept a cow. Having drunk their milk, and whilst the fitter was walking round the garden, and looking about, the old keelman went and cut a magnificent bunch of roses and presented them to his master, who was surprised, and said, "Why, Robin, where have you got these from?" "The garden," said Robin. "The garden, Robin, I never saw them." "No, maister, you might not see them, but they were there, they were hid amongst the nettles." The old keelman continuing said, "The sweetest smelling and the bonniest roses are found amongst the nettles. You see the roses are protected by the nettles till they come out in full bloom."

The last time I saw Robin's son, Tom, was, I think, in the year 1883 or 1884. I was at Coxgreen, and met with him. I told Tom the circumstance as related by my father. He said, "It's too soon for roses, but come away down to the cottage and see the garden, I will cut you as many wall flowers and what I have as you like to carry home." Two years later, and Tom Mushens went to his long home, aged eighty-two.

As we have already said, some of the keelmen were unlearned, yet you could hardly call them ignorant men.

One keelman went up to the running fitter's office to draw his running on money, when the fitter asked the usual question:—"Now, Parkin, how many tides?" "How monny tides, sir?" "Yes, how many tides?" "How monny tides av ah been, sir?" "Yes." After considering a little while, he said: "Ninety-ten, sir." "Ninety-ten, Parkin, how many is that?" "How monny is that, sir? why, ninety ten."

Parkin's tides were already in the books, and his money ready for him, and although he was a strong, energetic man, and a clever keelman, yet he could not count more than ninety—he did not know what one hundred was, and he called it ninety-ten. Ever afterwards he was nicknamed "ninety-ten." His wife kept a public house up a blind alley from the Low Street, on the east side of Ellerby's flour mill, which I think has been swallowed up by Forster's biscuit manufactory.

Amongst the persevering and thrifty keelmen was the late William Hopper, who latterly resided at Hurworth; at one time he was a keelman in John Hubbard's employ. Hopper, with rare exceptions, had a cast every tide he made, thus increasing his income. Then, the old keel he worked belonged to himself, and, as customary, so long as the old keel carried her cargo he received pay equal to the new ones. Hopper was a decent steady man; he then lived in Union Lane, in the lower part of a house between the cross street from Baines' Lane to Union Lane, and the Buck Lonnin on the west side of the lane. He joined the Primitive Methodists, and worked in the society as a local brother and class leader.

Every keelman used to carry his "bait," whether he was going up with his keel or going over land; whenever you saw him going over land he was always in a hurry, and if he met another going in a contrary direction he would sometimes walk past for about twenty yards, then stop and hail the man he had passed, and begin to shout their conversation, after which he would stump on as fast as he could. They often went overland in company, one waiting till his neighbour overtook him.

Miles Crosby and another, in going overland on one occasion, had passed Lawson's farm house, at the top of Hylton Bank, and were going along the road to Offerton. After they had got along the cart road, they had to cross a style and walk along a footpath through the next field. As it happened, an old tup was in the field along with the sheep, and seeing the objects, and hearing a noise, no doubt thought it was something interesting to him; he ran, made a spring, and before they were aware, butted Miley with his head, and down went Miley, while his friend, instead of helping him in his difficulties, cut and run, and soon put a thorn hedge between himself and the old tup, behind which he stood looking at Miley as he lay on the grass watched by the enemy. The tup retreated a few paces, but as soon as ever Miley attempted to rise, he was again charged and brought to earth, where he lay still for a short time, and thinking his foe had gone, rose up for a run, when his companion shouted "He's coming again, Miley," and before the tup got up to him he was again flat on the grass; and thus the affray went on, Miley running when he could, and his companion shouting "He's coming again, Miley," until he contrived to put the hedge between himself and the tup. Crosby's cognomen ever afterwards was "He's coming again, Miley."

THE ACT OF PARLIAMENT FOR INCORPORATING THE KEELMEN.

This Act was procured in the year 1792, and is an Act for establishing a permanent fund for the relief and support of skippers and keelmen employed in the coal trade on the river Wear, in the County of Durham, who, by sickness or other accidental misfortunes, or by old age, shall not be able to maintain themselves and their families; and also for the relief of the widows and children of such skippers and keelmen.

In pursuance of this Act the skippers and keelmen were to be formed into a society called "The Society of Keelmen on the River Wear," the affairs of which were to be conducted by forty-one gentlemen, who are styled guardians. An hospital was to be provided for the reception and maintenance of such skippers and keelmen as should, by sickness or other accidental misfortunes, or by old age, be rendered incapable of maintaining themselves or their families; and the guardians were vested with power to allow certain pensions to the widows and children of such skippers and keelmen, provided such children were not of the age of twelve years, or if of that age or upwards, and not capable of getting a livelihood by reason of lameness, blindness, or any other infirmity.

To raise a fund for these purposes each skipper or keelman employed in navigating and conducting a keel was required, during his employment, to pay, contribute, or allow such sum of money as the guardians or their successors should from time to time appoint, not exceeding, on the whole, the sum of one half-penny for each and every chaldron of coals carried in each such keel; which sum, the person by whom such skipper or keelman was employed, was authorised and required to deduct and retain out of the wages due to such skipper or keelman, respectively. The fund thus produced was to accumulate for the first two years for the purpose of purchasing and building a hospital.

With the terms of this Act, however, the keelmen refused to comply or pay one farthing towards the fund.

Garbutt, *pages 352-354.*

In 1792, the quantity of coals cleared at the Custom House, coastwise and foreign amounted to 260,200 chaldrons, which, according to the Act, at one half-penny per chaldron, would amount to the sum of £542 1s. 8d., or 4d. per tide off their earnings, which would really seem to be a large sum in these days.

In 1822, 30 years later, there were shipped from the port 395,269 chaldrons, of these 358,409 chaldrons were loaded out of the keels by casting, and 36,860 chaldrons were loaded at Nesham's spouts and Hetton Coal Co.

One half-penny per chaldron on the quantity loaded by keels, and chargeable by the Act, would amount to the sum of £746 13s. 8d., or an increase of revenue towards the funds of the charity of £204 12s., being an increase of nearly 38 per cent., or about 1¼ per cent. per annum. This amount of £746 13s. 8d. would have been about the largest sum that could have been collected by the Act in one year.

In 1822 John George Lambton purchased the Newbottle Collieries from Nesham & Co.

The same year records the first shipment of coals by the Honourable Archibald Cochrane & Co., at the Hetton Spouts, afterwards called the Hetton Drops.

In 1862, forty years later, the trade was extinct of keels and keelmen, after being in existence and flourishing for more than 200 years.

Could the Parliament of 1792 ever have foreshadowed or dreamed that a craft then a necessity, and being a real necessary of life, would in seventy years have become extinct—dead.

Beside the coal keel there was the ballast keel, which carried 50 or 60 tons. Every ballast keel was properly weighed and marked by the River Wear Commissioners, and licensed by them. On the stem and stern for every five tons up to the full quantity they were allowed to carry, a special mark and number was put, so that the captain of the vessel could look and see what quantity the keel had in, and what he would have to pay.

The ballast keel carried five hands, and would go alongside the collier to receive what ballast she had in. A ballast stage was rigged in the hold, and three of the men threw the ballast on to the stage, and two on the stage threw it out of the port into the keel, a portsail being always supposed to be nailed on the outside, to prevent any falling into the river. If no ballast had been thrown out at sea, the captain would agree for so many tons, according to what he had taken on board. In such case, the ballast keelmen were not particular about the portsail, because the more ballast that slipped into the river the less they would have to take out to sea; they had always to proceed beyond the ballast buoy to discharge or throw the ballast into the sea, if caught discharging inside the buoy they were fined. The ballast keel was propelled the same as a coal keel, with a square sail and sets. After crossing the bar, the sets could not reach the bottom, they were therefore provided with a small long warp, which was fastened to a kedge or anchor, which was dropped overboard so soon as the keel was over the bar, and as the keel sailed on the warp was payed out, until she was on a line with or beyond the ballast buoys, when the anchor was dropped. Having thrown the ballast overboard and cleared the hold, the anchor was weighed. When looking at her from a distance, you could see her moving towards the land, but no men were seen on the shuts or gunwales, they were all in the hold of the keel, hauling away at the warp they had payed out, three men hauling, one coiling away in the stern sheets, the skipper helping and looking on, sometimes going to the tiller to keep her in her proper course. Arriving at where they dropped the kedge it is weighed, and four of the crew take up the sets and puy her up the river, the skipper at the tiller.

If the weather was stormy, and vessels waiting to get their ballast out, then the ballast keels would go up the river, and discharge their ballast into carts belonging to private owners, who charged so much per ton. This method neither paid the owners of the keel nor the men, each party having to allow so much out of the different proportions of pay.

BALLAST.

There were different places on the river where it was discharged. On the North Sands ships had to be discharged into carts, which led the ballast up to the top of the bank. Monkwearmouth Church stood up the sloping bank, 150 yards from the high water mark. Monkwearmouth-shore Poorhouse, in our remembrance, stood quite in the fields, but Sir Hedworth Williamson kept leading up and depositing the ballast till the Churchyard was below the level of the deposits, and they likewise went on laying ballast around the poorhouse until at last it lay in a hole, the surrounding levels being higher than the chimneys of the house. It was at last pulled down, and the whole of of the space levelled up.

On the North Quay, there were two cranes, worked by horses, to take the ballast out of ships. The Lookout Hill, Cage Hill, and Palmer's Hill are only ballast deposits. Charles street, Barclay street and others were levelled up with ballast for house building. Afterwards a subway was constructed, an engine and cranes erected below the Ferry, the engine doing duty of discharging ballast and also drawing waggons to the top of the bank, where at first they were tipped into carts, and afterwards into waggons on a lower level, and thus the roads and streets from the Lookout hill to Roker were formed.

On the beach, above the Wreath quay, vessels used to discharge their ballast into carts, which carried their loads up to the higher ballast hills, where the Wearmouth Colliery ship their coals. There was also a quantity led out at Southwick, and also at Robert Reay's yard at North Hylton, the two latter principally from keels.

At Deptford, vessels used to lie on the beach and discharge their ballast into carts, which was led up the road, and formed what is called the ballast hills at Ayre's Quay, and also Lookout hill at Deptford. The Jews' old burying ground was, and still may be seen on the Ballast hills at Ayre's quay. Latterly ballast was discharged at the Gill by Gordon Black, which formed the Gill Cemetery. Gordon removed from Hardcastle's quay to the Gill. From Hardcastle's, Bowes' and Ettrick's quays, and from Thornhill's, Holmes' and Wylam's wharves, ballast was led all over the town, wherever required for paving and other filling in purposes, as well as to other places of deposit.

Contractors, when putting in culverts or sewers, are sometimes astonished to find London dredge sand with shells, and small dust coals, all mixed after being tipped, and sometimes flints are crossed in the same way, having come from the West of England as ballast.

The difficulty with the different owners of quays and wharfingers, after landing the ballast, was to find a place of deposit, and they often had a long lead to the spot.

COLLIERS.

A collier was a vessel of from two up to twenty keels of coals; the smaller ones were sloops or billy-boys, then schooners, brigs, snows, and latterly a few barques. She was a vessel with round bluff bows and square sterned; if the stern happened to be round or bluff she was called a pink—why, I cannot tell. The guard, or as familiarly called the gate boards, was a plank bolted edgeways on to the lower part of the paint streak, from eight to ten inches broad; these were to give a wider stretch to the rigging, and were also supposed to give more staying power to the masts. The deadeyes above the gate boards were fastened by a chain or long links, which were bolted to the top and blacking streaks below. The shrouds ran down to the level of or below the rail, with a deadeye properly seized on to the end of each. The upper and lower deadeyes were laced tight, at a short distance from each other, with a rope called the lanyards, and the whole, when complete, were called the shrouds. It was in the after shrouds that the sailor stood when throwing the lead, and calling out the depth of water that was under the vessel as she sailed along the coast, and turning up the Swin; and with a lump of fat stuck on the bottom of the lead the skipper divined whereabouts his ship was in the dark or in a fog, by the sand or shell sticking to the fat on the lead, and the depth of water thus obtained.

We will not go through the complete rig of the collier, but pass on to our purpose. If the vessel was a larger one, say, sixteen or eighteen keels of coals, then she would have three ports on each side for taking in coals, viz.: one under the gate boards fore and aft, and the midship ports. The rails and bulwarks in midships were movable. As the vessel got deeper in the water the side ports were caulked and lashed inside; the bulwarks and rails were unshipped, and the coals thrown on deck. Where a provision of six deck ports was made (three on each side—fore and aft and midships) for the coals, they were fenced with hatches, to keep the coals near the deck port, and prevent them spreading over the deck; when these were all filled up the main hatchway was the last, and the coals had to be shovelled from the deck into the hatchway.

If coals were expected, and the vessel was in the tier, then she would have to be hove between tiers, so that the the keels might get alongside to discharge; the lead had to be used to sound the level of the berth, for fear she might sit on a bank and break her back, or do herself damage.

When the keels came down, and were alongside, then might be heard the cry of "casters, oh! casters, oh!" At night, the foreman caster had his large iron fire grates, these were carried and lighted up with coals. In each keel there were 5 casters, and they were generally under two hours in casting a keel of coals. The coals had to be cast into the port-hole, at the edge of which, a coal stage was made fast with ropes, and underneath the stage, a portsail was nailed at the top, and fastened to the keel's gunwale to save the coals from falling into the river; on the stage was a boy or man to shovel or put the coals through the port-hole into the hold. The casters always kept time, with foot and shovel, so that the boy on the stage could clear away the coals before the next lot came, otherwise his hands or his shins would have suffered. In the hold was the trimmer with his candle.

If the flare from the fire grate did not give sufficient light to see the port, then a lanthorn was slung above the port-hole for light.

Imagine, in the black night, the weird light of the flaring lamps, the methodical manner of the casters in the keels, and the boys on the coal stages, and you will have a dim idea how colliers were loaded in the olden times, years ago. And here I would observe, that I have often seen four keels alongside a collier at the same time, that is to say, there were two keels on each side, and from these four keels there would be loaded on board the vessel eighty-four tons sixteen cwts. of coals in about two hours (so regular were they in time), which gave employment to twenty casters, four keelmen, four boys, and four trimmers, together with the running fitter and crew of the vessel. The twenty casters had two shillings and a pint of beer each; the keelmen received fifteen shillings per tide, *i.e.* ten shillings on discharge each tide, and five shillings lying-on money, which was paid half-yearly, the fitter being owner of the keel. If the keelman owned his keel, then twenty pounds per year was given by the fitter for the loan of keel, which, as times changed, was successively reduced to fifteen pounds, then to ten pounds, and ultimately, for both keel and tubs, one shilling per tide. Thus, for every keel of coals shipped, employment was given to one keelman, five casters, one port boy, and one trimmer. The cost of the fitter finding his own keel was as follows, viz.: keelman, fifteen shillings; casters, eleven shillings and threepence—total, twenty-six shillings and threepence, to which must be added the value of the keel in interest and repairs. When the keel belonged to the skipper, and the usual payment taken into account, the cost to the fitter, from staith to loading, would be one shilling and sixpence per ton, or rather more when the running fitter's salary and other things were taken into account.

The casters were paid in the usual manner at the public house, the publican paying them and supplying the pint of ale. At the end of the week he took his account up to the fitter's office and received his money; the keelmen were also paid their ten shillings per tide by him, the running-on money being paid by the fitter half-yearly.

IN THE YEAR 1818, AS PER CUSTOMS' RETURN,

There were shipped from the Port of Sunderland 389,354 chaldrons of coals coastwise, 312 chaldrons of cinders, and 15,838 chaldrons of coals to foreign countries, altogether 405,504 chaldrons, or 1,074,585½ tons; deducting 41,200 chaldrons shipped by Nesham & Co., leaves 364,304 chaldrons or 965,405½ tons brought down the river, which loaded 45,538 keels.

The following being the vend of coals from the 30th day of June to and with the 31st day of December, 1818, shews in what proportion the respective collieries on the Wear contributed to this exportation :—

John George Lambton, Esq.'s Collieries ....
Lady Frances Vane Tempest..........................
John Nesham, Esq., and Partners...... ....:....
W. M. Lamb, Esq., & Co. ....
Sir T. H. Liddell, Bart., and Partners.................
M. J. Davison, Esq..
John Humble, Esq...
John Carr, Esq., and Partners ....
William Russell, Esq. & Co. ....
William Stobart, Jun. ....
Thompson & Co. ....

    Half-year's Exportation ....

In the year 1820, as per River Wear Commissioners' Return, there were exported from the Port of Sunderland 421,061½ chaldrons of coals, or 1,115,812 tons. Unfortunately, the return does not show what quantity was shipped coastwise and what foreign, yet on the gross it shews an increase of 15,557 chaldrons, or 41,226½ tons beyond the year 1818. Further on we give the corresponding six months of 1820, and the name of John Carr, Esq., and partners, and Thompson & Co. do not appear from henceforth, Carr & Co. having no doubt arranged for the shipment of their coals on the Tyne.

Of the above quantity, 421,061½ chaldrons of coals,

There were shipped from keel on the river......	377,797½	chaldrons
From Nesham's Spouts	43,264	
		421,061½
Or in Tons loaded from keels in the river	1,001,163	tons
From Nesham's Spouts	114,649	
		1,115,812

Now, these 1,001,163 tons, or 377,797½ chaldrons would require 47,225 keels to carry the coals down to the colliers, and, according to their then carrying capacity, would load 7,439 of them.

The following is the vend of coals for the last six months of 1820 by the different coal owners, and at what staith loaded :—

	Chaldrons.
Sir Thomas H. Liddle and partners, loaded from Washington Staiths, N.S.	16,951
Morton John Davison, Esq., loaded from Fatfield Staith, N.S.	15,481
John George Lambton, Esq., loaded from Harraton Staith, N.S., and Low Lambton on the South Side	60,724
The Right Hon. Lord Vane Stewart, loaded at Dog hole and Pensher, on the South side	63,133
J. D. Nesham, Esq., and partners, loaded from spouts above Sunderland Bridge	22,153
Matthew Russell, Esq., and partners, loaded at Coxgreen Staith, a little below the ferry N.S., and at Pensher almost adjoining Lord Vane Stewart's	12,219
John Humble, Esq., loaded at Chator's haugh, N.S.	4,676
William Stobart, jun., Esq., loaded at Fatfield	12,111
Warren Maude Lamb, Esq. and partners, loaded at Low Fatfield, adjoining Stobart's staiths, N.S	16,642
	224,090

By the foregoing list, only one colliery owner shipped by keels loaded from the south side of the river, viz., Vane Stewart Two, Lambton and Russell, loaded on both sides of the river. At that period, Lambton was loading largely at the Harraton staiths, more than one half of the 115,438 chaldrons credited were loaded at Harraton, and allowing 60,000 chaldrons to have been loaded there, will shew that in the year 1820 more than one half of the 377,797½ chaldrons, or 1,001,163 tons of coals were loaded from staiths on the north side of the river.

The year 1820 seems to mark the highest tonnage cast into the colliers from keels, or 1,001,163 tons.

In the year 1821, only 391,110 chaldrons, or 1,036,441 tons were shipped in the total.
Deducting Nesham's 40,225 „ 106,596 „
Leaves casting from keels 350,885 „ 929,845 „

The year 1822 shews a slight increase over 1821, and 1823 shews a slight increase of coals shipped from keels over 1820, but I am not sure whether a portion were not lifted from the tub keels.

The shipment of coals from Sunderland in gross were in—

1820	....	421,061 chaldrons, or	1,115,812	tons
1821-	....	391,110 „	1,036,441	„
1822	....	395,269 „	1,047,462	„

1821 and 1822 were the years when the vends were on, and when the coal owners, by agreement, restricted the output to raise the price of coals.

1823	....	481,789 chaldrons, or	1,276,735	tons
1824	....	476,894 „	1,263,769	„
1825	....	502,042 „	1,330,411	„

Up to about this period, all the coals were brought out of the pit to bank in corves, as they were called. They were hung on the chain, and on arrival at bank, were landed by a particular jerk, the engineman watching attentively, hoisting or lowering as required; when empty, the corves were again hung on and sent down. At this period all the hewers and workers below were called pitmen, and had, in going down and coming up the shaft, to get into the corves. The pitmen at that time were rather a peculiar class; during the binding week, or what was called the signing of the pitmen's bond, holiday was kept. On Christmas week they would not work; bands of them would range the county as mummers and sword dancers. I hear that at some of the colliery villages the mummers still practice.

In the year 1818 there were cleared from the Port of Sunderland 7,078 vessels, coastwise; and 312 vessels to foreign parts. The average carrying capacity of these vessels at that period was—coastwise, $145\frac{5479}{7078}$ tons, and for foreign parts, $134\frac{164}{312}$ tons, or an average under 7 keels of coals, coastwise, and a little over 6 keels to foreign parts.

In the same year (1818) there were registered at the Custom House, as belonging to the port of Sunderland, 545 vessels, measuring 80,693 tons, an average of $148\frac{33}{545}$ tons register measurement, and employing 3,754 seamen and boys. A very large portion of these vessels, by their peculiar build, would, when loaded, carry 50 per cent. of cargo over and above their registered measurement in tons, dead weight. But to be on the safe side, by adding only 40 per cent. on the register tonnage, dead weight, would give an average carrying capacity of 207 tons. The difference in the average of 207 tons dead weight carrying capacity and of $145\frac{5478}{7078}$, the average on the whole is accounted for by the large number of small coasting vessels frequenting the port at that period, such as the Yarmouth sloops and schooners, Boston billyboys, and coasters to Whitby and Staiths, the latter only carrying two or three keels.

In the year 1886, there cleared from the port of Sunderland 6982 vessels, of the registered tonnage of 2,388,724 tons, or an average of $342\frac{880}{6982}$ tons, and carrying 3,945,434 tons dead weight in coals, or an average of 565 tons.

A great difficulty occurs in comparing the average register tonnage between 1818 and 1886, the former being under the old measurement scale of 94ths, the latter under the new measurement. Besides, it is not stated in the return whether the measurement is gross, or after deductions have been allowed for engine space and bunkers in the large screw steamers which are included in the return of 1866. The old register measurement was taken externally for the 94ths; the new register was taken internally, which increased upon the old mode, as against the shipowner, in all light and dock dues.

The first shipment of coals by the Hetton Coal Co. was in the second half of 1822, when they shipped 2,343 chaldrons. They had to team all their coals on to the staith, and they were then loaded down the spout by the basket, each basket being tallied. Waggons were afterwards used for loading.

Nesham's waggons were drawn by horses, on a high level, to the staith, which was a large, long, covered in building, on the high ground west of the Gill; if a vessel was under the spouts, then the coals were dropped from the waggons on the high level into waggons on the lower level, when they were run down the incline across the Gill, the loaded waggons running down drawing the empty ones up, the brakesman regulating the speed. If there were no vessels under the spouts, then the coals were teemed on to the staith, and had to be cast into the waggons when a ship was ready.

This mode of shipment, to the common mode of casting (whereby the coals were much more broken) was found to be so much superior that about the year 1822-23, old Will Paterson, the Marquis' engineer at the collieries, invented the floating drop, which, I believe, was the beginning of the tub keels. This, it was shewn, would enable the coal owners to ship their coals from keels in a better condition; each keel carried eight tubs of one chaldron each.

The floating drop was at first moored above the bridge, at the north side, where she began to load the colliers from the tub keels. It was afterwards thought better for the keels to come down than for the ships to go higher up to the drops, therefore the drop was moved down to opposite Noble's quay, where it was moored in the tier, with the collier out or off side, and the keel with the tubs inside.

Before beginning to load, a flat rope was passed under the bottom of the collier from the drop, and made fast at the opposite side of the vessel, so that when the crane or lifting power had hold of the tub, bringing the drop over towards the keel as though it wou'd capsize, the flat rope (technically called a bellyband) held the drop firm on the other side, so that when the tub was lifted, and passed from one side to the other to be discharged, the drop making a lurch towards the collier, the bellyband again held her firm; it was a first-rate contrivance and answered its purpose well. There was also a broad wooden flange on both sides of the drop, bolted on just level with the water, so that when lifting from the keel the flange between acted as a steadiment to the drop, and also when the drop canted to the collier on the other side; one side in either case was out of the water, acting as a balance, the other under the water, acting as a support or floating power. The gallows or drop by which the tub was raised or lifted worked backwards and forwards, and was guided by two circular collars, between which the tub passed, and on which the chain drawing the drop from one side to the other worked. It was sometimes found difficult to begin to load a large collier, because the drop would only lift the tub so high and stretch so far over, coming in contact with the covering board. The coals were dropped as close to the hatchway as possible, until the vessel took a list, and got lower in the water, when the tub would reach the hatchway. One advantage of the floating drop was, they could work at all times of tide.

In 1828, by neglect, one of the valves was left open, and the drop sank, when they had to send for the old engineer at Pensher, who got her raised and placed again for work. Unfortunately, at that time the River Wear Commissioners could not agree with the Marquis, the drop was complained of as a nuisance, and an impediment to the navigation.

Meanwhile, the Marquis erected two drops below the bridge, on the north side, the places are now occupied by Wilson's timber yard and saw mills.

The floating drop lay some time afterwards in the river, but on a heavy fresh coming down, it broke adrift with other vessels, and sank a wreck on the flat.

In November, 1828, the formation of Seaham Harbour was commenced, and in the month of July, 1831, the first shipment of coal was made from the Penshaw and Rainton collieries, and one or two years later, the shipment of the Marquis' coals by tub keels on the Wear almost ceased, and the drops below the bridge were given up; one of them was taken down, and the other was kept going sometime longer, if I remember right, by Russell.

Lambtons erected two drops below the spouts they had acquired from Nesham's trustees, and one below the Panns ferry, north side. This was soon abandoned, and the other two only kept going till the whole of the collieries could be connected with the Nesham line of railway, hence, the wooden bridge, called the "Bee's Bank Bridge," half a mile above Finchale Abbey, which brought the whole of their coals to be shipped at the drops, for the spouts had in their turn to make way for the drops as at present seen.

The drop above the bridge was called Stobart's drop, which together with the one on the north quay, seemed to suffice for the other shippers, whose total shipments amounted, in the year 1823, to 142,496 chaldrons; the larger quantity of these coals were cast by hand.

Taking the Marquis of Londonderry, and John George Lambton, Esq., as the largest shippers by tub keels, the full time they were used only averaged 12 to 14 years.

The collieries on the north side still continued shipping coals by tub keels some years longer, down to 1853 for certain. The keelmen state that Mr. Eden was the last that shipped his coals by tub keel*. One thing which seemed singular was, when a ship had to finish loading in the roads, to see the coals taken from the tub keel and dropped into an empty keel for casting on board in the roads. I have sometimes seen them casting from tub keels on board of ships in the harbour.

In 1830, the year before Seaham Harbour was opened, there were shipped from the Wear 1,387,420 tons. In 1832, the year after Seaham Harbour was opened, 1,203,802 tons, showing a falling off in the shipments of 183,618 tons.

1835 and 1844 seems to have been the worst years for shipments; in the former, only 1,088,829, in the latter 1,045,351 tons were shipped.

In 1840 the North Dock was opened, and some time afterwards began to ship coals. It was not till the year 1845 that the quantity of coals shipped from the port of Sunderland exceeded that of 1830, the quantity being 1,414,339 tons. Meanwhile, the Durham and Sunderland Railway had been made and opened for traffic. The old houses on the Low quay were pulled down, amongst which was the shop where I had served my apprenticeship, together with the house and blacksmiths' shop where the late Alderman William Nicholson wore his leather apron. His father before him lived in the house above the shop. Joe Adie's oyster pits were filled up, the tide flowed into them through openings in the quay wall, so that Joe's oysters got freshened twice a day. The old Custom House, in which Peggie Potts lived, and from which Winter went to fish, was also levelled to the ground. Through a cutting

---

*They were called Beamish, generally Mr. Eden's Beamish.

in Barrack street, from the Moor, the railway ran, close to the Barrack wall. On this ground the Sunderland cattle market formerly was held. Where the Old Custom House stood, the erection of the gearings began on which drops were erected for the shipment of coals in the river.

By means of the railway, Haswell, Murton, Shincliffe, Belmont, Whitwell and other Collieries were brought into shipping connection with the port of Sunderland.

From 1845 we find a steady increase of shipments. In 1849, 1,519,354 tons of coal were shipped. In 1850 the South Dock was opened, and in that year 1,718,427 tons of coal were shipped.

In 1856 the South Outlet was opened, and in that year 2,606,513 tons were shipped. The shipments were sometimes more, sometimes less, but on the whole a steady increase was maintained, so that in the year 1886 3,945,434 tons were shipped.

In 1860 there were shipped from the North Dock 90,515 tons. In 1886, 9,639 tons only. This decrease is explained by the preference of the North-Eastern Railway Co. for Tyne Dock. It might otherwise arise from the fact that vessels loaded at Tyne Dock could always get into the river and to sea, whilst at the North Dock, if a heavy sea ran, they could not open the gates.

From what we have written, it will be seen that from 1820, when the shipments of coals were 1,115,812 tons, the trade developed, until in 1886, when the quantity shipped amounted to 3,945,434 tons, or an increase of 2,829,622 tons. All this increase and ups and downs during a single lifetime. Who will prophesy what will be the condition of the coal trade seventy years after 1891 ?

A great deal has been said and written about Newcastle and the large quantity of coals and coke exported from thence, but very few people appear to know that two thirds of the coals, and nearly all the coke, that passes entry through the Custom House at Newcastle are Durham coals and coke.

HYLTON, SOUTHWICK AND MONKWEARMOUTH RAILWAY.

In 1866, February 9th, there is recorded the death of William Hay, timber merchant. His timber yard and beach was in the Rack, and extended to the east end of the Wreath Quay. The timber yard was purchased from the Dean and Chapter of Durham, in or about the year 1836. The beach to the east of the yard, including the banks, &c., he afterwards bought from Pemberton or the Colliery Company, and built the quay extending to and including the shipbuilding yard for some time occupied by Peverill and Davison.

In 1871, the Hylton, Southwick, and Monkwearmouth Railway Bill was passed. The Act is in 34 and 35 Victoria, session 1871, and received the royal assent on 25th May, 1871. The first waggon of coals for the locomotive used on the line came down from the west end of the line on Thursday morning, April 29th, 1875.

The traffic was first worked on the line by the North-Eastern Railway Company in the early part of 1876, although some traffic to Southwick was sent by the Hylton, Southwick, and Monkwearmouth Railway Company before that period.

The winter following the passing of the Act, i.e., 1871 and 1872, the writer, through Henry Coxon, then the agent here, tried to sell the whole of the property belonging to the executors of the late William Hay, including the timber yards, beach, etc. down to the lower end of the Wreath

Quay, to Sir George Elliot, who at that period was the managing partner of the Usworth Colliery Company, for the purpose of erecting drops for the shipment of their coals by the Hylton, Southwick, and Monkwearmouth Railway Company, at the same time pointing out that the foundation was of marl rock, and easily excavated to any depth for the loading berths. The yards above, belonging to T. Tiffin and Woods & Co, were then laid idle, and in the market for sale. The junction with the drops and railway would have been at or above Raven's Wheel. Mr. Samuel Bailey Coxon, the engineer and viewer at the colliery, came down and looked at the place superficially; the result was the site was not entertained, and the purchase declined.

On June 29th, 1889, after relating the above circumstances to H. H. Wake, Esq., engineer to the Commissioners, he said: "And now Sir George Elliot would give any money for the place. Two years ago Sir George sent for me to go up to London to discuss the matter with him, and see what could be done for the shipment of his coals from his different collieries; I never knew till now that you had tried to sell him that property."

The Wearmouth Coal Company subsequently bought the whole of the property belonging to the executors of William Hay, and also the property to the west of it, belonging to Tiffins, and also to Woods, thus closing the outlet for the shipment of coals by the Hylton and Southwick Railway Company in the Rack, or by drops at the Wreath Quay.

CINDERS OR COKE.

Cinders or coke used to be exported, for we find that in 1791, 844 chaldrons were shipped from the port, and in succeeding years, but not in any large quantities till later date.

The first coke ovens erected in this locality, were by Jeremiah Summers, south of the white wall on the moor, on the Hendon road to the sea; they were afterwards connected with the Durham and Sunderland railway. A coal landsale now occupies the site.

Some collieries in the south and west of North Durham ruined the original owners, they wanted household coals. These collieries were sold, the purchasers erected coke ovens beside the pits, and the coal which could not find a market, being used for cokeing, made the purchasers millionaires.

In 1891 thousands of tons were shipped weekly, instead of 844 chaldrons, as in 1791.

LIME.

Next to coals was Lime, the production and export of which employed many men.

We first notice the limekilns at the Sheepfolds.* From the same Quay, the lime from the Fulwell kilns used also to be shipped, the latter was sent in waggons down the Fulwell road on a horse tramway to a high level above the lime kilns, and sent down a spout to the vesssel's hold. This horse tramway was also used for supplying the kilns with stone from the quarries and for drawing the coals up to the Fulwell kilns. It was a very common occurrence to see three or four vessels loading here at the same time.

Above Raven's Wheel were Bowery's kilns, formerly Wake's; adjoining, at the west, were Stafford's kilns—both sets of kilns shipping from the quay, which ran in front of the whole. Sometimes you would see five or six vessels at the same time lying alongside loading. And further up,

---

* These kilns have been pulled down, and what shipment there may be has been diverted to the North Dock, from the Fulwell kilns.

on a higher level, were three kilns, and vessels loaded alongside the quay. Mr. Laing's graving dock now occupies the site where these three kilns stood.

These kilns were supplied from the quarries by horse tram roads to the top of the bank, and run down to the kilns by a reversal wheel and brake; the loaded ones running down pulled the empty ones up.

Above the potteries at Southwick, was a long range of kilns, called Brunton's, where four or five vessels might be seen loading at the same time. The Glass houses now occupy part of the site. Higher up were other four or five kilns, the vessels loading alongside the quay. These were pulled down to make room for wood shipbuilding. Jim Hardy built on the yard; George Clark's boiler shops now occupy the site.

These two last blocks of kilns were supplied from the west or higher end of Southwick, in the mode already described.

The ridge of limestone running from Fulwell up to the high part of Southwick, supplied the whole of these kilns with stone.

ON THE SOUTH SIDE OF THE RIVER,

The Gill had its lime kilns, the stone was wrought out of the Gill, and shipped at the Gill Quay.

At Pallion there was a long row of fifteen or sixteen kilns. The stone was wrought from the quarry at the back of the kilns, the annual quantity burnt was from 7,500 to 9,000 tons, both these works belonged to the Rectory, the latter was carried on by Mr. Thomas Baker. From twenty-five to thirty vessels of 40 to 100 tons each were employed in the trade.

At Pallion, the vessels could not lay alongside the quay for loading. Several gangways were therefore erected into the river for this purpose, along which the barrows were wheeled and tipped into the vessel's hold at the end.

The kilns highest up the river were on the quay below Claxheugh where vessels used to load.

Above Claxheugh rock the limestone breaks, and at Hylton, the freestone or sandstone crops up in high ridges.

Lime was always loaded into small vessels of 40 to 120 tons, they were loaded alongside the quay, and consequently lay dry on the ground at low water. They were compelled to be strong and tight, otherwise the lime might take fire, when the vessel might burst. I have seen two or three of these lime schooners with their cargoes on fire, laid on the beach, complete wrecks before the fire had burnt out.

Lime used to be sent both south and north, a large quantity going to Newport on the Tees, for agricultural purposes, long before Middlesbro' was, and all along the Yorkshire coast to Staiths, Whitby, and Scarbro'; and northwards to the Tyne and Scotland; a quantity is still sent to the latter place.

At the period to which the foregoing refers Sunderland really enjoyed a monopoly—and that in the lime trade, for she was the only exporting port from the Humber to the Forth.

GLASS.

A large manufacturing business in glass was conducted on the banks of the Wear. There was the crown glass, the flint glass, and the bottle glass.

CROWN GLASS—Messrs. Fenwick & Co. had two houses or cones below the Panns ferry (Mr. Alexander Wilson, one of the pastors of Sans Street Baptist Chapel, was engaged in these works). These works were closed, and the cones afterwards pulled down in order to make room for a patent slipway for S. P. Austin & Son; the Panns graving dock and yard now occupy the site.

Mr. Attwood's works were at Southwick, and these, after changing owners two or three times, came into the possession of Mr. Robert Preston; and after some ineffectual attempts to carry them on at a profit, were closed.

FLINT GLASS—These works were carried on at Deptford by Mr. Booth, they occupied the site between the bottle houses and a large warehouse on the west, and were afterwards enclosed in Featherstonhaugh's bottle works.

BOTTLE GLASS—There were two cones below the bridge, belonging to Messrs. Fenwick & Co., now standing in ruins; the road to them led down by the Panns ferry. The vessels used to lie alongside the quay, just above the ferry steps, when taking in the bottles.

Above the bridge there were two cones of houses, belonging to Horn & Scott, or the Ayre's Quay Bottle Company; the last of these cones was pulled down for the erection of the Railway Bridge which now crosses the Wear.

Then there was the Ayre's Quay Bottle Co., in which the late Mr. Philip Laing, John Hubbard, and others were partners. These works appear to be the oldest on the river of which we have any account.

In Bishopwearmouth Church, near the north door, entering the nave, is the following:—

Near this wall
Lies interred the body of
THOMAS WILSON,
One of the proprietors of the Glass Manufactory at Ayre's Quay,
Who died the 30th November, 1776,
Aged 55 years.

These works are still carried on by the descendants of the parties first named. Sixty years ago the vessels used to lie alongside the quay at the lower part and take in their cargoes.

Pemberton's Bottle Works were also at Ayre's Quay, at the corner of the turn of the river, and had a long beach offside the quay, so that vessels could not get alongside the quay to load. A gangway had to be run out into the river, at the end of which lay Pemberton's Dutchman, laid there for that purpose, which afterwards was an endless bone of contention with the Commissioners. These works were afterwards sold to Mr. Kirk, with the shipbuilding yard below, on which he erected new cones. The whole of these works have been laid idle for some years, and have now fallen to ruin and decay.

Featherstonhaugh's bottle works were at Deptford. At first the cones were only on the quay, then extended higher up the bank and further west, taking in the works of Booth. These are now all standing idle, and going fast to ruin; warehouses, gangways, railway, and even a large quay frontage unoccupied.

In 1877, except the Ayre's Quay Bottle Co., the whole of the above named glass works were closed and abandoned. Fenwick, Pemberton, Booth, Featherstonhaugh, Attwood, and Kirk have left the trade.

It is true that other works have been commenced and carried on since, such as Hartley's, Southwick Bottle Co., the works at Cornhill and Millfield, but these cannot compensate for the immense loss in trade for the port, and the number of glassmakers that have had to seek work elsewhere.*

---

* In 1818 there were exported from the Port of Sunderland 1543 cwts. 2 qrs. 24 lbs. of Bottles, 1296 cwts. 1 qr. 19 lbs. of Crown Glass, and 463 cwts. 0 qrs. 13 lbs. of Flint Glass. The quantities are given in cwts. and lbs. as the duty was payable in weight.

Whilst writing about glass, we would observe that there was also the trade of the glass cutter. Mr. Pyle had his shop in the Low Street, opposite Bee-hive Lane, and Mr. Haddock, in the Low Street, at Custom House Quay, nearly opposite the Fish Market. Tumbler glasses and glass bowls with different devices cut upon them, or your name or initials, etc., were purchased largely by captains, sailors, and strangers, to carry to their homes as presents, etc. It was something beautiful to see the grand arch of Sunderland bridge and vessels sailing underneath, cut on your tumbler glasses, and any other device you could wish. Has this art become extinct in the town?

EARTHENWARE.

There were five large manufactories on the banks of the river, or in close proximity thereto. A great number of hands, both men and women, boys and girls, were employed at each establishment.

There was Dixon's pottery, at the east end of High Street and at the top of the bank called Pottery Bank. In summer time there was always one or two vessels loading or discharging at the quay. The late William Dixon told the writer· "My father had always two of the cranes engaged at Thornhill's wharf, one for lifting coals out of the keels to be carted to the pottery, and also for discharging white clay from the ships; the other was for loading the heavy crates from the carts into the vessel." This was my experience before being confirmed by the son. When a vessel was loading, you would see both men, women, and children carrying crockery in their arms or on their heads from the pottery down to the wharf for shipment on board the vessel they were to fill up for stowage. The Pottery Buildings, and the ruins of the cement works, mark the place where the pottery once stood.

Scott's pottery, at Southwick, was a large place with a large export trade, and has descended in the family for generations, and is the only one out of the five named still carrying on the trade.

Since writing the foregoing the potters have been celebrating the centenary of Scott's pottery.

Moor's pottery adjoined Scott's, and had the right of shipment of goods from the quay west of Scott's, and of landing their coals and carting them up from the quay to the pottery. Each of these potteries received its coals from the river, and in summer time, when the vessels arrived to load for exportation, the quay line was almost blocked, what with vessels loading earthenware, keels alongside casting coals, and vessels discharging China clay. I have seen four or five foreign vessels alongside these quays loading for different ports on the continent. Moor's pottery has since ceased to exist.

Dawson's pottery, at South Hylton, had a long space of quay frontage to the river, with a high quay wall, the coals were carted from the beach at the west side of the quay and led up the slope to where required. On the quay were two or three cranes for loading and discharging. The burn ran at the east side of the works, and up the valley across the road; and by the side of the burn were extensive works, and amongst these were the kilns for burning the flints and the mill for pulverising or grinding the burnt flints into a very fine powder, to be utilized in the manufacture of their goods. I have seen the quay space fully occupied, some vessels loading, others discharging flints, and white clay from Cornwall.

At North Hylton, was Austin and Dixon's pottery; there was room for one vessel to load at the quay. Most of the earthenware from this pottery was sent down the river in keels.

The pottery at North Hylton belonged to Mr. Maling, grandfather or great grandfather of the present E. Allan Maling, M.D. The same Mr. Maling built the Grange. It was his custom to ride to the works at Hylton every morning on horseback, crossing the river by the horse ferry boat. The manufacture of earthenware was considered a grand paying business at that time.

It was curious to see the different builds and nationalities of vessels sent across for this trade, all of small size. There were old-fashioned Dutchmen, Norwegian, Prussian, German and Danish.

In the year ending January 5th, 1819, there were exported 292,142 pieces of earthenware, and of this quantity 145,092 pieces were exported to Holland. But, besides these exports, vast quantities were sent to different parts of the kingdom; Messrs. Scott, of Southwick, had a warehouse in London, to which they sent great quantities, and colliers trading coastwise also took earthenware; and, as will be seen by the tabular statement, Guernsey and Jersey took a large quantity, considering their size and population.

Out of these five centres of industry exporting earthenware, only one now exists, the trade with Holland collapsed years ago, the Dutchmen enticed our skilled workmen over, and the natives learned the trade, which is now extinct.

Note of exports of earthenware :

    To Norway ....
    ,, Denmark............................   ,,
    ,, Prussia ....   ,,
    ,, Germany...........................   ,,
    ,, Holland ....   ,
    ,, Guernsey..........................   ,,
    ,, Jersey ....   ,,
    ,, British Northern Colonies .... ,,

IRON STONE.

The workings employed several men and boys, the latter were called putters, and also several wherries to convey the mineral to the blast furnaces on the Tyne. Long before the Cleveland Hills were wrought for iron ore, we were producing from the Wear, iron stones, iron boulders, or iron ore from the mines or grub holes as they were called.

The largest workings were at White-heugh, the quay still remains; if you look up the bank side you will see large heaps of shale, which was called putt. These mines entered the bank side and extended up to Offerton, with shafts in the fields above, to admit air into the mine, or to bring up ore; between the railway and Offerton you will see mounds of shale brought to the surface. The iron ore boulders were taken to the mouth of the mine, and thrown down from the high level and shipped in wherries from the quay.

A few openings were worked on Robert Reay's estate, North Hylton, a little to the east of where the highway rises from the ferry to the bank; three or four grub holes were worked and the iron stone shipped into wherries from the quay. There were also some mines or grub holes below the yard where the late Edward Potts carried on business as a shipbuilder, and which was afterwards occupied by William Gales, and latterly by Willy Naisby; these mines were closed, and sawdust and rubbish thrown over the banks, covering the mouths of the mines from view.

I do not know the percentage of metal these iron stones yielded, but there is no doubt they were vastly superior in the quality of metal and percentage produced to the Cleveland mines. I suppose the cost of working and the small quantity of boulders secured, together with the opening out of the Yorkshire mines at Whitby, and afterwards in Cleveland, rendered the workings unprofitable. There is still the question whether the putt or shale could not be utilised for some commercial purpose.

GRINDSTONES.

Newcastle Grindstones were made on the Wear, and sent or sold by the merchants of Newcastle as Newcastle grindstones. The Sunderland merchants exported their own Grindstones. The quality of the grindstones made on the Wear was reckoned superior to any that was then made on the Tyne.

The quarries from which they were wrought were situated at North Hylton and Coxgreen. The quarries of the latter still produce stone suitable for grindstones. Quantities were sent by the colliers to London and the different ports along the coast.

In 1818, ending January 5th, 1819, there were exported from Sunderland 353 chaldrons of grindstones and 4,000 whet-stones.

To Norway	
Denmark	,,
Prussia	,,
Germany	,,
Holland...	
British Northern Colonies	,,
United States	,,
	353⅓ cha'drons.

This trade is still in existence, for I see entered for export in 1887, grindstones.

COPPERAS

Was another article of export. There were three copperas works, viz. : one at Deptford, one at Hylton, and the third at Coxgreen. The works at Hylton were carried on the latest. Copperas was manufactured from the brasses picked out from the coal at the colleries. Tons upon tons of brasses were laid together upon a level or platform to secure the drainage, which led to receivers for the liquor draining from the brasses after rain. These receivers were emptied into a large boiler and heat applied, after which the liquor was allowed to cool, and the water run off; the crystals were then gathered from the different appliances placed for the purpose, and packed into large casks or hogsheads ready for shipment. Brasses had to be replenished from the different collieries to make up for the wasting away, also to keep up the strengthened quality of the liquor. A crane on the quay was used to put the hogsheads into the keels, which were shipped off to London and elsewhere. In 1818 there was exported from Sunderland to foreign parts 96 tons, 9 cwt. 3 qrs., 18 lbs.

CHARCOAL.

The manufacture and burning of charcoal, and the distillation for acetic acid, was carried on at Deptford, and also at North and South Hylton. On the decline of wood shipbuilding, these manufactories died out. The one at North Hylton was the last. I suppose it was the low price paid to the shipbuilders for timber ends, slabs, cuttings and small wood which enabled the business to be carried on. The larger pieces of oak were used for cutting railway keys and pins, the refuse thrown into the oven for charcoal. The making of the acetic acid depended on the burning of the oak for the liquid or juice, which afterwards had to be distilled and dried, when the last pan gave the acid for the market, which was principally used for making white wine vinegar.

LAMP BLACK.

There were two manufactories on the river, one at North Hylton, the other at Fatfield. Lamp black was used by the painters solely for black paint. The lamp black casks were to be seen going in all directions, both to home and foreign markets. In 1818 there were exported to foreign countries 466 barrels. This industry has also ceased.

PRUSSIAN BLUE

Used to be manufactured, although it might be on a small scale. The factory was at the foot of Claxheugh Rock, where the run of fresh water turned almost at right angles in a full stream to the river. I think the building (when writing) is still standing, though now in ruins.

FIRE BRICKS

Were largely manufactured, and, together with fire clay, largely exported. This business is still carried on by some of the colliery proprietors, who also manufacture gas retorts, and other goods made of fire clay.

FLINTS,

Brought from the west of England, roasted in the kiln, and then ground into fine powder, were used for making earthenware, and used to be exported in bulk.

VITRIOL

Was manufactured in Monkwearmouth, the works being beside the North Dock.

NAILS.

Nail making was a branch of industry that flourished here about sixty or seventy years ago. Baglee, the nailmaker, had his shop in or off the Long Bank; he died in 1882, aged ninety-five years. Jacky Rodgers, in Pewterer's Lane, was considered a large maker; he had eight or ten fires; his shop was next door to the works; he made all kinds and sizes, from a ribbon nail down to a small tack. There was also Matthew, the nail-maker, and a lot of others. At the present time, I do not know of one shop in the town.

ANCHORS AND CHAINS.

Anchors and chains have been made for generations, but the large cable chains only began to be manufactured and used in my early days. Small chains were made in small shops, but some of the large manufacturers made their own small chain to complete the outfits, until they could buy the small chain cheaper than they could make it. The competition for these articles was very great; and whilst the manufacturers were competing amongst themselves for orders, they found that strangers came in and undersold them on their own ground. Although the men were told that the trade was sensibly slipping from their masters, under the heavy competition which they had to meet, yet, so blind were they to their own interests, and so callous to those of the masters, that the anchor smiths and chain makers insisted on maintaining their list of prices; and with what effect?

The trade has gone. Where once there were eight or ten manufactories in full operation, at the early part of the year 1887 there was not one left in operation at all, at that time all had ceased.

This extinction of the trade, had it only injured the men, must have been bad enough, especially when you take into account the families of these men who were depending on them for bread. But what of the masters? Every firm engaged in the manufacture of anchors and chains on the Wear has succumbed. No matter what the reputed wealth they possessed, they either failed in the first, or shut up in the succeeding generation.

THE WORKING CUTLER.

I have stood and watched him forge the blade for a pen knife, temper, polish, and fit it in the haft. If you broke your blade in your pen knife, and took it to Waddle's, he made a new one and fitted it for you. Waddle was famed for his blades, the very best tempered scrieve knives could only be had at Waddle's; the business had descended from father to son. I think it is now extinct.

ROPE MAKING.

In the olden days of rope-walks, the yarn was handspun, and laid or made up by manual labour, as partly described in our sketch of the Town Moor. From the Moor four roperies were to be seen at work, viz., Cockerill's, on the Ropery; Kirton's, in Ropery lane; Johnson and Willy Usher's, at the west end of the Assembly Garth, running from Coronation Street to Hendon Lodge. The former was in Sunderland, the latter in Bishopwearmouth Parish. There were twelve or thirteen of these roperies scattered over the town and across the water, and two patent roperies. The whole of these were kept well employed in fitting out new ships, and supplying the numerous colliers with what was required for wear and tear. The whole of the winding ropes for the pits, and the ropes required for drawing the waggons up the inclines, were then made of hemp rope.

It was not till towards 1852 that wire rope began to be used in this locality for the fitting out of new ships. At first it was used only for fore and aft stays and back stays. It was not till some time after that it came into use for lower and topmast shrouds, etc., and, latterly, for towing hawsers and mooring ropes of steel wire.

The winding ropes for collieries are now all made of steel wire, also the ropes for the inclines. Hence the heavy or major portion of the trade has been changed from hemp to steel wire rope, though the manufacture of hemp rope is not likely to be extinguished.

The result of the change is, that where there were thirteen rope walks there are now only one or two, and where there were only two patent roperies there are now six large establishments. Hand spinning has almost entirely ceased; the ropemakers purchase largely of the imported yarns from St. Petersburg, on which there is no duty.

SAIL CLOTH

Was largely manufactured, and still continues to be, but not to the same extent as it was. The keen competition of the Scotch makers, and the revolution from sailing to steam vessels, has caused a diminution in the make; first on account of the low price, and second on account of the falling off of the demand.

FURRIERS AND SKINNERS.

There were two manufactories, employing a number of hands. The old factory was at the bottom of Queen street, Bishopwearmouth, entered by large gates from the street. It has since been converted into dwelling houses. The new factory was built in the same street, by the late Thomas Mounsey. They were generally called coney cutting factories. Valuable skins were imported from all parts, both home and foreign, many from Russia, and the famous beavers' skins from the far north-west. The business must have been flourishing at one period, or Mr. Mounsey would never have built the large new factory. A few years after it was built, silk hats were introduced, and these did away with the famous beaver, consequently, the business was closed. Mr. Edward Capper Robson's flour mill was converted from the furrier factory to its present use.

HATTERS.

The different hatters in the town made their own hats, and sold them in their own shops, and for some time after the closing of the furrier factories they continued still to do so. One or two of the hatters commenced to make hats, as well as the felt or beaver hats; but these old-fashioned tradesmen have all passed away.

TANNERS.

In Bishopwearmouth there were two tanneries, viz.: Clark's and Richardson's. You may look in vain now for the tan pits, the drying sheds, the store room for the bark, and the warehouse for the leather; these have long since ceased. The enlargement of Messrs. Richardson's flour mill, and the building of Green Terrace, occupy the places of the tan yards, and also the sites of the houses in which the master tanners lived.

CURRIERS.

The trade of the currier or leather dresser seems to have followed that of the tanner. No hides, therefore no leather to dress. There were several curriers' shops about the town; I remember seeing four or five of them when young. Where are they now?

CORDWAINERS

Were a numerous class in the town; they supplied all the inhabitants with home-made boots, shoes, and wooden clogs, the latter were generally called cloggers. Every master had his own workshop, and also outside hands, who took the material with them and worked in their own homes; there was also a class of women workers called binders, who did the light work in or on the upper leathers. Sunderland was noted for its boots and shoes; sailors, both Scotch and south countrymen, purchased their boots and shoes when here, and also those for their friends. The boots and shoes were made, not manufactured.

In the year 1818 there were 277 pairs of shoes exported to the American Colonies, and 224 pounds of leather clogs were sent to Norway. Considering the population of the town at that period, the "knights of St. Crispin" were very numerous. They had their different lodges, where the brotherhood assembled, and Cobblers' Monday used to be a common expression, denoting the purpose to which it was devoted. One of the chief or principal lodges was held at the Queen's Head Inn, Queen Street, Sunderland. Sometimes the lodge broke up early, but, as a general rule, you would see the brethren leaving the lodge linked arm in-arm, digging their elbows into each other's ribs in a friendly manner, just helping each other to keep their legs. They were a queer lot in their ways, and yet a jolly lot, the sons of St. Crispin.

In the jubilee year of George the Third, 1810, the knights and squires, and others of the order, had a grand procession. I have not seen it recorded in print.

On the 23rd June, 1887, I met an old friend, Mr. Telford, in Holmside, Borough Road, and whilst talking of the Queen's jubilee, I asked him if he recollected George the Third's jubilee? "Nicely, nicely," he said, "That was in 1810. I was nine years old. The cobblers had a grand procession." "Nay, nay," I said, "Not cobblers, cordwainers, or the knights of St. Crispin." "Yes, yes," he said, "You are right. Mr. Ramsey, who had his shop just opposite the Methodist chapel, below the Quakers' meeting house, and next door to Barney Sharp, the hosier's, headed the procession on horseback, and was clad from head to foot in complete armour, having a sword by his side and a lance in his hand; and Mr. Bell, who had his shop in Church Street, wore his regalia, and carried a white wand in his hand. Mr. Bell, who was a tall, very stout man, and called Daniel Lambert, headed the procession on foot. The knights of the order followed first, the esquires bringing up the rear, and whilst the procession moved on the trumpets sounded and the bands played. The people, and especially the boys, were hurrahing and shouting 'Here comes the king of cobblers.'"

CHAPTER X.

COLLIERS.

The collier being loaded, and ready for sea, the difficulties of navigation were so great that a great deal of care and attention had to be given, on account of the many sands and shoals described elsewhere.

Should the wind be from the west, and plenty of water, she would sail out of the harbour, with the coble alongside, or towing astern. If a light wind from the east, smooth sea and spring tides, then she had to be warped down the harbour into the roadstead, from the loading berth, wherever she might be taking in her cargo, whether at the spouts, drops, or by casting from keels.

If the collier belonged to the fitter, a fine spun small warp, 180 to 200 fathoms in length, kept specially for the purpose, would be coiled in the after part of the coble, before going up to the ship. At Panns Quay, one end would be made fast to a ring, and the coble, with the tide, was pulled up to the ship above the bridge; this was done to save time, for the vessel had to be warped down to the flat, before or at high water. There was always something to which the line or warp could be made fast, either to a ship in the tier or the buoys. After the flat was passed, the ship had to be warped down the harbour by kedging. Outside the bar, there were placed, at certain distances, wooden buoys, swaling to and fro, with large holes through the top ends, which appeared above water, through these the warp was rove and made fast by the men in the coble. This continued from buoy to buoy till the vessel was in the roadstead. Should several vessels be warping out at the same time, the coblemen would race to the buoys, as there were only two holes through each buoy to make fast to. In such case, the kedge was kept in the coble, for use if required. If a vessel drew much water, and there was any fear of her grounding on the flat or striking the bar, then one or two keels of coals were sent to sea with her, and cast on board in the roads, the vessel laying at anchor for the purpose. The keelmen and casters got double pay for what was called a sea tide. If the tides were taking off, the ship would go out and wait for the coals in the roads. I have known vessels thus waiting, when a gale has sprung up, and if they could not get the anchor, slip it. If the gale blew from the south-east they would make for the Tyne or Leith Roads; if from the north-east, for London or any other port with what cargo they had on board.

If the wind was from the north-east the vessel would be warped down to the North Pier, and a rope run ashore up the stone steps, and a few hailers set on to draw her slowly down whilst the sailors were setting the sails; as soon as she felt the wind on the sails, and got steerageway, the rope was let go, and away she went.

The light colliers coming to the port used to cast anchor in the roads or Hendon bay, to discharge or cast their ballast. Running down with a light southerly wind, they would be casting their ballast as they ran along the coast. All the sailors had to help to cast the ballast; if the pilot had boarded, then the coble's crew had to assist—this was the rule in summer time or in calm weather. Should there be a strong wind blowing, though fair, then the ballast would be kept on board, and afterwards discharged into keels, or at the different wharves, quays, or beaches.

With a gale of wind from the south-west, ships would sail as far up the harbour as they could fetch; they would then luff the ship in order to get her head towards the south whilst she had steerageway; if she lost her steerageway, and the strong wind blowing her out of the harbour, then the anchor had to be dropped until the sails were clewed up and a warp run to the South Pier. If a handy coble's crew were in attendance, a thick warp would be run to the pier and made fast to a post (posts were placed on the pier for this special purpose, with a certain amount of space between them), while the sails were being clewed up and stowed away; the running fitter or the owner would then hire or call so many men for a hail. Should the vessel be at the mouth of the river, and hard to start, then one of the large capstans under the shed on the pier would be used to heave her to windward; once started, the hailers would clap on to the rope and haul the ship up to the hailing house, after which the sailors had to warp her up the harbour, and the hailers would run down the pier for another hail. These men had their numbers chalked on their hats, which they shewed to the running fitter or to the person who paid them. The shipowners often engaged and paid the hailers.

They were a motley lot, these hailers—cobblers, tailors, hodmen, casters, or any man that might be on the spot and willing to earn a shilling.

It often happened that before the first vessel could get hauled out of the way, others following would not be able to pass. If the vessel coming in was well up in the wind the hailers would have to stop and slack their warp; and, meanwhile, their ship might drift down, or others come athwart hawse; then would come a crash—bowsprits, bulwarks, sterns, main booms and what not would be carried away.

A squall of wind would sometimes take the vessel while the men were hauling on the warp, and she would drift astern; and, if the hailers could not hold the vessel to the wind, they would take a round turn to one of the posts on the pier until the squall eased. It sometimes happened that the warp broke, when all the hailers would fall on the pier one on another, and the ship would drift into another one coming up astern, and carry away her bowsprit or catheads, and also smash in her own stern, in which case the anchor, whether hanging in the hawse or at the cathead, would be let go, in order to bring the ship up till another warp was run on to the pier; then the anchor had to be weighed before the hailers could start again to get her out of the way. Should the wind be from the east or southeast, with a strong sea, then the pilot would board the vessel within the piers, when there would be quite a scramble amongst the pilots to get down as far as they safely could, some cobles at one side, some on the other, but the pilot who first got over the rail on to the deck claimed the ship. If the way was clear, he would shorten sail, and bump the vessel on the North Sands, when she would swing round with the tide and wind and drop up the harbour. Otherwise, the anchor would be dropped below the Sand Point or on the Flat for the vessel to swing round, when the sails would be clewed up, and the anchor got as soon as possible, to clear the way for other vessels following; if the anchor was not got in time the next ship would likely get athwart her hawse and do damage, whilst the continual run of vessels made it worse. The number entangled, one with another, was sometimes great, and all that followed made the confusion worse—there was no road past, the river was blocked. Ships following would then drop anchor lower down, opposite the Potato Garth; and should they get fouled in the same way, the wind would drive them on to the garth; and often, if the vessel would not luff to the wind, she would be driven on to the Potato Garth, and, if a very heavy sea was running, would be wrecked there.

The great difficulty in taking the harbour was not the narrow entrance, but the want of water in the middle and on the south side. The deep water channel then lay close to the North Pier, and the difficulty was to keep the vessel to the windward in turning the ground inside the South Pier, which was dry half-way across the river at low water. If the captain or pilot tried to keep to windward, the chances were that the vessel might strike on the sand and become unmanageable, until a few more seas would wash her over the sand, and very likely drive her on to the Potato Garth, a little higher up to leeward.

A great deal depended on the activity of the crew in clewing the sails and in dropping and weighing the anchors; sailors and apprentices belonging to the port were always found to be more active and useful than the south country men. It must here be remembered that the cables were of rope, and a boy had to hold on with the half watch tackle, which had to be flitted when so much of the cable was on board; the cables were afterwards one of rope and one of chain, being the transitional state from rope to chain cables.

The anchors could only be lifted by the windlass and handspike; all hands had to keep time. There were three stages in the half turn of the windlass, which the sailor had to accomplish, viz.:—First, to place the handspike in the hole of the windlass, then rise to the perpendicular, and, with one foot on the windlass, catch the end of the handspike and swing for a turn, this would probably come one-third down; secondly, to jump up, close to the end of the handspike, and swing his weight upon it, which brought the handspike below the level of the breast; and, thirdly, to press the handspike down to the deck so as to place the square of the windlass on the top, so that the rise, as for the first, could be taken. These motions had all to be done, every man keeping time with his neighbour by a shout given by one of them, and sometimes by all in chorus.

At the time of which we write patent windlasses were not known here; only the windlass for the anchor and heavy work, and the capstan, were in operation. But there were men then to man the colliers, and boys were trained up to be men on board of every collier sailing along the coast.

Vessels inwards had always to take a pilot, but the running fitter generally took them out to sea; this was a sore bone of contention—pilots insisting on piloting vessels out as well as in, as piloting out was an easier, shorter, and better business, but as many of the running fitters were at that time also pilots the matter dropped.

Sunderland at that time was considered a creek to Newcastle, and the pilots were licensed by the Trinity House of Newcastle, who received or derived the benefit of sixpence per ship from the pilot for each one he brought in, and sixpence for each one he piloted out. The running fitters were equal in proficiency to the pilots, but they must be running fitters and pilots, because anyone acting as a pilot, without a license, was liable to be heavily fined. A "Branch" was a parchment document issued to the holder by the Trinity House of Newcastle, as an authority to act as pilot. It stated the number which the pilot held on their roll. The pilot's number was painted in large figures on each side of the coble's nose, and each pilot had to pay sixpence per vessel to the pilot ruler in Sunderland for his branch and privilege. Originally, the branch was for life and competency. The brethren at Newcastle thinking that correct returns had not been given, issued new rules as to pilotage, and demanded a yearly payment for the license; the whole of the old branches were called in. Some of the older pilots objected to the new rules, and refused to give up their original branch or license, and still continued their vocation. The brethren did not enforce their new order on the old pilots; why, I do not know, but they were evidently in a fix and dare not try to compel them to give up their branches; the old pilots really had their vested interest in the matter. Guy Potts was pilot ruler or master at the time.

Rarely any vessel went to sea without a piece of beef and a few biscuits being put into the coble for the running fitter and the coble's crew. If she was a Lynn or south country vessel, then it was usually a lump of cold boiled corned beef and biscuits; if a Sunderland vessel, a piece of fresh beef (to be cut into steaks and fried) and biscuits tied up in a piece of canvas or a handkerchief, or put into the coble dish. And on coming ashore, no matter what time of night, they would go to their house of call, rouse the landlord out of his bed to have their beef cooked, drink their ale, and divide the foy before they went home. It was the custom—they always expected the beef and biscuits to be put into the coble, even when the shipowner himself was on board.

The colliers were all steered by the long tiller, stretching from the rudder head over the skylight and close to the cabin funnel, behind the binnacle at the back of the companion. The binnacle held the two compasses, and the light was placed in the centre, so that the man steering could see the compass, and thereby regulate the vessel's course. A rope passed from rail to rail, through a sheave on each side, and with a round turn over the tiller, close to the end, enabled the steersman to pull up to windward, and in heavy storms he would be lashed to the helm, in case a sea should break over the quarter and wash him from his position, hence the chorus of the song

"Lashed to the helm, should the sea overwhelm,
I'll think on thee, my love."

Next in time came the wheel, which was placed behind the companion, and was worked by a couple of sheaves on each side of the rail, one on either side being on a line with the wheel, and the other so placed as to brace the tiller hard up. Afterwards came the short tiller and patent steering gear, etc.

There were a certain number of apprentices on board each collier. Should the Fair be on, and the vessel going to sea in the evening or early morning, you would find all these youths and sailors on board, also the pilot, the coble alongside, all the moorings cast off, and yet the vessel would not move, all seemed to wonder, but could not tell why. The apprentices appeared to be doing all they could, nay, even excelling the crew in their anxiety to get to sea, but they knew very well it was only for an hour. When the tide turned, the ship had to be moored again; and grumbling at not having got to sea, went ashore, laughing at what they had done. They would then go for a night's jollification, and dance to the tune of the fiddle at the fair. The truth was they had already lashed the ship for the purpose of getting away. Such a course would sometimes be pursued by the sailors, for reasons unknown to the pilot or owner.

Goods were brought down from London for tradesmen in fast sailing colliers, called packets; thus there was the Sunderland packet, the Wear packet, the Durham packet, etc. They carried coals (and goods, if there were any) to London, and brought in return what goods or merchandise there might be at the London wharves for them. The different wharfingers were interested in the packets. Some of the larger tradesmen would also have shares, and they always had their goods sent down in the packet in which they had an interest. This was then the only way in which heavy goods could be brought from London.

Afterwards, the General Steam Navigation Co. ran their boats twice a week to Newcastle, and the goods were sent here from Newcastle by waggon.

During the fruit season, the Lynn colliers brought hundreds of baskets of fruit on top of the ballast, apples, pears, plums, damsons, etc. They used to lie at the Bull Quay to discharge. Dannet's apple loft was in the Low Street, corner of Holmes' wharf, and opposite Spenceley Lane. The women carried the baskets of fruit on their heads from the ship to the apple loft. The vessel would sometimes make a rapid run down, and deliver the fruit in good condition; if long, a large portion was spoiled.

In winter the freshes had always to be provided against, on account of the ice coming away after a thaw. There were so many sands, and so little depth of water in the river, that the vessels felt the full force of the waters as they rushed down. Keels would come down with the fresh, having broken adrift in the upper reaches, when cobles and boats would be in requisition. Running fitters, with their men, could be seen with warps trying to stop and sheer them into a place of safety, while some would drift out to sea and be lost. The writer's father once stopped his keel when she had got down as far as the North Pier; some drifted amongst the ships, got squeezed and sunk, and only a remnant of them left to tell that they had been. As the fresh subsided, one morning on looking out of the window on to the flat, our ballast keel showed only her stem and bottom, the rest was all gone. Part of the warps, anchor and chain were saved, but the keel was a total loss, uninsured. At another of these freshes, whole tiers of colliers were swept away. Some grounded and sunk on the Flat, and thus prevented others from going to sea. When the waters subsided, there were upwards of twenty ships and keels lying there, some complete wrecks, and were abandoned as such by their owners, whilst others were more or less damaged. The amount of damage done by the fresh in one tide, when drawn for by the insurance clubs, amounted to 8 per cent. on the whole capital. We have no such casualties now, though the volume of water is as great, the bed of the river having been deepened by dredging, so that with more space the fresh runs quieter to sea.

Dredging? yes! At that time a small dredger was generally occupied in keeping the low tier clear of the caunch, or the caunch from filling up the low tier. But then the dredger could not always work for want of hoppers; these, at that period, were sailing schooners. If the weather was rough they would not get to sea; and if the wind did not suit, they were in the same fix. There were only four or five of the sailing hoppers; they were generally manned by old sailors, who did not care to venture out if there was not a good prospect of getting in again. When any tier was silting up, then the spooning keel or the dredger would be sent to deepen and level the bottom of the tier. The dredger was called the "Quiam."

It often happened, if a ship lay badly, she would set up her bilge or break her back, and then she would have to discharge and go into the graving or floating dock for repairs, or be hauled up in a primitive way on the North Sands yards. If a ship required her keel seam overhauled, her butt ends caulked, or her bottom cleaned, then she would be laid on the hard, or on the caunch; and ship jobbers, such as Joe Bell, John Spence, Tommy Hall, and others were always ready to undertake the job.

On the 1st April, twenty or more vessels would start on their voyage to Quebec, with ribbons and garlands flying on the stays and rigging, when both Piers would be crowded with friends and sight seers, watching them off and waving their farewells—this was considered a splendid sight.

On one occasion I was standing watching a fleet of light vessels coming into the harbour; the wind was from the east—a good topsail breeze, with a heavy roll of sea; one vessel, further out than the ballast buoys, seemed to be coming in at a prodigious rate; at first we could not understand it. She passed all the others as though they were at anchor. On looking, we saw that one huge wave had caught, and given its impetus to, the ship, which was poised on the top of the rolling wave, which held and carried her on to the beach behind the North Pier, leaving her almost dry on receding.*

It would be about the years 1823-24 that the Seamen's Loyal Standard Association was established.

The first president elected or chosen was the late Capt. William Patterson, retired from the sea, and who was then a teacher of navigation in Pewterer's lane. The Secretary's name was Atkinson. The society was formed for mutual benefits, by payments to shipwrecked seamen, their widows or children. For two years or so the society prospered, both in the number of members and also in its funds. In 1825, an agitation arose amongst the members for a rise in wages, and a general meeting of the members was called to consider and discuss the question. At the meeting, the president deprecated a strike, and counselled accordingly. On the other hand, the secretary supported the strike movement. On the resolution being put to the meeting, it was carried for a strike, to obtain a rise in wages, whereupon the president resigned. A strike did take place, afterwards called the great strike, and a fierce struggle between owners and seamen occurred; the funds, which had been accumulating since the establishment of the association, were soon exhausted. As the strike continued, some of the sailors went round the country, amongst the villages

---

* I have only seen such a sight once in my life.

and farm houses, seeking support, sometimes bringing home potatoes or other produce, and perhaps a chicken or duck. Scant sympathy was shown them by the town's people in general. Stopping the ships going to sea was almost blocking the whole trade of the town and port, and tended very much to ruffle the temper of those whose livelihood depended on trade. Meanwhile, gangs of men kept visiting all the tiers, and overhauling the different ships, and taking the crews out of the vessels. Indeed, the struggle had become so acute that owners, who had secured crews for their ships, found great difficulty in getting them to sea, for the river at tide time swarmed with boats, filled with men on strike, seemingly determined to prevent any vessel going to sea, and when the vessels came abreast the Sand Point (*the channel at that time was close to the point), they were boarded, when a struggle or fight took place to get the men out of the ship, and showers of stones from the Point fell on board the ships. The military were called out, but the sailors still continuing the riot, the magistrates read the Riot Act, calling on the rioters to desist, but taking no heed of this, the soldiers were ordered to fire, which they did, aiming above the heads of the sailors, when the shots took effect amongst the crowd on the Sand Point and on the shipyards, where several men and women were wounded, and two shot dead. The effect of the firing was the dispersion of the mob, and the dis-

---

* An old captain, John Firth, speaking of the strike, said, "I know I had not been long at sea, and they came and took the men out of our ship at the Ferryboat Landing tier, and I could not tell what they had done it for. I was apprenticed to Mr. Ralph Laws, who was a lawyer, and also magistrates' clerk at the time, and when we came back from the voyage, the girls, *i.e.*, the servant girls, told me that a large piece of rag or cloth had been thrown over the back wall, steeped in blood; they supposed the sailors had done it to frighten the master."

Captain W. Lambton said, "The sailors great strike was in 1825, it would be in September or October, we were on the Scotch coast, coming from Quebec, and arrived a day or two after the men were shot."

Neither the wounded nor those shot dead had taken any part in the riot, they were only lookers on.

appearance of the boats and rioters ; other feeble efforts were made to continue the strike, but they failed, and the sailors had to give in.

In 1825, the year of the strike, there were registered at at the Custom House 588 vessels belonging to the port, and of the registered tonnage of 94,582 tons. The number of sailors was estimated at 4,205, exclusive of the apprentices.

One institution in connection with the collier was the harbour boat, the owner of which generally kept a marine store. Patchy Canny was a well-known one, his shop was at the foot of Chancery Lane, in the Low Street ; old Moor, at the foot of the Long Bank, and others. The boat was let out on hire, the charge being three shillings and sixpence for the time the vessel was in the harbour, no matter whether it was three days or three weeks. Captains and owners preferred to hire rather than risk the launching of the ships' boats, which might get squeezed or otherwise come to grief, and perhaps stolen, for if the apprentices wanted to be aboard, and the watch was asleep, it was no uncommon thing to break the chain or pick the lock of any boat in order to get on board, and then let her drift—to have fastened her to the ship would not do. They were a queer lot of boats—strong thofts with knees tarred all over, always causing trouble to the apprentices who had them under their charge. The boys had always to take off or put on shore any person hailing the ship. Should she be moored ashore with a short chain, she might, and would sometimes, sink on the flood tide, and then she had to be bailed out. As a general rule they were always leaky ; and on a morning, as a retired captain tells it, one of us would be sculling and the other bailing out. The places for mooring these boats were—Hardcastle's Slip, Custom House Quay, Mark Quay, Drysdale's Entry, Black Bull Quay, and the foot of the public way above Wylam's Wharf, as well as at other places on the North Quay. There were also the "taggerine" boats plying up and down the river, ready to exchange crockery, or whatever else they might have, for old rope, iron, chains, etc.; his stock-in-trade included crockery, mops, brooms, scrapers, etc.

In the year 1820, there were cleared from the port of Sunderland 7,523 vessels coastwise and 246 to foreign parts, making 7,769. These vessels had to come in as well as clear out. The larger classs of vessels could only go to sea on spring tides, and if the sea was heavy, had to wait till next springs, so that the number of loaded vessels accumulated, and the south-east winds, which brought the light vessels down, prevented the loaded ones from proceeding to sea; thus the harbour got crowded, and some of the light vessels had to go up as far as Deptford, until room could be found in the tiers for them to load. To regulate the movements of traffic for so large a number of vessels, the Commissioners appointed three harbour masters. The harbour was divided into three districts, over which each one had charge. From the piers to the ferryboat landing, Thomas Davison, senior, had charge; he lived in Bank Street. From the ferryboat landing to the bridge, Guy Potts had authority; he lived in his own double cottage on the road to the pier. John Stafford's district included all above the bridge; he lived above John Christy's public house, facing Hardcastle's Quay. Each harbour master was provided with a coble and man to pull him about the river.

DREDGERS.

In the year 1823 or 1824, the Commissioners built a second and more powerful dredger, working on both sides. She was built between Rochester's house and Shotton the boatbuilder's shop, and which stood close by the public road leading from the town to the sands. The ground belonged to the Commissioners, and when ready it was launched into the sea; whilst the machinery was getting ready and fitted, which was slow work in these days. They built three or four hoppers on the same ground, which were also launched into the sea. It would be about 1825 before the dredger got fairly to work. At first the hoppers were towed to sea by hired tug boats; afterwards, in 1826, the Commissioners built a tug boat, and called her the Sea Horse, which was employed for the special purpose of towing the hoppers to and from sea.

The "Wear" steam boat was built and launched from the corner now occupied by Blumer & Robson's yard, over the Potato garth, in 1825. She was commanded by Billy Burton. The "Dragon" was built on Thompson's raff yard, at the foot of Beggar's Bank, and launched November 29th, 1825. Tom Boys was captain.

The "Neptune" was launched from the same yard in 1826, and several other tugboats were built, as well as others which plied on the river. The deepening of the channel and the loading berths by the dredger, and the using of the tugboats, caused a complete revolution in the navigation of the port—the warping down and out to the roads was gone for ever.

The price of towage at first was 2/6 per keel, with 2/6 gratuity to the captain; afterwards it settled down to the charge of 1/6 per keel, and either 2/6 or 1/6 gratuity. Offices were opened to take the colliers on turn for towage to sea.

In 1825 the number of vessels belonging to the Port of Sunderland was 588, with a registered tonnage of 94,582 tons, or an average of $160\tfrac{502}{588}$ tons. In 1828 there were 604 vessels registered, with a tonnage of 103,529 tons, or an average of $171\tfrac{245}{604}$ tons; so that from 1825 to 1828, both years included, the average tonnage had increased about

6¾ per cent., thus showing that the clearing out of the channel, with the increased depth of water, together with the use of the steam tugboats now established, gave greater facilities for despatch ; but these improvements did not in the least improve the position of the shipowners, the ships performing their voyages more quickly by not being detained in the harbour.

On July 10th, 1833, Mr. Henry Tanner, in his evidence before the Select Committee of the House of Commons, when asked question 6640 : " Does not a ship perform her voyage more quickly than she did fifteen years ago ? " says : " I believe she does." Question 6641 : " In what proportion should you say ? " " I cannot answer that question ; but the facilities of steam vessels must increase the number of voyages ; in former years a vessel would lie in Sunderland harbour perhaps six weeks before she could get to sea, now she scarcely ever lies six days." Question 6642 : " So that with the same amount of tonnage there will be a great deal more work done ?" " Unquestionably." Question 6643 : "So that, although the actual amount of tonnage may not be increased, there may be too much tonnage for the work to be done ?" " Yes."

So that, as we have already shewn, the tonnage had increased from 1825 to 1828, the facilities were greater, and ships made more voyages ; yet, unfortunately, the shipments of coals had fallen off.

In 1825, 521,796 chaldrons of coals were shipped coastwise. In 1828, 509,567 chaldrons only were shipped, shewing a falling off of 12,229 chaldrons.

During 1825, 15,531 chaldrons, and during 1828, 22,941 chaldrons were shipped foreign, shewing an increase in 1828 over 1825 of 7,410 chaldrons, but a decrease upon the whole export of 4,819 chaldrons.—*Burnett.* The River

Wear Commissioners, in their return for December, 1886, shew that in 1825, 1,330,414 tons were shipped, and in 1828, 1,326,593 tons, being a decrease of 3,821 tons.

The Commissioners' returns have only lately been made up, but in either case there was a decrease in the exports. Thus, the better facilities, shorter voyages in time, and keener competition, caused a lower rate in freights, and this depression continued for some years. Some owners, possessed of the larger class of vessels, say from 260 to 280 tons register, sent them out to Canada and elsewhere, and, if profitable employment could not be obtained on their return, they were laid up. Some of them were laid up for six months in the year 1832. Other vessels were also laid up for months together; but even the laying up of the ships did not improve the position of the owners much, for at that period, as at present, the whole savings of a lifetime of some owners was in the ship, their living depended on the ship. When Mr. Tanner was asked the question (6614): "Is there great distress among the shipowners at Sunderland?" his reply was, "Very great." Question 6615, "Many insolvencies?" "I am afraid there are." Question 6616, "Do you know whether any considerable portion of shipping belonging to Sunderland is under mortgage?" "I am afraid there is a good deal." Question 6617, "In consequence of losses?" "Yes, and the want of remunerative freights. A man that has a ship of 200 tons, and nothing else to depend upon, is gradually going to ruin."

Thus, according to Mr. Tanner's evidence, small shipowners, in bad times, with nothing else to depend upon, were gradually going to ruin. Even in good times, shipowners with borrowed capital could rarely make it pay; and in after years, when the vicious system became more general, ruin almost invariably followed. The borrower had little or no chance; he had to pay 8 or 10 per cent. per annum for the loan, and taking into account the depreciation of the vessel at 7½ per cent., and the insurance at 10 per cent., in effect 20 per cent. per annum on the value of the vessel had to be paid, without taking into account the depreciation of the vessel's value, before any profit was left for the owner. Thus the small owners, whose vessels were mortgaged, and whose whole living depended upon the profits of the voyage, could hardly be expected to weather the times.*

In all cases, when a vessel was mortgaged, the mortgagee had to give an undertaking to the clubs or insurance associations, guaranteeing any or all calls made by the clubs, that in case the owner of the vessel failed to pay the calls, he undertook to do so, in order to secure to him or them, in case of loss of the vessel, the payment of the insurance money from the clubs to them.†

*In after years, the same system prevailed, not only in small colliers, but in larger vessels. A sailmaker, being wishful to enlarge his trade, wanted to purchase a vessel, he could not be credited for such a large amount, and a lawyer in fair practice was the guarantee for the due payment of the bills. It was known and understood that a mortgage would have to be got, and the full amount of this money was to be paid to the sellers, and for the due payment of the bills a second mortgage was executed to them. Thus the sellers thought they were secure with a respectable guarantee and a second mortgage. The first mortgagee was a noted London merchant, the advance was nominally to be for £4,000, but from this had to be deducted the whole of the year's interest, paid in advance, at 10 per cent., i.e. £400; then there was the insurance for 12 months at 8 per cent. on Lloyds' rules £320, then the lawyer's charges, so that for the nominal sum of £4,000, only £3,250 or thereabouts was advanced. The vessel sailed to the East Indies, the voyage was unfortunate, none of the acceptances were honoured, and when the vessel arrived in London the mortgagee put his bailiff on board, just 12 months after the vessel had started on her first voyage. The sellers had to pay the £4,000 and expenses to secure possession under their mortgage; both the sailmaker and the lawyer went through the bankruptcy court, and after putting the vessel in order and re-selling her, on winding up the accounts, the sellers found they had lost the full amount of money advanced by the first mortgagee, viz., £3,250.

† If a small shipowner lost his vessel he generally received his money from the clubs at six or nine months; and, as this was his business, the money was almost invariably re-invested in shipping.

The withdrawal of the Marquis' coals, for shipment at Seaham Harbour, in 1831, tended to diminish the export of coals at Sunderland. But the opening of the Durham and Sunderland Railway, in 1836, helped in some measure to recoup the loss.

The Railway Company pulled down the old Custom House and all the houses on the Low Quay from the Fish Market up to Noble's Quay, and erected coal drops on a high level for the shipment of coals.

In the years 1834 and 1835 the export of coals got less and less. In 1833, 1,349,058 tons were exported; in 1834, 1,111,760 tons; and in 1835, 1,088,829 tons; thus, at this period, 1835, there seems to have been the least quantity shipped, for in 1836, 1,155,414 tons, and in 1837, 1,331,438 tons were exported.‡

In 1836 a boom in shipping seems to have taken the old shipowners by surprise. Shipping Companies were being established all along the east coast—on the Tyne, Wear, and Tees, and also at other places. The managers were generally selected from captains that had been successful as captains, so that their experience might tell on investors as to the efficiency of management.

By the establishment of these companies, a complete rage for vessels took place in the market, new vessels were contracted for, and old ones bought up, as the requirements of the companies had to be satisfied.

---

‡ The Durham and Sunderland Railway was opened on the 7th day of August, 1836, which accounts for the increased shipment of coals in that year, and the further increase in 1837, and years following. By this railway the following collieries were brought into connection with the port, viz.:—Haswell, South Hetton, Belmont, Shincliff, Whitwell, Hetton, and Rainton.

One shipping company, managed by Capt. Murray, of the "Market Hotel," Coronation Street, determined to call all their new vessels by the letters in the Greek alphabet, beginning at Alpha and ending at Omega. This company made rapid progress, and got, I think, to the seventh letter. Other companies were also contracting for new vessels, the results were, shipbuilding became brisk, and, in order to supply the demand, shipbuilding yards were established in almost inconceivable places; in quarry holes, on the edges of the banks of the river, or the clay dug out to make a hole to build the vessel in. Working men left their employment to become master shipbuilders, and such energy was put into the trade that the supply of vessels soon overtook and distanced the demand. Speculation in ships became rife, some ships were sold twice or thrice over, even before they were launched, and sometimes three or four times the value of the vessel was floating on paper before she went to sea. Indeed, literally speaking, a man with a decent looking face, and goodly appearance, could become a shipowner without paying more than a five pound note to clinch the bargain. He having bought, his next move was to hurry off and sell his ship to somebody else. The payments were often at 3, 6 and 9 months' date. If the purchaser could get a little barter shoved in, so much the better for the buyer and also the seller; the former thought he made a profit on his goods, the latter that he was reducing his risks by having something in hand. Meanwhile, the rapidity of production far outstripped the necessities or the demand. But I must not here anticipate, suffice it to say the bubble of the shipping companies burst, the majority of the vessels were brought to the hammer, no one seemed to be any the richer except the managers, and many lost the savings which they had invested. And yet times became worse than ever for shipowners. In 1842, the exportation of coal fell off from the previous year. In 1841 1,348,980 tons were shipped; in 1842, 1,242,051; in 1843,

1,194,723, and in 1844, 1,045,351 tons, which was the lowest quantity since the year 1821, when the total quantity shipped amounted to 1,036,441 tons, and in 1822 to 1,047,462 tons. The small quantity shipped in 1844 is perhaps justly attributed to the long strike of the pitmen in that year. Nevertheless, this goes to show the extremely hard conditions under which the shipowners laboured or suffered, especially in the coal trade, and how hard it must have been for small owners, having a mortgage on their vessels, to eke out a living.

In 1842, employment for shipping was difficult to be had at any rate of freight, *i.e.* remunerative. The "Ringdove," belonging to the late William Potts, made a coal voyage to London; she was chartered from Quebec to Sunderland, with liberty to take a cargo of coals on her way out. After performing the voyage, on her arrival at Sunderland, she was taken off the clubs for a month—a remunerative freight could not be had. "I don't care," said the owner to the captain "if you can only get two sixpences for a shilling; I don't want to lay her up yet; go, and see what you can do." The captain tried, and ultimately a freight to a French port was obtained; from there she went to Cardiff and loaded coals for London, and then she came to Sunderland, where she was laid up for the winter. When the whole of the year's work was balanced, the owner said to the captain, with a smiling face (for the old gentleman always had a smiling face): "Now, what do you think she has made?" The captain said: "I am sure I cannot tell." "Well, then, she has left on the year's work twelve pounds." "Only twelve pounds?" "Yes, twelve pounds left to pay for management, interest on the capital, $7\frac{1}{2}$ to 10 per cent. depreciation in value of the vessel, and for the yearly overhaul, and the fresh supply of stores to pay for to start next year's work."

In 1842 we reached the lowest depression in shipping. At the close of the year five ships sailed from Liverpool in search of the island called Ichaboe, where, it had been surmised, a large deposit of guano would be found; the instructions given to the captains must have been imperfect, for four of them returned, not being able to find the island; the fifth one, the "Ann," of Bristol, was nearly in the same predicament, when, by accident, the island was found.

The arrival of this vessel, in 1843, loaded with guano, and the cargo selling at a high price, caused a good deal of excitement amongst shipowners. The guano was to be had for carrying on board the vessel. The principal things the owners had to do was to supply the vessel with sufficient provisions and water, together with wheel barrows, picks, shovels and bags, for the guano to be dug out of the mass, and carried in bags or wheeled in barrows to the boats. Planks and spars had also to be sent, to erect a gangway to where the boat lay afloat outside the surf to receive the cargo. Early on the rush, some enterprising Yorkshiremen erected a gangway some 300 feet in length, for the use of which they charged, and made a fortune out of the adventure. Amongst the number of vessels, from different ports in the kingdom, flocking to Ichaboe, Sunderland sent her portion, several of the shipowning firms sent out vessels, amongst whom were Andrew and Richard White, Greenwell and Sacker, and others. The success of the first venture stimulated for the second. During the run, there sprung up a lot of guano merchants, willing to charter at good rates of freight, the shipowner finding all the necessary requisites for loading the vessel; and brokers were running after the shipowners, with the charters—already signed by the guano merchants—in their pockets. Several shipowners were actually prevailed on to send their vessels out under these charters, supposing they had a responsible person on whom to fall back in case of non-success.

On the arrival out of some of these vessels no agent was to be found; the 800,000 or 1,000,000 tons of guano had either been already shipped or was claimed by the different captains on the is'and, and no cargo was to be had; the result was that the vessels had either to return in ballast or run on for the Cape of Good Hope, or stretch across to South America for a cargo. On the return of these vessels the charterers could not be found. It afterwards transpired that a large number of these charters had been signed by a shoemaker living in an attic in Liverpool, and who had received a certain sum for every charter he signed.

In 1844 the whole of the guano was about cleared off the island. The year 1845 witnessed the run of nitrate of soda, also said to be found on the African coast. Nothing to do but load the nitrate of soda as fast as you could! This run was more from the west coast. There was at least one Sunderland shipowner who sent a vessel out on this venture—Ralph Hutchinson. The captain said: "When the ship arrived out there were hundreds of vessels lying along the coast ready to load the nitrate of soda. But when I landed with the boat I saw at once it was all a sham; there was a thin salted crust on the top, the under part all sand; it might be said to have been at one time covered by the sea. I left the coast and visited several small islands, and contrived to bring home a cargo of guano, though not of first-rate quality."

The guano and nitrate of soda run, by reducing the surplus tonnage (for which no profitable employment could be had in 1842), shewed itself at once by the stiffening, and also the rising in the freight market all round. Besides these the general trade of the country was better.

The development of the railway system was also helping on the improvement, so that in 1843-4-5 there was a general revival in shipping; more enquiries for new vessels were in the market, and though for a time the trade was partially speculative, yet ships were paying better ; carpenters' wages had risen to 18/- per week, and in 1845 to 24/- per week. Freights also rose in 1844—Quebec to Sunderland, 37/- per load, which was a good payable freight. 1846 was the first year of the Irish famine, and freights, Quebec to Sunderland, reached 45/- per load, and in 1847, 45/6 per load ; meanwhile, the freights from Odessa to Cork or Falmouth for orders, ran up to from 80/- to 90/-* per ton for tallow ; and those owners who had vessels suitable for the trade made large profits. Some owners, whose ships were not sheathed with yellow metal, had their bottoms coated with a mixture of brimstone, arsenic, and blacklead, running all risks with such a coating, of their vessels getting wormed, so tempting were the large profits then made. This spurt in freights was only temporary—to fill up a present demand, and no more. Yet, still it had the effect for the time being of raising the freights all round. In 1847 ten pounds per keel was given from Sunderland to Quebec ; and in June, 1847, a vessel called the "Blessing," was chartered to carry 50,000 fire bricks from the North Dock to Quebec at thirteen pounds sterling per keel of 7,000 fire bricks. The foregoing seem to have been the highest rates the shipowners obtained during the period of the Irish famine.

In 1848, the extra demand had subsided. Freight to Quebec fell—coals were £8, fire bricks £10 per keel of 7,000 bricks ; showing a fall in outward rates from the previous year of 20 per cent., whilst the homeward freights (Quebec to Sunderland) fell from £2 5s. 6d. to £1 14s., a reduction of 25 per cent., yet this was not the lowest. In 1849, £7 10s. per keel was paid coals, Sunderland to Quebec, and in the same year £1 13s. per load was paid,

---

* It was said that some of the ships that went out seeking were chartered at 120/- per ton, tallow.

Quebec to Sunderland; and, freights still falling—in 1850, £1 12s.; in 1851, £1 10s.; and in 1852, £1 8s. per load was paid Quebec to Sunderland.

The year 1852 seems to have been a bad one, for several heavy failures occurred among shipowners, and also several other firms, previously of good standing.

The downward course, previous to 1852, as before related, was progressive, and that in the face of times when there was an expectation of improvement, for in 1848 the gold diggings in California were before the world; in that year 6,000 emigrants entered the field. It is stated that in 1849 no less than 100,000 emigrants entered California—80,000 Americans, and 20,000 of other nationalities. It was thought that this immense number of emigrants would absorb a large amount of tonnage, and thus cause a rise in freights. But, then, the carrying capacity of the American mercantile navy was such that it really had little or no percepible impression on the freight market here, on the east coast; they did all, or nearly all the then carrying work amongst themselves, without any regard to the British shipowner.

In June, 1851, the discovery of the gold fields at Mount Alexander and Ballarat, in the Province of Victoria, Australia, was the cause of a great demand for shipping. In the year 1852 there were landed in Victoria, 94,664 emigrants. So large a number of emigrants required a proportionate amount of shipping space for transport, this tonnage was removed out of the market for at least twelve months. The withdrawal of this large amount of shipping was not felt much in 1852. A large percentage sailed in the summer and autumn of that year. But when the engagements for shipping had to be made for 1853, the scarcity of tonnage became apparent. The result was, freights rose in some instances 50 per cent. and upwards; and freights which, in 1852 (Quebec to Sunderland), were done at 28/- per load, opened out in the spring of 1853 at £2 2s. per load, *i.e.* 50 per cent. more than in the previous year; and from Stettin, £1 3s. per load oak was paid. On March 3rd, 1852, 21/6 per ton was paid, Sunderland to Rio de Janeiro. On April 1st, 1853, from Newport, Monmouth, to the same place, 35/- per ton was paid, showing an advance on the Sunderland freight of 60 per cent., without considering the relative positions of the two ports for the same destination. In August, 1852, 60/- per ton, tallow, of 20 cwts. gross, was paid from Odessa to London; other goods as per printed rates.

So great was the scarcity of tonnage that outward vessels were chartered in advance homewards; and four pounds per ton, dead weight, for sugar, saltpetre and seeds was given, Calcutta to London, to a ship then on her way to Aden from Sunderland with coals.

In 1852, two emigrant vessels sailed from the port; they were both new ships, built here, viz.: the "Lizzie Webber" and the "Emigrant."

The owner of the "Lizzy Webber," together with his wife and family, emigrated in his own vessel. Webber had been a farmer and English timber merchant, at that period these two trades were often linked together. The captain was a Sunderland man, named Rowntree, whose wife and family also sailed in the ship; they intended to employ the vessel in trading in Australia.

The sailing of this first emigrant vessel from the Port of Sunderland, on the 31st July, 1852, direct to Melbourne, caused a great sensation, not only in the town, but also in the surrounding districts; as several of the emigrants came from these districts, a large number of their friends had come to see them off, and take the last farewell. The Piers were crowded. As the vessel left the Docks and went out of the Harbour, with garlands hanging and colours flying, the hurrahs were loud and continuous, the waving of the handkerchiefs and the gesticulations many. When she was leaving the entrance three loud cheers were given by the crowd on the Piers, then the three return cheers from the ship, and one more from the friends on shore; but the last cheer was not so hearty and loud as the first; to some of the spectators it was the last look—the last farewell to loved ones dear; and many a throbbing, beating heart, and many a lump-choaked throat, and many a briny tear was dropped from the eye whilst they remained watching the vessel as she sailed away, until the white sails only were seen reflected by the shining sun.

The second vessel, the "Emigrant," 405 tons, commanded by R. Williams, sailed from Sunderland on the 11th day of September, 1852. A portion of the emigrants went on board here, the remainder embarked at Plymouth. Some of our noted tradesmen went with these two vessels, amongst others was Brown Young, the sailmaker, who was a prominent Wesleyan, but left the old connexion during the purging by the fly leaf controversies. He was one of the principal men in the erection of the South Durham Street Tabernacle. Mr. Snaith, a well-to-do merchant tailor, with his wife and family, were amongst the number that embarked at Plymouth. After remaining some years he found means to return to the old town, and commenced business as an auctioneer; also, William Stephenson, the painter, with his son William and one of his daughters. He had a good business, and was considered fairly well to do in the trade, but nothing could deter him from going, so off he went, leaving his wife and part of his young family behind. Years after, one of his daughters went to service at Mrs. Love's, at Durham, and being a comely looking girl, young Love married her. Her husband was the heir to upwards of one million pounds sterling. The son William, who emigrated with his father, has risen in position and station, and in the year in which we write, 1887, is chairman or president of the Wesleyan Conference in Australia.

This rise in freights took place before the breaking out of the Crimea war, and was principally caused by the sudden withdrawal of so large an amount of tonnage from the general trade; a great impetus was also given to exports to Australia, in order to supply the demand for necessaries for the emigrants, which further reduced the available amount of shipping for present use or need.

In the latter part of September, 1853, in anticipation of the Crimea war, £1 10s. per load freight for fir timber, and £1 12s. per load for oak timber was given from Memel to Sunderland.

In the spring of 1854 the Crimea war took a further quantity of tonnage out of the market for transports, etc. This withdrawal was not so much felt, because the war closed the trade to the Black Sea, and also to the Russian Ports in the Baltic and White Seas. Yet still, on the opening out of the shipping trade for 1854, freights from Quebec to Sunderland rose from £2 2s. to £2 13s. per load, or an advance of 25 per cent. upon those of 1853, and 90 per cent. above those of 1852.

In 1855, after the war, freights from Quebec to Sunderland fell to £1 17s. per load, or a drop of 30 per cent. 1856 freights ruled the same as in 1855. In 1857, Quebec freights dropped to £1 12s. per load—a further fall of 15 per cent.; and in 1858, ships were chartered from Quebec to Sunderland at £1 6s. per load, being a further drop of 20 per cent., this rate was 2/- per load, or 7 per cent. less than the lowest rate in 1852.

Thus, from 1852 to 1854 freights rose 90 per cent., chiefly on account of the tonnage required for emigration to Australia in 1852-53, and for the tonnage required for transports for the war. The return of the emigrant vessels and the closing of the war, together with the enormous increase of new tonnage added (to be hereafter touched on), caused a complete stagnation in the freight market, and, consequently, freights fell, between 1854 and 1858, to less than they were in 1852 by 7 per cent.

Before the Crimea war, any extra supply of wheat, both for France and England, was drawn largely from the Danube and Black Sea. The war with Russia not only stopped the supply, but the partial harvests in the southern provinces of that country (on account of non-cultivation and other causes) were required for the support of the Russian army; consequently, wheat became scarce, and in the early part of 1856 the French Government paid, through their agents, as high as £6 10s. per ton freight for wheat from Bombay to Havre, which was placed in the government stores.

What we have already written will show the uncertainty of profits in shipping, and any calculation as to profits should be taken and estimated over a series of years, not forgetting to take into account the annual depreciation in value of the vessel.

SHIP CAPTAINS.

Some owners refused to purchase a ship until they had secured the services of a captain whom they could trust. When the vessel was once out of the reach of the owner, all depended on the captain, who had it in his power to make or mar the owner; hence the necessity of having your property in the hands of a captain you could trust. An owner might plan, lay his vessel on for something which he considered good, and sure to leave a handsome profit; but his profits, as estimated, might be swamped, and a loss recorded in his books, owing to the incompetency and want of common sense on the part of the captain. Yet trusted captains have been turned out of their employment because they were uncertificated, and very incompetent men in every respect put into their places, to the great detriment and heavy loss of the owner.*

---

* A ship 1000 tons, 13 years A1, had performed a successful voyage from Sunderland to Calcutta and London. When the Indian Mutiny broke out, in 1857, she was taken up by the Government to convey troops to Bombay, the poop was filled with officers. When ready for clearing out, the owners were informed that the captain could not go, being uncertificated. A captain holding a certificate was engaged at £20 per month. After a very long voyage, he found his way to Bombay, amongst the last of the transports. At Bombay, she was chartered by the agents to load rice at Rangoon at £3 15s. per ton for London, this freight would amount to £4,500, upon which the owners paid a commission of 5 per cent. The vessel should have made the round in twelve or thirteen months. On the arrival of the ship at Rangoon, the captain was induced to cancel the charter, and to accept instead a freight to Hong Kong for rice, at a dollar a bag, the gross amount of this freight was £3,500. On arrival at Hong Kong no freights were to be had, he had to take in ballast, and the vessel laid at Hong Kong for six months, when she was chartered at £2 per ton from Woo Sung to London. The whole of the £3,500 was spent, and the captain drew upon the owners for the balance of his expenses £140. The ship came home with 500 tons of stone ballast, and only discharged 1,400 tons of tea instead of 1,700 or 1,800 tons. The homeward freight was £2,800, thus the gross amount of freight earned was £6,300, or £800 more than the direct freight home, less £140 drawn on the owners. For this amount of £660 net, the vessel was detained and occupied on the whole round upwards of two years, as against 12 to 13 months as before stated. Thus, when the accounts were made up, instead of making a profit of £2,000, by coming direct home as chartered, the loss, including insurance for 18 months, interest on capital, depreciation of property, portage bill, etc., was £4,677, making a difference to the owners of £6,677. On the vessel's discharge in London, when the captain's accounts were presented, they shewed a balance due to him of £850 odd. The gross amount of his wages for two years, according to agreement, was £480. These accounts were left for arbitration, and instead of £850 odd were reduced to £440, or £40 less than his gross wages. This man, on the spur of the difficulty, took the place of an honest man and careful captain. The owners, after making enquiry, found that they could get no redress against this certificated captain.

To shew the contrast—a portion of the vessel was sold to a captain who took the command by agreement ; his remuneration was £10 per month, and 1/3 cabin freight. The ship was taken off the A1 clubs, and insurance effected at Lloyd's—out to Calcutta, whilst there, and home at 75/- per cent. The owners were fortunate in again obtaining government employment ; the vessel sailed, and on her arrival at Calcutta the captain succeeded in obtaining invalids home. The voyage was completed in nine months, and after paying insurance and all charges, left a nett profit of £5,300.

These illustrations shew how much the profits on investments in shipping depended on the captain, in whose possession, for the time being, all authority and power rested.

CHAPTER XI.

CUSTOM HOUSES AND TIMBER DUTIES.

Tradition affirms that the Custom House was on Bishopwearmouth Green. An old low two-storied house is said to be the one which was occupied by the Customs authorities centuries ago.

According to our local historians—Garbutt, Burnett, and Summers—the tradition comes out during an action at law by the evidence of a witness.

It appears on the records that the copyholders held that they had the right, and had been in the habit of quarrying and leading stones from Building Hill from time immemorial, without hindrance and without payment.

Teasdale Mowbray wanted to levy a charge on the copyholders for the stones thus quarried and led, which the copyholders resisted and would not pay. Amongst the copyholders was Mr. John Thornhill; and in order to compel payment, in the year 1767 Mowbray commenced an action at law, which stood—Teasdale Mowbray *versus* J. Thornhill; the case was tried, and the decision of the jury was in favour of the copyholders; and, amongst other things brought out in the evidence at the trial, was the following:—"An old man deposed that he had heard old John Richardson say that the market was on the Green, and that he shewed where the cross and the stalls stood; that the Sunderland people *had stolen the Custom House*, then the Market, and would steal the Church if they could carry it." What a pity it is that when old John Richardson shewed where the cross and the stalls stoods he did not

As the trade of the port increased this house would, no doubt, be found too small and inconvenient for the purpose of the Customs. A large house was consequently rented, which stood about 200 yards to the east of the old house, facing Bank Street and the Pottery Bank, with a large open space at the back running down to the river's side. The customs were removed to this house in the year 1748.*

As the other Custom Houses, which were occupied both before and after this house, are still to be seen, while this house seems to have gone out of memory, we will describe it as it was about seventy years ago, or in 1822-3:—Bank Street was held up by a high, broad, buttress wall. The house stood at a distance from the street, and the entrance from Bank Street was over an arched-way; and between the house and the sustaining wall flights of stone steps led down to the lower parts of the building, known as the Out-door Officers' Departments, and out at the back into a large yard, and thence on to the quay at Hardcastle's Slipway, now the Low Street. This house stood by itself, it was a square brick building, three stories in height, and always went by the name of the Old Custom House.†

---

* This Custom House, which we call number three, appears to have been built by a man named Smithson, who belonged to Monkwearmouth. Smithson appears to have been a speculative builder, and had got hold of a parcel of freehold ground, on which he built this house and afterwards mortgaged it, as appears by the deed of 1768, wherein it was described as being then used as a Custom House; and again by a deed of 1799 we find it to be used as a Custom House; and in a deed of 1815, as lately used as a Custom House.

† There were no houses to the west of it until you came to Mrs. Hutchinson's property, where a flight of stone steps led from the top of the banks down to the quay. At the east of these steps were the two ashpits (in common) for the tennants. Mr. Penman's garden at the back of his house, together with his workshops, looked over the banks on to, and far beyond, the river. The banks were at that time partially covered with coarse grass, upon which the children played.

In the rooms of this Old Custom House Peggie Potts lived during her early married life, and a comely good-looking woman she was in her youthful days. Her husband's name was William, commonly called "Bill," but amongst his intimate associates he was generally called "Winter,"—Winter being his nick-name.

After the passing of the Durham and Sunderland Railway Bill the Old Custom House was pulled down to make the railway from the Moor to the drops in the Low Street and on the Quay for the shipment of coals; the railway was open August 7th, 1836.

The Customs were transferred from the old Custom House on the 10th October, 1813 (corrected date), to a large double three-storied house, originally erected in 1727, by a Mr. Edward Brown, for his private residence, at the end of Fitters' Row, facing south, with a large garden or garth running down to the ropery on the Moor, and to Silver Street on the west.†

George Robinson, Esq., was collector, this gentleman resigned in 1822.

During the period of Mr. Robinson's collectorship no vessel was allowed to clear at the Custom House until the whole of her cargo was on board; and when the loading

---

The last time I saw the old woman was in the summer of 1875, at the head of Lambton Street, in the High Street, at Turnbull's shop corner, dressed as usual—with a clean apron on, and looking about in what the poor folks would call a rather dazed manner, with a kind of unrest about her. I stopped, and simply said to her: "Peggie, how many years is it since Winter died?" Immediately, the old woman's memory flashed back to the days of her young and married life; she laid her hand on me by the arm, "Winter!" she said, "and did you know Winter, sir?" "Yes, Peggie, I knew him very well." "Mister, and you knew Winter?" "Yes, Peggie." "Why, sir, Winter was my husband; who are you? and you knew Winter; do tell me, sir, who you are." "Yes, Peggie, I have often heard him sing his favourite song: 'Gloomy winter's come again.'" The old woman's thoughts went back to her early days of married life; her heart seemed full of the olden days, and tears trickled down her old cheeks, when she asked me again, "Do tell me, sir, who you are; and you knew Winter. Ah! my poor Winter." A few months later and the rolls of death contained the name of poor Peggie, who died on the 10th October, 1875, aged eighty-six years. She was buried in the Sunderland Cemetery, and with a respectable funeral. The writer saw her buried, and received a memorial card from the family. The late W. W. Robson also saw her buried, but neither the writer nor Mr. Robson were amongst the funeral cortege.

† Thomas Street now occupies a large portion of the garden, and the offices of the Board of Trade and the Shipping Offices now occupy the south portion of the garden facing the Moor.

had to be completed in the river or in the roads the captain had to come ashore and clear the ship, and go off again in the coble before he could start on his voyage; for this purpose a room was rented, and occupied by a clerk called "a night clerk," whose duty it was to clear vessels loaded in the river or in the roadstead after custom house hours. For the performance of this duty an extra fee was charged, which went into the private pocket of the collector, he paying the clerk for attendances and sevices.

It was openly stated that the collector's overtime fees were more than double the amount of his fixed salary. The Board of Customs, without any intimation, sent down Commissioners to make enquiry into the circumstances. The collector was asked to state to them the amount he received per annum, including his salary and the extra fees he received for clearing after Custom House hours; fearing to state the full amount of extras he received, in case that he might have to refund a large sum, he named £750, or thereabouts, which sum was really not equal to one-half the amount he had been receiving. The Board of Customs took the collector at his word, raised his stipend to the amount he named, abolished the fees, and thus hushed up the matter.

After the resignation of Mr Robinson, in 1822, Sir Cuthbert Sharp was appointed collector; meanwhile, the neighbourhood in which the Custom House stood had been and was deteriorating very fast. Houses, which were at one time the large mansions of the fitters, were let out into tenements; and the approaches to the Custom House being by way of the Hat Case or through open alleys from Silver Street, which were also inhabited by a lower class population, made the situation anything but pleasant to approach.

The merchants and shipowners, who were the parties principally interested in doing business at the Custom House, accordingly presented a memorial to the Commissioners of Customs, requesting that a more eligible situation might be appointed; this memorial was presented before the year 1830. After waiting for several years the present Custom House was erected, and opened for business on the 5th October, 1837. It is built facing the river; the main or principal entrance is from the High Street, where Chancery Lane* was; the house is built where Canny's Square or Place was, and also the site where Patchy Canny's house stood, where he lived and carried on the business of a ship chandler and marine store dealer.

The Customs Authorities had had the memorial of the merchants and shipowners before them for nearly ten years. Meanwhile, the Durham and Sunderland Railway Company had for their purposes acquired the Low Quay and the houses thereon; and after pulling down the houses and strengthening the quay walls, had erected the wooden gearing and drops for the shipment of coals, as previously stated, in 1836. So that when the Custom House was opened, in October, 1837, the upper story or long room looked on to the railway gearing and drops, whilst the lower stories were over-shadowed by the erections, leaving only the narrow cart way between, in the Low Street.

Since the opening of the South Docks, in 1850, the whole of the wooden gearing and drops have been removed, and now the Custom House really faces the river. It is a building of three stories; the long room in the upper story is on a level with the High Street, and runs the full length of the building, from east to west; the offices below, facing the river, are light and airy; the offices facing south look on a blank retaining wall, are consequently dark, and cannot, by any possibility, have a glimpse of the sun. The

---

* Chancery Lane communicated from the High Street with the square by a short flight of steps from the end of the lane to a wooden gallery running to the west side of the square, and thence by another long flight of steps to the square and the Low Street.

communications from the long room to these lower offices are by a broad flight of stairs and passages, terminating at a step above the level of the Low Street. On this lower flat the outside officers—tide waiters, boatmen, searchers, timber measurers, and other officials were located; and at each side of the passage are the Customs' warehouses, with large gates opening into the Low Street.

At the date of the opening of this Custom House (5th October, 1837,) Sir Cuthbert Sharp was Collector, Mr. Smith, Controller; and Mr. John Blakeston, Landing Surveyor.

So great had been the increase of the trade of the port that the accommodation in the new premises was completely occupied; this increase was especially the case for materials in wood shipbuilding, viz.: in hemp, tar, and oak timber, as well as in the bulk of trade generally, for whereas in the year 1818 only eight loads of oak were imported from Germany, in 1837 and following years, thousands of loads were brought in, which gave employment to a great many officers and extra or outside men. All things seemed to work smoothly and even between the merchants and the Customs; the merchants knew what duty had to be paid, and were also acquainted with the different classes of wood and the different modes of measurement, and generally had a person to check the Customs' Officers in their measurements for duty.

In the years 1845 and 1846 this harmony was disturbed; an altogether new and different manufacture of oak was imported from Stettin, which was denominated as oak plancons, and also hewn oak logs. This class of wood being irregular in its growth and make, it was found that there was no rule laid down in the book of instructions by which the wood could be callipered and brought into cubic feet for duty (except by the quarter girth line measure), but this was not to be thought of, the timber had to be charged duty as per calliper measure. The officers, accordingly, measured the logs the extreme size, and required the merchants to pay the duty on this measure as callipered; to this the importers demurred, and declined to pay. They said the duty was only payable on 50 cubic feet of timber, *i.e.*, a cubic foot of 1728 cubic inches, and that the officers, in calliping the wood and working the same out on the rule, had included so many cubic feet of the atmosphere, for which said air they declined to pay 7/6 per load duty. In fact, the logs were all irregular, each one having a wane of several inches, more or less, on the four corners; the Landing Surveyor's (Mr. Charles Lemon) attention was called to the matter, and he at once admitted that they could not legally charge duty on wood when it was not there, and, after considering the matter, gave instructions to the officers that the defective angles should be measured and the amounts deducted from the gross measurement of the logs, and the duty to be charged on the nett. The average allowance thus made would be about 12 per cent., had the timber, however, been measured by the tape quarter girth, the difference would have been from 25 to 30 per cent.*

This mode of measuring, by allowing off the defective angles, was continued without question, until merchants at other ports began to import the same class of logs; these importers, hearing of the allowance at Sunderland, naturally claimed the same allowance for the defective angles, as at Sunderland; this was not allowed, and the question was ultimately referred to the Board in London. The Board called or required Mr. Lemon, the Landing Surveyor, to account for his conduct in making such allowance, and, after some correspondence, he sent the drawing of a log, shewing

---

* It is a fact that for irregular wood, such as English Oak, Elm, etc., in all cases for their own uses, the government always bought by the legal measure of 1728 cubic inches to the foot, by string measure, quarter girth.

the defective angles, up to the Board—this took place in 1852; the Board then sent down their head measurer to inspect the wood and report. He came down and inspected a cargo which was then discharging in the South Dock, and which had been brought in by the original importers of this class of wood, and he, on his return, reported to the Board. Meanwhile, the Board made enquiries amongst their old Landing Surveyors, amongst whom was Mr. John Blakeston, whose report upheld that of Mr. Lemon, the Landing Surveyor.

After consideration, the Board ordered that the logs should be measured in full, and 6 per cent. allowed off to compensate for the defective angles. The trade considered the order of the Board as unjust.* However, the importers did not feel themselves justified in withstanding the order for the general benefit of the whole trade.

---

* This unjust decision of the Board was also productive of great evil and loss to the merchants otherwise. The Board's order, as stated for this class of wood, was used by the Port Authorities and the Railway Company to over-ride the common law.

The Port Authorities charged their dues under this order, and the Railway Company charged their rates of carriage under this order, and only 6 per cent. was allowed. Thus the merchants and consumers were made to pay more than 19 per cent. for port dues and railway carriage than was rightly due; and no remonstrance or protest, made from time to time by the merchants, had any effect, till on February 7th, 1881, the Railway Company wrote: "I beg to inform you that it has now been decided to charge Stettin Oak Logs and Memel Wainscot Logs tape measurement. The square timber rate with Derby is 12/6 per ton, not 10/10, as heretofore.—Signed, Wm. Bryans."

From the date of the receipt of this note the merchants forwarded all their hewn oak logs tape measurement, which gave 30 per cent. and upwards in comparison with calliper measurement, which they continued to do until the second note was sent, which shews that the company almost regretted the former, and offering to carry the logs 25 per cent. under calliper measurement.

But it was not until June, 1882, that is thirty years after the Board's dictum, that the North-Eastern Railway Company, notified as follows:

"North-Eastern Railway, South Dock Station,
Sunderland, June 13th, 1882.

Gentlemen—I beg to inform you that it has now been decided (when the correct calliper measurement is given) to allow 25 per cent. off calliper measurement on Stettin Oak, and to charge at the square timber rates.—Signed, Wm. Bryans."

The order of the Board, as regards the allowance of the 6 per cent., still caused the merchants to pay duty on 19 per cent. for wood which was not in the log.

So long as any duty was collected the allowance of only 6 per cent. in the measurement was deducted off this class of logs.

In the year 1860 the duty on foreign timber was reduced from 7/6 to 1/- per load.

In the year 1861 all colonial timber and East India teak, which had previously been admitted free of duty, was also charged 1/- per load duty.*

The Board's order, so far as the Customs were concerned, ended ten years after, on the repeal of the timber duties in 1862, but it enabled the Port Authorities and the Railway Company to continue the unjust scale of charge for twenty years after, viz. : from 1862 to 1882.

One firm in this line of business, during the space of eleven years, had been overcharged, and had paid to the North-Eastern Railway Company an amount of between £2,700 and £3,000.

* Colonial timber and East India Teak not being measured by the Customs, disputes often arose between the shipowner and merchant as measurement for freight ; the owner could always employ a measurer on his own account, but this never occurred without grumbling.

When the duty was reduced to 1/- per load on foreign timber, the writer, in a letter to W. S. Lindsay, M.P., suggested that, in order to do away with cavilling and unpleasantness between shipowner and merchant, 1/- per load should be charged on all Colonial timber and East India Teak, which would enable the shipowner to get his certificate of cargo when discharged from the Customs, and which would also pay the Customs' expenses for measuring and leave a balance for the Treasury. This letter was shewn by Mr. Lindsay to the Secretary of the Treasury, who adopted the suggestion, and the budget for 1861 declared the duty of 1/- per load on all timber imported. This suggestion, at the time, was made in the interests of the shipowners.

In 1861 a large and influential meeting of shipowners was held in the Large Hall in the Freemasons' Tavern, Bishopsgate Street, to ventilate their grievances. Mr. W. S. Lindsay and the writer representing the Sunderland Shipowners' Society (by special request), were both on the platform, together with Mr. Charles Alcock and Mr. Holmes, late wharfinger. The meeting was the most noisy I ever attended. W. S. Lindsay, our M.P., was literally howled down, and had to take his seat before finishing his speech. The representative from Sunderland also spoke, and, amongst other things, stated that the foreigner could then build a ship, put all the outfit on board complete, bring her over to England, sell her, and obtain an English register, without paying a shilling duty ; whereas if the merchant brought in the same class of

This gave the officers more work, for previously they had not measured wood which was free from duty. This was the last spark of prosperity to the measurers and men interested, but it was only for a short period, for in 1862 the timber duties were abolished. The officers' duties as timber measurers had become a thing of the past; it also threw out of employment a number of outside men, who were taken on when required, but were not on the permanent staff of the house.

raw material of which the foreign ship was built, on that material or wood he would have to pay duty, and illustrated this as follows: at Sunderland, on one occasion when a strong south-east gale of wind was blowing, with a heavy sea running and breaking on the bar, a very large fleet of light vessels ran into the harbour, and several were driven on to the Potato Garth, which was within the mouth of the harbour, and some lives were lost; a number of the vessels were wrecked, amongst them being several foreign vessels, some of which were sold as wrecks. When the storm abated, efforts were made to get them off. The foreign vessels that were sold and got off were registered at the Customs, no duty being chargeable; whilst other foreign vessels, which could not be got off, had to be broken up, and the buyers had to pay duty on the broken up wood of the old ships. The "Times," and other London papers, commented on the inconsistency of such a state of things. In the next Session of Parliament (1862) the whole of the duties on timber were abolished.

CHAPTER XII.

PRIMAGE DUES.

Sunderland had been held (as the phrase runs), from time immemorial, to be a creek of Newcastle, and was said to be so styled in the Charter granted to the Trinity House of Newcastle-on-Tyne.

The Guild or Fraternity of the Blessed Trinity of Newcastle was the ancient name under which they were known. The brethern or fraternity elected their own officers and filled the vacancies amongst themselves as they occurred.

It is said that the Guild and its successors had been in existence for about 500 years—probably at or prior to the period "when Richard the second, in 1384, on account of his devotion to St. Cuthbert, granted leave to export the produce of the mines in the County of Durham without paying any duties to the Corporation of Newcastle."—*Burnett, page 129.* And is supposed, in its earlier days, to have been formed for mutual aid and charity.

It may be, as alleged, that from times prior to the date of 1384, they had power or authority to collect monies for charities, to place buoys and beacons, to erect lights, and rule the pilotage. At the trial in Carlisle, in 1851, no documents as to having such authority and power were produced. It was then stated to the court, by counsel for the Trinity House, that the oldest and most ancient of their records had been consumed or burnt by a fire on their premises many years ago. The date of the fire was rather problematical.

Newcastle and the Tyne.

About 1592, in the reign of Queen Elizabeth, the old name of the Guild or Fraternity of the Blessed Trinity of Newcastle was dropped, and they received the name of the Masters, Pilots, and Seamen of the Trinity House of Newcastle. Under their new name or title their authority was still confined to Newcastle and the Tyne, and it was not till fourteen years later that their jurisdiction was extended.

"On the 18th January, 1606, King James I., on the humble petition of the Companie, Misterie, Brotherhood, and Society of Shipmasters, Pilots, and Seamen within the towne and port of Newcastle-upon-Tyne, in the Countie of the said towne of Newcastle-upon-Tyne, extended their jurisdiction to Blyth, Sunderland, Hartlepool, Whitby, and Staiths (commonly Steays, in Yorkshire), and granted them the duties called Primage, that is to say—twopence of every tunn of wine, oil, and other goods, wares, merchandizes, and commodities rated and accompted by the tunn (fish killed and brought in by Englishmen only excepted); and threepence for every laste of flax, hemp, pitch, tarr, or any other goods or raff wares, merchandizes and commodities whatsoever, rated and accompted by the laste."—*Brand's History of Newcastle, vol., ii., pages 325 and 696.*

Summers in his history, commenting on the aforegoing, says:—

"We are not going to question the King's right (however questionable that might be) to grant these dues at Whitby and Staiths to the Trinity House of Newcastle-upon-Tyne; but he clearly had no right to make such a grant at Sunderland, Hartlepool, and Blyth, within the Palatinate of Durham, where his kingly authority was a dead letter, except by his act of usurpation, whereby he gave away that which was not his to give."

During the wars between Charles I. and the Parliament Sunderland became of great importance, for in 1642 the Parliament ordered Sunderland to be garrisoned, and they sent down their Commissioners, who took possession of the whole sources of revenue and removed the Custom House from Bishopwearmouth to Sunderland.

"In 1643, May 12th, an ordinance of Parliament ordained that there be a free and open trade in the Port of Sunderland, in the County of Durham, to relieve the poor inhabitants by reason of rapines and spoyles these enemies, of Newcastle, have brought upon them, they being in great want and extremity."—*Gardiner's Grievances—Burnett, page 129.*

Just thirty-seven years after the date of the Charter of James I., the primage dues were abolished by ordinance of Parliament.

In 1644, Newcastle was besieged and captured by the Scottish army; and the Trinity Corporation of Newcastle have no documents in their possession from the date of 1643 to 1660 shewing that primage dues were collected by them at Sunderland, or any of the outlying ports, or even at Newcastle itself during that period.

Under the ordinance of 1643 the dues had fallen into desuetude, and for eighteen years had ceased to be collected in Sunderland.

After the restoration of Charles II., the brethren of the Trinity House petitioned the Crown for the restoration of what they considered their rights, which had been lost to them by desuetude or non-payment for many years. On account of the loyalty of the town to his father, Charles granted them, *i.e.*, the Trinity House of Newcastle-upon-Tyne, a supplementary Charter confirming the provisions of the old Charter of James I., which empowered them to again collect the primage and other dues which had ceased to be paid.

By the granting of this Charter Sunderland was again made to pay primage, which continued for a further space of two hundred years.

At the time of granting the Charter probably the primage dues would only total a moderate amount. In later times, when Sunderland became the first shipbuilding

Thus Mr. Brown, on account of his continued illness, appointed Messrs. Wright to conduct the trial conjointly with himself; as a consequence, Messrs. Wright took their instructions from the Merchants' Committee, and looked to them as their paymasters.

It had previously been agreed by the merchants to support each other in refusing payment of the primage dues, holding and believing that Charles II. had neither power nor right to grant a charter to any Corporation empowering them to levy on other ports or persons any money dues for which no equivalent was received in return.

The Commission opened at Carlisle on the 4th day of August, 1851. The case was the Trinity House of Newcastle-on-Tyne *versus* Bradley and Potts, to compel payment of primage dues, which they alleged had been collected by them and paid to them under their several charters from time immemorial. The solicitor for the plaintiffs was Ralph Park Philipson; for the defendants, Mr. Robert Brown and Messrs. Wright; and Serjeant Wilkins, one of the most able and eloquent counsellors at the bar, was retained for the defence. A special jury was empannelled to try the case.

The pith of the case rested on the charters granted to the Trinity House. What purported to be the original document of James I. was a mere rag of a document, entirely undecipherable, but so valuable that the solicitor, Mr. Philipson, refused to allow it to be handed round amongst the counsel, and after handing it up to the judge for inspection, returned it again to its safe keeping. I think there was a copy of the supposed charter in court.

The confirmatory charter of Charles II. was a very small document, written very close in Latin.

After the production of the charters, and other evidence as to their continuity in the possession of the plaintiffs, Serjeant Wilkins addressed the court and jury in a most learned and eloquent speech for the defence; after which the court held that the charter of Charles II. did not create or give any new power to collect primage dues, that it only confirmed the powers the plaintiffs had possessed from time immemorial, or under the charter of James I. Verdict for the plaintiffs, with costs.

Summers, in his history, says of the trial:

"On the trial of the cause at Carlisle Assizes, August 8th, 1851, before Mr. Justice Sir Edward Vaughan Williams and a special jury, between the Master and Brethren of the Trinity House of Newcastle-upon-Tyne, plaintiffs; and William Orton Bradley and another, of Sunderland, defendants, respecting the claim made (and subsequently upon very doubtful evidence established) by the plaintiffs to primage dues at the Port of Sunderland. Mr. Edward Peele, managing clerk in the office of the Dean and Chapter of Durham, produced the enrolment or confirmation by the prior and monks of the Monastery of Durham, from the muniments or records of their successors the Dean and Chapter, on behalf of the defendants in the cause, in proof of the ancient royal power of the Bishops of Durham in their Palatinate. Also the charter granted by King Henry III., in the year 1247, produced at the trial by Mr. Thomas Edlyne Tomlins, of Barnard's Inn, London, to his borough of Warnemouth, which concluded thus: 'Wherefore we will and strictly command, for us and all our heirs, that our aforesaid burgesses of Warne-mouth, and their heirs for ever, may have and hold all their liberties and acquitances aforesaid, together with all other liberties and free customs which the burgesses of Newcastle-upon-Tyne had at the time of our ancestors, when they better and more freely had them well in peacefully and wholly in all places and things as is aforesaid witnessed.

Given under our hands at Woodstock, the twenty-sixth day of April, in the year 1247."—*Summers, pages 223, 234 and 235.*

In the trial the validity of the charter of James I., which was very questionable, was taken for granted, the dues having been collected for so long a period.

The abolition of the impost, along with others, by ordinance of Parliament, 12th May, 1643, together with the desuetude of the collection of the dues for eighteen years, were not brought before the court, neither was the legality of the charter of Charles II., or his power and right to grant such a charter challenged or brought prominently before the court.*

The result of the trial was so unsatisfactory that it was resolved by the Merchants' Committee to move for a new trial in the Superior Courts, and after arguments before the court the order for a new trial was granted. Meanwhile, the Shipowners' Committee, through their secretary, informed the Merchants' Committee that they had withdrawn from the case after the verdict of the jury.

On receiving this communication, the Merchants' Committee did not feel themselves justified to carry on the new trial on their own responsibility, and stayed all further proceedings.

When application was made to the Shipowners' Society for their proportion of costs, Mr. Brown, the secretary, wrote as follows :—

"Sunderland, 5th January, 1855.

Dear Sirs,
Yourselves, ats Trinity House.

The Shipowners' Society, as you are perfectly well aware, had nothing whatever to do with the second action. As my agent and myself are largely in advance, an early settlement would be a great convenience ; and I shall feel obliged by your paying my proportion of the bill of costs (*i.e.* one-half,) into my own hands.

Yours truly—ROBERT BROWN.
To Messrs. Bradley and Potts."

---

* Many years afterwards, meeting with Mr. Brown, and in conversation with him, the writer asked why, at the trial, they had not brought forward the plea of desuetude for eighteen years—the abolishing by solemn ordinance of Parliament, and challenged the Charter of Charles II. on public utility and rights. Mr. Brown said that there certainly was some force in the position named ; that the desuetude for eighteen years, and the question of the power of Charles II. to grant or resuscitate a payment that had been lost and abolished ought to have had prominence in the case ; but really he had never thought of it, indeed it never struck him in that light.

On receipt of the foregoing a meeting of the Merchants' Committee was called, and the chairman instructed to reply as follows :—

"*Primage Dues.*

Sunderland, 10th January, 1855.

To Robert Brown, Esq., Solicitor, Sunderland.

Dear Sir,

The Committee do not seem to be so perfectly well aware as you about the Shipowners' Committee withdrawing from the action after the first trial; and having been brought into the action originally by the shipowners, we cannot see how we could be left equitably or legally to fight the remainder of the action after having succeeded in obtaining a new trial.

But, supposing we were to admit the legality of their withdrawing after the first trial, which the Committee do not admit, you must acknowledge the Shipowners' Committee are liable to their one-half of the costs in the action, which we have paid to R. P. Philipson, up to the period of the time at which you allege they did withdraw from the action. And, further, if such is the determination of the Committee of Shipowners, to go no further than you state, the Merchants' Committee are at a loss to conceive how the shipowners can expect the merchants to bear one-half of their costs, which they had incurred by getting legal opinion, and other extra charges, before they were ever called in to support the shipowners in the trial, and long previous to any arrangements being made by the Committees. Therefore, if the Shipowners' Committee think that they could equitably withdraw after having drawn the merchants into the net, the merchants consider that the shipowners are at any rate liable to their share of the costs in the action up to the time of their alleged withdrawal; and if the shipowners think that they could honourably withdraw, the merchants consider in that case that they are not, and certainly ought not to be called upon to pay any share of the costs entered into by the shipowners previous to their joining to try the case. The merchants would, therefore, beg to suggest that the shipowners appoint a number (say three or four) of their committee to meet a like number of the Merchants' Committee, and try to amicably arrange the whole matter.

I am, sir, your obedient servant,
TAYLOR POTTS,
Chairman of the Merchants' Committee."

On January 11th, 1855, the following reply was received:—

"Sunderland, 10th January, 1855.

TRINITY HOUSE.

Dear Sir—I must decline, as Secretary to the Shipowners' Society, to take any step. Mr. Philipson could have been arranged with after the first trial, and the payment of the fresh costs avoided. I took pains at that time to apprize you of your position, and that the Shipowners' Society had no funds at their disposal to justify their further interference. In fact, the money they have spent is much beyond what was originally contemplated. My view of the question was that it was simply a point of law to be submitted to the Court on a special case, as was done with regard to the Ramsgate Harbour Dues, where I got a favourable decision for £100. You called Mr. Wright in without asking the Shipowners' Society a question upon the subject, and I must add, without much consideration of courtesy towards myself. Mr. Wright thought it a case for the jury, and the result was the adoption of a totally different and much more expensive course of procedure. The accuracy of my original opinion has been verified; but, notwithstanding that, Mr. Wright's great experience entitles his advice to great deference, and it is but fair to say that the case might have taken such a turn as to have justified it. The whole proceedings were subsequently conducted by the merchants themselves, not by the joint committee originally appointed, and there seems to me to be something supremely ridiculous in you taking the matter into your own hands, and appointing another solicitor, wholly independent of the Shipowners' Society, and carrying on the proceedings after you had notice they had discontinued them, and then asking them to pay debts which you, without their authority, had incurred.

With regard to the costs of the preliminary cases, these cases contained the whole of the facts and evidence on which you went to trial. Not one jot was added to them, and if you look to the terms of the original resolution you will find their payments were thereby provided for. That is a matter settled and complete, and cannot be re-opened.

I shall certainly not move the Shipowners' Society upon the question, and shall give my most decided opposition to their entertaining it.

I am, dear sir, yours truly,

ROBERT BROWN.

To Taylor Potts, Esq."

Thus the merchants, who were supplicated by the Shipowners' Society to aid them in this matter, were left to pay the costs.

The merchants' agreement amongst themselves was to pay *pro-rata*, according to the amount of primage dues paid by each firm, in proportion to the whole costs, which were upwards of £3,000.

There was only one firm of merchants who did not subscribe to the costs of this trial.

As will be seen in the sequel, Thomas B. Horsfall, Esq., Chairman of the Select Committee of the House of Commons, when this matter was brought before them, asked whether the case had been brought before the House of Lords, in such a manner as intimating that it ought to have been brought before them.

In 1858–59 a bill was introduced into the House of Commons to abolish passing tolls and local charges on shipping, and for other purposes.

In support of this bill a public meeting of merchants, shipowners, and other inhabitants was held, when the following resolution, moved by Taylor Potts and seconded by T. B. Simey, was agreed to :—

"That the petition now read to the meeting be signed by the chairman on behalf of the meeting and forwarded to Henry Fenwick, Esq., M P., for presentation to the House of Commons ; and that Mr. Hudson and the members of the County be asked to attend and support its prayer."

To the Honourable the Commons of the United Kingdom of Great Britain and Ireland in Parliament assembled.

> The petition of the Merchants, Shipowners, and other Inhabitants of the Port of Sunderland, in public meeting assembled.

Humbly sheweth—That your petitioners observe with gratification that a Bill has been introduced into your Honourable House to abolish Passing Tolls and Local Charges on Shipping, and on goods carried in shipping.

That the passing of the said Bill will greatly promote the welfare of your petitioners, and advance the interests of the Port of Sunderland.

That the said port, in addition to the charges levied generally on shipping, and on goods carried in shipping, is burthened with the payment to the Trinity House of Newcastle-on-Tyne of a tonnage duty on goods imported, called Primage, which operates invidiously, and is prejudicial to the commerce and interests of the port.

> Your petitioners therefore humbly pray that your Honourable House will be pleased to pass the said Bill into a Law, and especially to provide for the speedy and total abolition of the said Primage Duty
> And your petitioners will ever pray, etc.

In 1860 the House of Commons appointed a select committee to enquire into the burdens pressing on merchant shipping, of which Thomas B. Horsfall, Esq., was chairman.

Mr. R. M. Hudson and Mr. Taylor Potts were summoned to give evidence before the committee, and amongst other burdens pressing on the merchant shipping, the Primage Dues were named.

On May 8th, 1860, Mr. Potts, in answer to Mr. Lindsay's question 4160—Mr. Hudson mentioned, on the part of the Sunderland Shipowners, a charge of the Trinity House of Newcastle levied upon the Sunderland Shipowners, which amounted to, I think, some £600 or £700 per annum, for which they received no equivalent; has the payment of that charge ever been resisted? You refer to Primage?

4161—Yes. Yes, it has been resisted; my partner and I resisted the payment of it some years ago, at the cost of £3,000, and the trial has never been really settled, because instead of coming to the House of Lords the lawyers contrived amongst themselves to settle the matter; we continue to pay yet. I believed then that it was an illegal charge, and I believe the same yet.

4162—Chairman : But still you continue to pay it rather than go to the great cost of contesting it before the House of Lords? We cannot go to the cost of contesting every small item to the tune of £200; law suits continually going on, we would sooner pay than go to the cost.

The Select Committee reported to the House of Commons, and upon the evidence taken by them, an Act commonly called "Milner Gibson's Act" was passed.

VICTORIA REGINA.
Cap. xlvii.

An Act to facilitate the construction and improvement of Harbours by authorising loans to Harbour Authorities; to abolish passing tolls, and for other purposes.—(1st August, 1861.)

WHEREAS it is expedient that provision should be made for the construction and improvement of Harbours by authorising loans from the public funds to Harbour Authorities; and that provision should also be made for the abolition of passing tolls, of tolls levied on shipping for the purpose of charities, of differential dues on foreign shipping, and of compensation payable in respect thereof out of the public monies; and for making arrangements for the preservation of the rights of creditors, and for other purposes : Be it enacted by the Queen's most Excellent Majesty, by and with the advice and consent of the Lords, spiritual and temporal, and Commons in this present Parliament assembled, and by the authority of the same, as follows :—

PART III.—ABOLITION OF DUES LEVIED BY CHARITABLE CORPORATIONS.

6. All Rates, Dues, Duties, and Imposts (hereinafter included in the term Shipping Dues,) leviable by any of the Charitable Authorities named in the first schedule annexed hereto on ships, or on goods carried in ships, shall, except so far as the same may be required for the execution of such shipping purposes as have hitherto been executed by means of the said dues, cease to be levied on and after the First Day of January, One Thousand Eight Hundred and Seventy-two.

7 Whenever any of the Shipping Dues, leviable by any of the said Authorities named in the first Schedule, are applicable to shipping purposes, but such shipping purposes are not for the benefit of ships or goods carried therein, at the port or place at which such dues are levied, such dues shall cease to be levied on and after the First Day of January, One Thousand Eight Hundred and Seventy-two.

FIRST SCHEDULE.

NAME OF AUTHORITY.

The Trinity House of Kingston-upon-Hull.
The Trinity House of Newcastle-on-Tyne.
The Fraternity of Hostmen of Newcastle-on-Tyne.
The Society of Keelmen on the River Tyne.
The Trinity Corporation of Leith.
The Guildry Incorporation of Perth.
The Fraternity of the Masters and Seamen of Dundee.

By this Act Sunderland achieved her independence, and could no longer be called a creek of Newcastle.

The £3,000 and odd pounds expended by the defendants in connection with the trial at Carlisle, in August, 1851, was not lost, its value was more than received; by the passing of the Act in August, 1861, not only were Primage Dues abolished, but also the collection of all monies from ships, or goods carried in ships, by the other charitable corporations named in the first schedule of the Act.

There were seven of these so called charitable corporations which were abolished, four in England and three in Scotland; of the four in England three of them were located in Newcastle, viz.:—The Trinity House of Newcastle-on-Tyne, The Fraternity of Host-men of Newcastle-on-Tyne*, The Society of Keelmen on the River Tyne.

From this it appears that Newcastle must have been the most beggarly port in the United Kingdom. Yet, Newcastle, through the passing of this Act, received the

* In 1661, the Host-men of Newcastle, jealous of its increasing consequence, procured an impost of one shilling per chaldron, in order to shackle its coal trade, upon all coals exported from Sunderland.

most and largest benefits. It freed the mercantile community from payments to these three charitable corporations for ever. And the outlying ports from Blyth to Whitby were also freed from Primage Dues.

Three of the members serving on this Select Committee of the House of Commons were local members, viz.: Mr. Henry George Liddle, member for South Northumberland; Mr. Hugh Taylor, member for Tynemouth; and Mr. W. S. Lindsay, member for Sunderland.

Primage Dues, under the Charter of James I., 18th January, 1606, were collected for thirty-seven years.

By ordinance of Parliament, 12th May, 1643, they were abolished, and ceased to be paid and collected for eighteen years.

Re-established under Charter of Charles II., 1661.

Abolished under Act of Parliament 1861.

Ten years' grace being allowed the Trinity House of Newcastle to arrange their affairs, the collection of Primage Dues finally ceased from the 31st day of December, 1871.

Primage Dues were collected from the date of the Charter of Charles II., 1661, to their final abolition in 1861, two hundred years. And to the end of their grace, December 31st, 1871, two hundred and ten years.

And from the date of the Charter of James I., 18th January, 1606, two hundred and fifty-five years. And to the date of final collection, December 31st, 1871, two hundred and sixty-five years.

The two latter, less eighteen years, from 1643 to 1661, when they were abolished by ordinance of Parliament.

In 1849—The amount of Primage Dues collected at Sunderland was £502 18 1½

„ 1851—August 4th, the trial was at Carlisle.

„ 1860—May 10th, before a Committee of the House of Commons, Mr. R. M. Hudson stated that the amount collected at Sunderland in the previous year was between £600 and £700 say....................................... .... 650 0

„ 1861—August 1st, an Act of Parliament was passed, abolishing the dues on and after the 1st day of January, Eighteen Hundred and Seventy-Two.

„ 1851—Hartlepool was then an old port, West Hartlepool not then dug out.

„ 1891—Forty years later, *i.e.* after the trial at Carlisle, the import of wood goods into the three ports, viz., the Tyne, Wear and the Hartlepools were, according to the returns for 1891, just now at hand, 692,867 loads of timber and deals, which, according to the Primage Dues paid in 1851, viz., 2½d. per load, would have amounted in 1891 to the sum of..... 7,217 7 3

Apportioned thus, viz,:--

	LOADS.		£	s.	d.
The Hartlepools	365,999 at 2½d.,		3,812	9	9
„ Tyne	169,011	„	1,760	10	8
„ Wear	157,857	„	1,644	6	10
Loads	£692,867		£7,217	7	3

7,217 7 3

In 1849—Sunderland paid Primage Dues amounting to £502 18 1½

„ 1860—Sunderland paid Primage Dues (say average) 650 0 0

„ 1891—Sunderland would have had to pay 1,644 6 10
Or more than three-fold paid in 1849.

„ 1891—The Tyne would have had to pay 1,760 10 8

„ 1851—Old Hartlepool was only paying a trifle, West Hartlepool was only then being dug out, would in 1891 have been chargeable with 3,812 9 9

£7,217 7 3

These dues are irrespective of other goods then chargeable to the Primage Dues, and are only estimated on timber and raff goods.

PILOTAGE.

Although, as already stated, the Act abolishing Primage Dues was passed on August 1st, 1861, yet the brethren of the Trinity House of Newcastle still continued to exercise their jurisdiction over the navigation of the River Wear; the passing of the Act of 1861 did not withdraw or overthrow their authority as to pilotage.

In 1865, the passing of the Sunderland Pilotage Order Confirmation Act, 28 and 29 Victoria, cap. 59, to which the royal assent was given 29th June, 1865, deprived them even of this shadow of authority.

By this Act a Board of Commissioners was appointed, consisting of fourteen persons or members, to be appointed by the different parties supposed to be interested in the matter, viz. :—

  2 by the Board of Trade.
  1 ,,   Admiralty.
  4 ,,   River Wear Commissioners.
  5 ,,   Shipowners; and
  2 ,,   Pilots.

And, as at present constituted, consists in rotation of—

Board of Trade—Edward John Weatherley and Thomas William Pinkney.

Admiralty—Edward Capper Robson.

River Wear Commissioners—R. M. Hudson, John Firth, G. R. Booth, R. H. Gayner.

Shipowners—John Sanderson, Joseph Horan (chairman), John Hopper, Thomas Stockdale, and Robert Todd Nicholson.

Pilots—Paul Wayman and William Thurlbeck.

Pilot Ruler—Fairley Downes.

Clerk to the Commissioners—John George Morris.

SUNDERLAND TOWN MOOR

Faced the sea on the east, and extended from the white wall on the south to beyond the hospital, and on to the battery on the north. On the north it was bounded by the Barracks and Cockerill's ropery up to Church Walk, then by a cabbage garden and the Churchyard on the north and west, and by the Churchyard on the north, and on the south and west by the road from Church Street, which went down to the beach at Hendon to the south of the white wall.

From the north end of the white wall to near the Church yard was a stunted thorn hedge, with a gate leading to the horse pond; the hedge was trodden down here and there, with large gaps in it. By the Churchyard wall, on its south side, there was a cart road leading to the manure depôt; a ditch between the road and the wall went right round the angles of the walls and the cabbage garden, up to the end of the Church Walk on the east, there was also a cart road cutting off the angles or indents, by which the farmers used to load the manure from the depôt. From the Church Walk to Cockerill's rope house was a stunted thorn hedge, almost trodden out of existence, and a ditch on the side of the Moor. Two thorn hedges ran at right angles straight across the Moor to the banks, with shallow ditches on each side; the north one started from the east side of the ropery house, the other opposite Chapel Street.

Two water courses drained the Moor, one of which cut the banks opposite St. John's Chapel, which was carried under the roadway by a small culvert. The other drained the Moor from the north-west, west, and south-west; this was the principal water course, and it emptied itself into the sea by Lauder's Dene, which was about opposite to Nesham Square; the high end of the dene, on the Moor, was spanned by a long culvert, through which the boys used to run, and a footpath wended down the dene to the sea beach by the side of the water course or ditch. About midway between Lauder's Dene and the white wall was the horse pond; it took up the drainage from the south part of the moor; cattle tracks and a rough cart road led to the pond. The pond was literally washed away, the Moor banks having fallen by the action of the waves, when another pond was made, further inland, on the Moor.

At a short distance from the edge of the banks ran a broad track from north to south over the culverts, which was altered as the banks washed away.

Let us now look at the town from the Moor. It is early morn—the bugle calls, and we proceed to look at the Barracks; the Hospital stands outside, some distance off, about the spot where the Gladstone Bridge was; the banks were washing away, and the Hospital had to be pulled down. The Battery, which was built of brick and stone, stood at the east of the Barracks, with a very broad space or way between, and by the side of the Battery was a deep ditch.

The Barracks were enclosed with strong wooden palisading, cut three-cornered ways, with three-cornered cross pieces inside. The officers' and soldiers' quarters were all built of wood; and the garrison was supplied with water drawn from wells within the palisading. Walking west, we pass the ropery premises, and look along shell hill; the canteen is on the right hand, and a soldier keeping guard at the gate; and, in the distance, a large open space with low hillocks of shells opposite the main entrance to the Barracks.

Passing St. John's Chapel we come to Chapel Street, containg four or five houses with pear trees in front, in one of which lived Dixon the potter; beyond was a garth from which the pottery owners got their clay. West of Chapel Street we see an open garth stretching up to the back of Stafford Street or East Street, and backing to the Fitters' Row, the rear of which was planted with trees. At the south end of Fitters' Row stood the Custom House, with a large garden running down to the road by the ropery, with a cross piece of ground facing Silver Street. Except the houses facing the Moor, there was then no Moorgate Street, no Thomas Street, and part of the east side of Silver Street belonged to the garth or garden. Then we come to Burleigh Street, with its splendid three-storied houses and grand mansions.

Looking down Vine Street, the apple blossoms were beautiful in the garden at the back of the large house facing the High Street, where one of the Lilburns once lived; the gardens extended from the house to the cross street from Burleigh Street to Vine Street; facing this cross street, in Vine Street, was a house with a garden in front, where old Mr. Pringle, the painter, lived. In Vine Street, a vine really grew in front of one of the houses.

Looking down Maling's Rig, you could see the quaint old chapel on the east side, and on the west side the apple trees and blossoms, which overtopped the back walls of the houses facing Nesham Square, with trees growing in the front of them. At the north-west corner of the square you could see the tall trees growing between Maling's Rig and Ropery Lane; this open garden, with trees, ran down to the head of John Street; and, at the end and back of the old Workhouse, facing the Church Walk, a lot of tall trees grew up to the workhouse wall; and looking at Hendon Lodge, at the south-west of the Moor, the high trees overtopped the mansion, while the flower garden was hidden from view by a wall. Then there was the Octagon Cottage with its beautiful flower garden, the burn ran past it to the sea; at the west of the cottage, a country road, which led to the Hendon Baths, on the west side of which was a stone wall, with a gate opening into the field, and with thorn hedges on the east side, with a low wall nearing the baths, looking into the field was a gate.

The houses looking on to Cockerill's ropery, from Nesham Square to St. John's Chapel, with one exception, had pear trees trained up the front. In the house at the south-west corner of the square, facing the Moor, with a pear tree against the wall, my aunt Mary lived. My strongest recollection of her, is of seeing her go to a drawer and bring out a stocking, the foot of which was filled with guineas. At that period ladies kept their gold in stocking feet.

In the house at the south-east corner of Silver Street, Mr. Mordey, shipowner and fitter lived, he was also a spirit merchant; the shop and office is still in Silver Street, above which he lived prior to removal to the house already named. The name of one of his captains was Douglass, and he had a little boy named George, who was a favourite with the Mordeys, and was allowed to climb up the pear tree to gather the pears. That little fellow is now to be seen in Alderman Douglass.

ROPE MAKING.

At early morn the ropemakers were busy; at dawn the yarns were trundled on the ground, separated, cleared and counted; as many yarns as were required were twisted into a strand, then three strands were fastened at each end, the one next the ropery house on to three separate hooks, there being a man at the handle of each hook, turning and twisting in time.

At the further end of the rope walk was the machine, with the three strands fastened on one hook, twisting them into a cable; this machine had a drag behind to keep all tight. As the rope advanced in the make, tailors or wipsters were set on to aid and assist the twisting process. Both men and women were employed at this labour, as many as twenty persons and upwards being engaged in the early morning; whilst the spinning wheel still went round, and the yarns were being spun. The same or similar work was going on at all the rope walks terminating on the Moor.

Looking across the Moor, and over the sea, we see the sun rising in all its splendour, making such colours and tinges in the clouds as it alone can give, whilst to the naked eye the water appears to be dropping off his beautiful face like large pure diamonds, the ocean meanwhile reflecting the rays and colours from the clouds, and between the two, and over the waves, you see the fishing boats making for the harbour on the early tide, and the pilot cobles sailing south. In Hendon Bay, three or four vessels are at anchor casting their ballast, there are also several in the roadstead waiting for the tide; the sun meanwhile shedding its rays of glory over the whole.

The voice calling the cows home has long ceased, the horses have been led off to carry on their daily toil. We go home to breakfast and return.

From the harbour, the loaded colliers are going out, the small Scotchmen north, and the light draft Lynnmen south, other larger vessels are making for the roadstead, having two or three keels in tow, loaded with coals to complete the collier's cargo when anchored, the casters all ready to commence as soon as the keels are secured alongside.

Over the Moor women are spreading their washing of clothes on the grass. There is a breeze blowing from the south-west, and as every piece of the washing is laid down a stone is placed upon it to prevent it blowing away; then, when all is laid, the mother leaves a little girl or boy to watch them; and, to shelter themselves from the wind, the clothes basket is set on end, inside of which the little watchers sit.

Meanwhile, the fishermen's nets are spread out to dry, and the fisherman's wife is there with netting needle and mesh, to take up any stray loop that may have been broken; the husband often performed this work. The nets are all tanned by the fishermen, as well as the cobles' sails.

This morning the tide suits, and mothers and children are wending their way across the Moor to the beach, by way of Lauder's dene, to bathe, and others are going down the road to Hendon. On looking over the Moor's edge, the bathers in the water are only to be seen disporting themselves; but on the beach quite a commotion is going on—two or three tents are pitched, and the proprietors (generally old women) charged twopence each for accommodation. The children are then, as now, "plodging" and enjoying themselves. Those who do not care to pay the twopence for tent accommodation are dressing and undressing close under the banks. Gentlemen walking along the beach, supposed to be looking at the waves, were allowed to walk along; but woe to the "loafer" that should try to pass—he was ordered back, and, in case of refusal, stood a chance of being stoned.

At the Hendon Baths two bathing machines were kept; the beach there was nearly always stony, and only a few people used them.

Men and boys used to bathe from the South Pier to the Battery, and from Hendon to Sandy Banks. At low tide, the Dove Rock and the Frying Pan were used. There were no bathing costumes in those days.

Returning to the Moor, we see the ballast keels leaving the harbour to discharge their ballast in the roads (there were five men in each keel for this purpose), the kedge has been dropped, and the warp has been paid out for the return. The light colliers are running down under easy sail, and anchor in the roadstead.

In the evening the Moor began to have a more bustling appearance, both young and old Sunderland are let loose. Some of the young hie to the horse pond to sail their ships, some are playing at "stealy claithes," others at "spel-an-ore" or "buckstick," some flying their kites, others playing at bat. On the hard ground on the ropery, several groups are playing at marbles. Every player at marbles had to keep his knuckles on the ground, the marble was shot by the finger and thumb; if the hand was raised off the ground that was called "fullicking;" if the opponent called out "knuckle down stump," then the player had to fire his marble so as to touch the ground before it reached the marble at which he was firing. Marbles had different values, the standard was the common pottery clay marble, a "stoney" was worth so many common ones, a "Jack ally" so many, an "ally" so many more, and a "blood-red ally" was the most valuable of all. Some lads, who were good players, after they had beggared the others, used to sell the marbles back again, according to the value before mentioned.

Quoits were played by the men; the foot had to be kept steadily against the hob until the quoit was thrown, there was no running half way over the ground before throwing, as I have seen done in the present day. Then a quoit was a quoit, now you see them playing with a flat ring which they call a quoit. Foot races were also run on the Moor.

BOWLING.

The bowling course ran from north to south. Each bowler had his tracker. A tracker was a person who walked and pointed out to the bowler the best or most convenient spot for the bowl to beat on when thrown. Wherever the bowler picked up his bowl his jacket was laid, and from that spot he must give the next throw, and so on to the end. Bowlers generally made their own bowls, they were made of blue stone, which they picked up off the beach and which had fallen out of the clay banks as the banks fell to the action of the waves; you would often see them with their little hammers tap, tap, tapping away, until they got them perfectly round and smooth to fit their hand. They had bowls of different sizes and weights, according to the skill of the players.

On the Moor, on a summer's evening, the town's people seemed to congregate. There were delights for the young; there the old ones found pleasure—no one to interfere; there were scenes for the painter's canvas and themes for the poet's song.

The sun's rays bring the Yorkshire highlands into view; the nearer cliffs appear as a darkish blue, but as we gaze steadily, trying to trace them in the distance, they become lighter and paler and lower, until lost to sight in the far-out sea. Souter Point stands boldly out in the shadow, whilst from the harbour the fishing cobles are seen scudding away to the fishing grounds, and a few light colliers are sailing down.

The sun has set to rise in the morning, as the old fisherman said—" dripping wet."

Uncle Bob came into grandfather's one evening with a smirk on his face, saying: "I have had a queer confab with some fishermen on the Moor, and in conversation I said the earth went round and the sun stood still, when an old fellow said: 'Don't believe that, I tell you the sun goes round the world; have I not seen him rise in the morning out of the sea, dripping wet, and at night go beautifully down in the west, and next morning come up out of the sea again, dripping wet; I say the sun goes round the world.'"

The incidents in connection with the Moor are numerous. There the early followers of the Wesleys held their first congregations in Sunderland.

It is said that when Whitfield preached on the Mill Hill, which is close by (now Minorca), that the people in Monk-wearmouth-Shore heard part of the sermon.

On the Moor the Primitives first took their stand when they came to the town, and it was on the Moor that their first camp meeting was held.

It was on the Moor that the sailors, during their strikes, assembled to discuss their grievances; and it was there the keelmen met in public meeting. At one of the meetings of the keelmen, it is said that they had some difficulty in getting a chairman; having succeeded, the chairman, in opening the meeting, is reported to have said, "Now, my canny fellows, I'm not going to make a long speech, and my advice to all of you is, 'ye that knaw nowt, say nowt.' Now, let's to business." What a deal of time would be saved in all our public and private meetings if the keelman's advice was followed.

I think it was in the year 1821, or somewhere thereabout, that many thousands of people, from the surrounding country, stood on the edge of the Moor to see the *man walk on the sea*. Looking at the Moor from the sea close to the beacon, it seemed as if a wall of human beings had been built, and on the sea some hundreds of boats were rowing to and fro. I was snug in the coble's nose, looking over the gunwale, seeing all that was going on, indeed, on several occasions I could have touched him. The man kept walking on, whilst his friends were collecting money from the thousands of people on the Moor and in the boats. I never heard the amount of the collection. He had a kind of machine or float, it was composed of 4 planks, 2 length ways and 2 cross ways, on which was erected a light frame, in which he stood or sat ; on his feet were fastened pieces of wood or floats, and as he splashed these floats in the water the machine moved slowly on. The whole was a dead sell on the public.

It was on May 29th, 1822, that the last bull bait was in Sunderland. The sport was got up by the running fitters and keelmen. Robert Gowland, Joe Charlton and two or three more were the promoters. The bull was borrowed from one of the butchers, and the place where the sport took place was adjoining the north-east corner of the Moor, at the south-east corner of the Barracks and at the south-west end of the battery.

The anchor or kedge was sunk into the ground, close to the palisading of the Barracks, with the ring above the ground, to which the bull was fastened with ropes. The circle in which the bull was baited was staked round with ropes, and no person was admitted inside the circle except the owners of the dogs, to set them on or call them off ; the betting was on the dogs.

Campbell, John Harrison, Joe Charlton, and several others had their dogs. The crowd outside the ring, consisting of men, women and children, stood looking on applauding the while (the writer was among the crowd and close to the ring). After the sport had gone on for some time the bull became fagged and would not run, when the dogs were called off, and the bull was led away to the slaughter house. The only fancy dogs in Sunderland at that period were the Bull dogs. The late Mr. Wealands

Robson, in accordance with his ancient ideas, had his bull dogs. Indeed, bull dogs had been specially bred for the purpose of bull-baiting.

In his history of Bishopwearmouth Green, Summers says, in its centre (*i.e.* the centre of the Green) was a stone, and a large iron ring fixed in it, to which the ropes were fastened, when the barbarous custom of baiting bulls was enforced by a legal enactment, binding butchers, under a penalty, not to sell bulls unbaited ; this enactment was in force till a late date.

The following presentment was made at the Court Barron at Sunderland in the year 1681 : "Anthony Hodgson and others, for selling their bulls unbaited, to the damage of the leige people, and against the form of the Statute, etc., fined 39/11," This was the highest fine the Court Barron could inflict.

On the occasions of bull baits the windows of the houses on the Green were always filled and their roofs covered with spectators. The last bull-bait held on the Green was in the year 1788.

The old building facing Church Walk, and at the west corner of the Moor, was a haunted house ; the loft or top story was used as a Lancastrian School. An officer's leg, mounted on horse back, used to ride round the school, and you could hear, when standing outside, the rattling noise he made on his rounds.

It was in the winter of 1824–25 that persons going along the Church Walk at midnight thought they saw corpse candles burning on a grave, and ghost-like shadows walking and flitting amongst the tomb stones ; at other times only a dim blue shaded light was seen, and on any exclamation or shout from those who saw it, the dim blue light went out, and the ghosts or shadows, like great black dogs, were seen hopping and running about. On these things becoming known the whole town and country side was in commotion. It was at first whispered, then afterwards broadly asserted, that some dead bodies had wriggled themselves out of their coffins and had quietly dropped over the churchyard wall, and slipped away over the Moor. The excitement was great; the graves of one or two of the persons who had lately been buried were opened, the lids of the coffins unscrewed, and sure enough, when taken off, the dead bodies were gone. The ground on and around the graves was closely examined—it did not appear to have been interfered with, and one remarkable thing was, as the bodies came into the world so they left their coffins—naked; their grave-clothes were all left behind, even to the face covering. The excitement became intensified, and no one would go singly on to the Moor or near it.

One person was buried, and the mourners went to have their tea, as customary; and at ten o'clock they went in a body with lanterns to inspect the grave and see that all was right. The upper sods did not seem to be exactly as they had left them; they ran for spades, and dug down to the coffin. On opening it they found that their dear departed friend had given them the slip—no holding them in the spirit world. It seemed marvellous that so many dead bodies had risen and still were not.

One singular thing was that they nearly all preferred slipping over the wall on to the Moor in the dark, they never ventured through the churchyard gates. One of them tried to get over the palings into the Church Walk. A drunken fellow walking along, stopped, and asked him what he was doing on the top of the spikes—with that he fell down; not receiving any answer, he went up and touched him through the railings, saying: "Thou's very cauld, better get back again into thy coffin." One or two people were coming up at the time, so they called up the sexton, who lived above the Cage (or lock up at that date), and the corpse was restored to the place from whence it came.

This circumstance becoming known, and the scare intensified, no person dare go along the Church Walk for fear of seeing a dead body climbing over the railings. It was always in the dark these dead people tried to slip out of their graves.

About this time it was said that one or two persons were missing. One dark night, between nine and ten o'clock, a fearful scream was heard from the Moor, when it suddenly ceased; several people ran towards the place from whence the scream was heard. On drawing near, some figures were seen vanishing in the darkness, but they found a female, who had been attacked. A pitch plaster had been clapped on her face, which prevented her further crying out, and it was only by the timely arrival of these people that her life was saved.

After this no female dared to venture out alone for fear of the plaster, and this fear lasted for a long time. Children would not stir out after dark, except in numbers, even then, any suspicious looking person caused them to run for their lives. I remember once running until I almost fell down breathless from fear.

My uncle George died in 1825, the date is on his tombstone now. I was at the funeral, and saw him buried; the grave was very deep. Several coffins had been broken up and the contents shovelled amongst the soil. I saw the coffin lowered into the grave, seven feet below the level. On the top of the coffin a thick broad plank was laid, at the head and foot of it long sharp stakes were driven into the ground, and securely fastened to the plank on the top, so that he had no chance of getting out. In general, these peculiar people wriggled out either at the head or foot of the coffin, hence the long stakes were driven deep into the ground.

Having fastened him in so securely, still they were not satisfied. At ten o'clock, my father, with a companion, armed with large horse pistols and swords, went and kept watch till the morning dawned. Next night other two kept guard, and so on every alternate night for a fortnight. At that time they dug down to the coffin to satisfy themselves that uncle had not given them the slip, and finding him still in it they left off watching. I am perfectly satisfied that if they had seen anyone helping him out of his grave they would have fared badly.

A wooden hut was afterwards put up in the churchyard, for the accommodation of any future watchers.

In another case a middle-aged female was buried; proper precautions not having been taken to secure her, she got wriggled out of her coffin, and slipped over the Church yard wall, got into a light cart, with a fast stepping pony, and drove off to Newcastle so as to be in time to take the early coach for Edinburgh. As she was booking at the coach office she seemed to say: "Not on the coach top, in the boot;" so she was placed in the boot and carried to her destination, where kind friends were waiting to receive her; these friends gave her a ride to the Hospital, where she was carefully handed over to the hospital officials, who, after examining her, paid liberally for the care that had been taken of her. After this she was carried in and laid on the dissecting table in the centre of the room, and thus rested for several hours, as though saying to herself: "This is beautiful, nice and warm here; what a change from the cold grave."

Whilst musing thus within herself a student enters with soft tread; he had large lustrous eyes, rather thick lower lip, an aquiline nose, with a thin and rather cadaverous-looking face. On hearing his foot draw near, the corpse on the dissecting table seemed to give a wink of the eye; but it was not certain whether it was the student's eye that winked, as a tear drop stood in one, when the corpse seemed to murmur "I have only come to shew myself, don't I look beautiful?" Aghast he stood, whilst fixing his gaze upon the corpse, he exclaimed, "My poor old nurse. Good God! and is it your body that I have bought to come under my dissecting knife? No, not on thy body, not on thy body, my poor old nurse, would I try to discover the secrets of my profession." The old nurse's body was re-interred.

Afterwards, the student received a letter informing him of his old nurse's death; so expeditiously had the body been sent.

In the winters of 1824 and 1825, from 7 to 11 o'clock at night, might be seen in the old market place, at the foot of Queen Street, a man with a clean white apron on, looped over the neck and tied round the waist. He had a large tin apparatus, with a charcoal fire inside. He had a loud shrill voice, which could be heard from Queen Street as far as Beggar's Bank, and every now and anon you could hear his shrill cry "Chelsea bons, Chelsea bons, hot Chelsea bons; pies all hot, smoking hot, hot mutton pies." He was often accompanied by a thick set middle-sized man, rather bull-necked. He was there in all kinds of weather, ready to sell hot mutton pies, and was a very obliging man, who had a kind word for all his customers. I have stood beside him, passed by him, heard his voice on many nights and seen him sell his pies.

It afterwards turned out that these two men were the cause of all the fright and terror in the town and neighbourhood. They were Burke and Hare, the principal body snatchers or resurrection men; and when the night watching in the churchyard became continuous and severe, and the danger of apprehension imminent, the cry of "Pies all hot" ceased. It was Hare that sold the pies.

Thus two or three body snatchers kept the whole town and neighbourhood in fear.

Burke was afterwards tried at Edinburgh, along with a young woman, December 24th, 1828, for three cold-blooded murders, perpetrated on unsuspecting victims, whom they had allured into their den, in order to murder them and sell their bodies. Burke no sooner heard the verdict of the jury, which found him guilty and acquitted the woman, than he threw his arms around her neck and kissed her, saying "Thank God, Mary, you are saved," thus shewing some sign of goodness in the worst of criminals.

Subsequently, it was ascertained that sixteen persons had been murdered by them, and their bodies sold.

On the Moor—the fading light betokens a storm, the sea gulls have fled inland, a cold, thick, driving mist from the sea covers the Moor, not a star to be seen, the heavens seem to have dropped on to the grass, murky blackness covers the whole.

Female forms are seen issuing from the ends of the streets, through dire necessity, with pails in their hands, across the Ropery, emptying their contents on the Moor, and running back by the light of the oil lamps, in the midst of the driving mist; they look more like shadows from another world than respectable housewives, who could only perform such duties under the cover of night.

Meanwhile, the gale has increased; all the oil lamps hanging at the corners of the streets have been blown out. The blast increasing, some of the crew of the lifeboat are in their oilskins and sou'-westers, and have stationed themselves at the lifeboat house. One boat is outside, lashed to the bogie with high wheels, ready to be run down to the sea.

As the night wears on, the wind blows like great guns, the sea is lashed into mountains, the roar of the waves as they break upon the shore is deafening, whilst the heavy deep thud of the blast overhead in a measure drowns the roar of the waves. Several figures are seen close to the edge of the Moor, shading their eyes with their hands, striving to pierce the black darkness. Suddenly a flash light is seen, then all is blackness. The lifeboat men have been hastily summoned to the boathouse. Davison, the captain, is there, whilst the cry is heard and echoed, "a ship in distress." A flaming light from the vessel shews her drifting on the shore. Meanwhile, with willing help, the lifeboat is run down to the beach and launched into the angry deep. Every man at his place, many a throbbing heart wishing them God speed. Whilst bending to their oars, a heavy sea strikes and almost upsets her, the two men at the after sweep strive hard to bring her head again to the sea, and seeing every now and again the light rolling and sweeping fast on to the rocks. Those watching on the Moor see the light close to the Beacon rocks, and, whilst eagerly watching, the light takes a higher leap than heretofore, when suddenly a heavy thud and crash is heard and the light disappears. The masts have gone by the board, and as wave succeeding wave rolls in, lifting her up, she goes down on the rocks. The crashing of her timbers is heard where the watchers stand; but above the roaring of the storm, and the crashing of the wreck, a cry of despair is heard; it was from the crew, their last cry. A lower moan was thought to be heard; none lived to reach the shore. The lifeboat's crew meanwhile lost sight of the light, they heard the crashing of the timbers, the last cry of despair, but they could not render help, the raging sea over the rocks would have holed and swamped their boat and dealt death to them. They had to dodge on and off till an opportunity occurred to beach the boat.

What a sad sight was seen on the Moor in the morning, women carrying coals in their baskets, men with lumps of wood in their arms—shattered portions of the wreck; but, saddest of all, was the sight of four men carrying a shutter with a poor drowned sailor stretched upon it, and this repeated during the day, as one after another was found.

It was known the night before that two ships were at anchor in the roads, and the names of the vessels had been mentioned by the knowing ones. When the morning broke, many, with anxious eyes and tired feet, were seen wandering over and searching the rocks, perchance it might be for the body of one they loved. One scene will suffice, a shutter had been brought from the street, and a drowned corpse was laid thereon, four men carried it, whilst others walked beside, talking low and watching. But there was one poor desolate woman, she looked at the corpse on the shutter, he had been her only hope, she could not weep, a lump rose in her throat, she staggered and fell down unconscious. She also had to be carried to their humble home. When she revived, she murmured, "My God, be to me the husband to the widow and the father to the fatherless," when the fountains of her eyes were opened, and the hot briny tears rolled down her cheeks, easing her aching heart. She afterwards became calm. When the storm came on, there were two ships in the roads, one of which parted from her anchors, and was lost with all hands. But what of the other?

When morning dawned every spy-glass was directed towards the place where the ships were seen at anchor the night before; at last a speck was observed tossing about amidst the rough sea, and as the light of day crept on the hull of the vessel was distinctly seen, and afterwards the crew were observed on the deck.

To save the vessel and their lives the captain had cut away the masts to ease the ship, and by so doing the vessel rode out the storm. I saw her afterwards, she was brought into the harbour and laid alongside Hardcastle's Quay. Both these vessels seemed riding in security on the evening before the gale broke; in the morning one was a total wreck, crew all perished; the other little better than a wreck, crew saved.

On another occasion I have seen ten wrecks lying on the rocks and beach, extending from the South Pier to Hendon, under similar circumstances. The vessels had run down to the roadstead in the evening, cast their ballast, and when the gale broke they were perfectly helpless, and drifted ashore.

Old Neptune was always attacking the Moor, either by his calm lipper, when he was washing away the marl from between the rock and the clay, or by his heavy blash against the banks. But did not the Moor help him in his attacks? The water was always oozing out from the top of the clay and trickling over the face of the bank, making a puddle bank, in fact softening the clay, so that being undermined and puddled it was prepared to fall, either by a storm or a frost. No matter what amount of clay fell, the action of the waves washed it all away, except the blue stones which fell embedded in the clay, so that the beach itself was none the more able to resist the waves; especially when the blue stones themselves were gathered by the Town Commissioners to pave the streets. The Moor seemed to suffer on every side; the Churchyard was a large nip off. It was said that Hendon Lodge and its gardens was another portion. But the Barracks was the largest nip of all. The fishermen built their houses on a portion of the Moor, believing that it belonged to them; and when the fairs came round they used to let the ground, collect the tolls from the booths and shows, and divide the money.—But I must pause.

Go, look at the Moor now, and compare it with what it was. Is the long wall, with coal waggons beyond, steaming locomotives, docks, drops and what not, to be compared with the tall trees, apple and pear blossoms, the rabbit warren, and nearly all the rural simplicity that nature gives?

CHAPTER XIV

THE PIERS.

In 1669 Charles II. granted letters patent to Edward Andrew, Esq., to build a pier or piers, and erect a lighthouse or lighthouses, to cleanse the harbour of Sunderland, and to raise contributions for that purpose. Burnett in his history, page 31, says "After Charles had granted letters patent to Edward Andrew, Esq., the pier was erected," but does not say where Andrew's pier was. No trace of it can be found.

In 1706 a proposal was submitted to Parliament for the improvement of the river Wear, &c., when it was opposed by the master and brethren of the Trinity House of Newcastle.

In 1716, when a bill was introduced for the improvement of the river Wear, &c., the Mayor, Aldermen and Common Council of Newcastle petitioned against it. Notwithstanding this opposition, an Act was obtained in 1717, 3rd George I. It appointed Commissioners for 21 years, who were charged with the conservancy of the harbour, and they were empowered to raise money by a tonnage duty on ships entering the port, for the purpose of making the river navigable to New Bridge, and building a Pier at its mouth.

The Commissioners, after their appointment, appear to have applied themselves to their duties. They had the river surveyed, and the mouth of the harbour map'd.

There appears to have been little or nothing done to improve the river between the years 1659 and 1719. An old plan is in existence, shewing the state of the mouth of the harbour at that date, previous to the improvements by the Commissioners. It shews the quay on the Sunderland side of the river, then terminated a little below the Custom House. The banks eastward formed the verge or boundary of the Town Moor. The channel of the river was diverted towards the north by high rocks, until it came again in contact with Dame Dolly's rock on the northern side, where a beacon was erected. The channel then proceeded eastward, passing another beacon erected on the western end of the north rocks, near the low water mark. The bar was situated still further to the eastward, and caused the river to diverge into various channels at its confluence with the sea.

There was also a swatchway through the stell caunch, the waters of which found their way to the sea in a circuitous manner through the sands. The highwater mark at that time approached within 150 yards of the east end of Monkwearmouth Church; it is now 420 yards distant from it, when measured in the same easterly direction, consequently a great portion of what is now dry land, and formed into streets and shipbuilding yards, was then overflowed by the tide.

About the year 1723 the Commissioners commenced to build the South Pier. At the inner or shore end it was founded on the limestone rock, which was dry at low water. During its progress, when the rock was found to be too deep for the purpose, piles were driven in, on which the masonry was laid. The object of the Pier was evidently to direct the current of the river against the bar and the adjacent shifting sands.

In 1737, by authority of the Commissioners, Messrs. Burleigh and Thompson's map of the river, from the sea up to New Bridge, was published.

The South Pier was then one thousand feet in length, and thirty feet broad at the top, with a parapet on one side.

This Pier was built solid as far down as the east of the low shed or shelter. Under this shed two large capstans were fixed with their palls. At the upper part or top piece of the capstan were square holes in which to fix the long capstan bars, which were always kept ready under the shed. More than thirty or forty men could be employed at a time at one of these capstans, which had a towline round, and two or three men holding on to start the ship to windward.

From this Pier-head or end all subsequent improvements for the Pier, according to the prevailing ideas of the then engineer, seem to have radiated.

In the year 1748 Mr. Charles Lebelye, the engineer of Westminster Bridge, in his report to the Commissioners, described the river downwards (after passing the Custom House of that day), as widening gradually and the depth increasing until it arrived at the stell and stell caunch, from whence it chiefly ran in two channels, the one passing the two beacons, the other nearer to the South Pier. And in order to cover the haven better, and to secure the ships from being endangered by great seas and violent winds setting right up the harbour, he proposed a North Pier, which he thought would greatly contribute to its security. The head of this Pier was to be placed exactly north (by the compass) off the South Pier, because—

1st—Such was the setting of the tides.

2nd—If the said head was placed eastward it would stop part of the flood and ebb, and soon gather vast quantities of sand within it; and if it stood to the westward it would not shelter the haven so well.

3rd—The position recommended agreed with the experience and practice of all good engineers.

The distance between the two pier heads he thought should be about 200 yards; the North Pier might be built full as high all the way as the South Pier, with a parapet on each side, the breadth might be 20 or 25 feet, the top battering full one sixth of its height. Mr. Labeyle concludes this part of his report thus, "After all, as no man can foresee all the consequences that may attend the erection of a north pier, if it should happen to occasion visibly (which I hope it will not) a greater obstruction to navigation than it removes, it must be unbuilt and taken up." Mr. Labeyle further says "Before the conclusion of this report, one caution more is thought necessary, which is that the Commissioners may never harken to any proposal for erecting sluices or locks across the river in any place which the tide reaches, for let the pretence for such work be ever so specious, and the reasons ever so plausible, be assured that the infallible consequence of all such projects would be the utter ruin of the harbour and navigation in a few years."

Labeyle's judicious view as to a North Pier, upon which the safety and maintenance of the harbour chiefly depended, was left in abeyance for forty years.

In 1752, Mr. Vincent, of Scarborough, was appointed engineer to the Harbour Trust. His attention seems to have been immediately turned to open out the old sledway, and to make it the navigable channel. To assist in doing this he sunk several old keels, drove piles, and adopted other means to stop up the north channel at the Stell.

Mr. Richard Oliver, now aged 88 years, told me in July, 1891, that he remembered his uncle telling him about the engineer sinking the old keels and driving piles in order to divert the channel to the south side of the river. His uncle, he said, recollected the incident quite well, and told him when he was a youth.

In 1755 Mr. Robson was appointed engineer to the Commissioners. Complaints appear to have been lodged with them to the effect that the position of the Pier head forced the current from the improved south channel too far to the northward, so that ships, in southerly winds, could not reach the harbour, but were driven on shore amongst the rocks at the north side. Mr. Robson therefore recommended that the ruinous part of the pier should be taken down, and a new length erected in an E.N.E. direction, which would alter the course of the channel, and direct, in a better manner, the set of the ebb upon the bar. This work was commenced in 1757.

In 1758 the Commissioners examined a plan projected by Mr. Robson, for building moles upon the north and south rocks, with a view of obtaining a depth of 12 feet at low water at the entrance, and they were so well satisfied with the design that in 1759 they petitioned Parliament to grant them powers to carry it into execution. The Parliamentary Committee made their report in favour of the petition, and the Act was passed.

Nothing appears to have been done under this Act for some time, but a report, addressed by Mr. Robson to the Commissioners on the 6th of May, 1767, states· "The constant operation of dredging, harrowing and cleansing to keep up an indifferent channel over the flat ground without the pier, and on the bar, appears to have been attended with considerable expense, and yet the said bar and flat ground has been constantly increasing in height, and expanding further to sea." And to strike at the root of this perpetually growing evil he recommends the erection of a pier upon the south rocks, pursuant to a plan laid before Parliament in 1759.

Before engaging in a work of such magnitude, the Commissioners took the opinion of Mr. John Wooler, who disagreed with Mr. Robson as to the quality and quantity of the limestone with which the pier was proposed to be built, and also the estimate. Mr. Wooler's estimate far exceeded Mr. Robson's; but, notwithstanding this, the Commissioners appear to have had confidence in the opinion of their own engineer, who forthwith proceeded to build the pier in the manner projected by him, with the stone chiefly quarried from the adjacent rocks *(thus removing the barrier which nature had provided for the protection and preservation of the Town Moor).*

Considerable progress was made with this work, for some portions of it remain at the present day on the outer rocks. Many of the stones were subsequently removed to build the extension of the South Pier. The reasons for abandoning the work do not now appear. In 1780 the mole* was in a very ruinous condition.

In a retrospective view of Sunderland harbour, from the year 1755 to 1774, it is stated "That the channel at the mouth of the harbour was so very narrow and shoal, that ships drawing only six or seven feet of water were often prevented from getting out to sea. When it blew hard from the south, which generally brought down the largest fleets, it was hardly possible, with the most laborious efforts, to get more than six or eight ships, and these of no greater burthen than six or eight keels, or about 149 tons, into the harbour in one tide. If the sea happened to run high, even these few were in the greatest jeopardy of being bulged on the Ham Sand, on which the sea ran most violently, and of receiving other considerable damage by beating one

---

* "Such extensive moles could only have been undertaken by national funds, and were ill adapted to such a small income as that of the port of Sunderland. It is the province of the engineer to prevent his employers being led into error, and particularly so in such an important work as the building of piers, which are costly in their construction and cannot be easily undone. With regard to those projected by Mr. Robson, there can be no doubt that the enthusiasm of the engineer carried him far beyond the bounds of prudence."—*John Murray.*

against another as they struggled to get over the Stell, a contracted shallow part of the channel." In northerly winds, the sea rushed so furiously into the harbour that it was with much difficulty ships lying in the lower part thereof could be held, with all their cables out; and such as lay in the upper part, and at the North Quay, were often sunk upon their own anchors, which were obliged to be carried out to hold them. Many keels suffered the same fate when dropping down to their respective ships on the ebb." Such was the state of the harbour in 1735.

In 1774 a regular channel was formed and brought near the pier, but they had serious obstacles to surmount before they could effect this, for it was necessary to cut four feet and a half through a rock extending five hundred feet in length and one hundred and eighty in breadth; then by opening the mouth of the harbour, and altering the direction of the pier, the sea, which ran so violently into the haven, was now diverted and thrown upon the north shore, below where its strength is broken and exhausted. Substantial moorings have been contrived and deposited in proper places in the haven to hold the ships fast, thereby superseding any further use of the anchors, &c." It is then observed that "considerable progress has been made in that important and approved, though critical undertaking of building a pier from the main shore to the sea, in order to form a new basin, as well as to check and turn aside the large quantities of ballast and gross matter which are perpetually washing out of the roads, that they may not lodge upon the bar nor be driven into the harbour, which purposes have been in a good degree answered." It is further observed, "The great advantages the building of the pier has done to the channel of the river, and how easily ships now go out of the harbour, without that danger and difficulty they formerly did. The channel is now laid open, and turned in a tolerable course to the south-eastward, which enables ships of various sizes to come in and go out of the harbour, even to the number of eighty or one hundred in a tide. They then observe the prodigious saving in the expense of keel dues, trimming, and the immense quantity of coals which inevitably drops down and are lost between the ships and keels when casting at sea."

This document shews how much gratified the shipowners were at the improvements of the harbour within the nineteen years—from 1755 to 1774.

In 1771 there was a great flood in all the rivers of the North of England (at this time Newcastle Bridge was carried away), seriously damaging the harbour, making a great breach in the Pier, and endangering a large portion of the foundation.

In 1779 Mr. Robert Shout was appointed engineer to the Commissioners, and he submitted to them in that year a plan for rebuilding and extending the old South Pier. On this project the Commissioners asked the opinion of Mr. John Smeaton, who reported: "That as a considerable part of the old Pier, from the head inwards, appears shaken and its foundation sapped, I see no more easy or proper mode of repair than that of re-erecting it on a new foundation." As the foundation was composed of loose sand it was thought necessary to drive piles; but after a large number had been driven, and the masonry had been raised to some considerable height and extent, the work was abandoned.

Probably the old Pier, which was damaged by the land flood of 1771, was found not to be in so dangerous a condition as had been anticipated, and therefore the hope of maintaining it with some slight works may have induced the Commissioners to repair it, and thus save a considerable outlay of capital in building a new Pier.

In 1786–87 the North Pier was commenced by erecting a series of timber frames or carcass work loaded with stones.

In 1788 the North Pier was begun; but, owing to the nature of the ground, which was a loose shifting sand and gravel, the work proved extremely tedious and expensive. Before the death of Mr. Shout, in 1795, a length of nearly 700 feet of solid Pier, built upon piles, was completed. Mr. Pickernell, his successor, added 115 feet, and near the termination of the Pier, in 1802, built the lighthouse, with a stationary light at the height of 78 feet above high water (ordinary spring tides), and it has been exhibited nightly ever since, from sun-set to sun-rise.

The first portion of masonry in this North Pier having failed, or having shown strong symptoms of doing so, from the strength of the ebb current striking upon it and undermining the piles upon which it was founded, a strong buttress, called the outshot or jetty, was built in front of the Pier.

The South Pier was also lengthened 327 feet. This was done with timber or carcass work solid to the height of high water, but of open framing above.

On the 28th July, 1794, Mr. Ralph Dodd made a report to the Commissioners on the river, harbour, and piers. Speaking of the upper navigation of the river, he says:—

"There is one way by which you might have a constant depth of water for your upper navigation, which might be accomplished by throwing a stank across the river at the most convenient place, making two tumbling bays, and gates to block up at half ebb; which, to be done in a workman-like manner, would not cost less than £900. Your keels would then have sufficient water to the staiths, and up and down at all times to your lock gates; the times of passing which must be the last half flood and the first half ebb. By this process you would have less water at low tide in your harbour, and at the last half, little or no current down, for which reasons I would advise you never to think of such a thing, for believe me, gentlemen, the very existence of your harbour depends upon your ebb tides; and when they are so happily conducted as to run counter to your flood the greatest benefit is to be derived therefrom."

"In surveying the mouth of the harbour," he continues, "I then proceeded to the South Pier, now in ruins; while I was walking on its scattered fragments—'what,' thought I, 'could induce any engineer to recommend its erection with another from the north?' the two nearly forming a segment in the open sea, where the united powers of Neptune and Boreas so oft in hoary winter lash these northern shores."

Speaking of the ruins of the Pier, he says: "The remaining timber here, I perceive, is nearly destroyed with worms." And then he propounds an extraordinary remedy: "Should they attack the timber work at the New Pier, it must be filled with *scupper nails*."

He considered that the new line of carcasses at the South Pier end would have been better if they had curved more to the south, as it would have given the flood a free entrance, and not have made such an eddy, which caused the accumulation of sand inside. But the leading feature of his report was the conversion of what is now called the Potato Garth into a wet dock of upwards of thirteen acres in extent, with two pairs of gates. The lower entrance was to enable ships to get out to sea at almost all times; and the upper entrance, as near the west end as possible, to allow ships and keels to pass to and fro.

In speaking of the sight, he says: "The first moment I cast my eye here in a survey it struck me for the purpose I now mention it; for nature, you see, has formed two sides of it already. I never saw a place better adapted, considering the local situation of your harbour."

In speaking of the trade of the port, he says: "Does any one wish to have a just idea of the extensive trade of this port? On a sea-tide, let him go where I once stood, the Pier end. No sooner there, than casting my eyes to the south-east, over the crystal flood, as Homer* beautifully

---

* Though I here quote a great poet, I know none equal to our own English bard on sea subjects, the unfortunate Falconer. The sea, as claiming him for her own, entombed him in the deep. Government sent him and others to make astronomical observations in the Southern Hemisphere, and they were all drowned in the "Aurora" frigate.

observes, I saw a wood of ships, a zephyr was gently fanning them to the port, all sails drew, and their streamers were waving to the wind.

This prominent point where I stood, stretching in the sea, soon became thronged. Here, with glad steps, came some of Eve's fairest daughters, some hung on their arms the cherub form, and by their side their tender offspring led. What glittering eyes of gladness were fixed on this fleet; some to parents, some to husbands, some to lovers. Does the artist want a subject of nature to paint joy and gladness by? He cannot be better served than here; and for sadness on the days of departure. He would see the half closed eye, with the crystal tear dropping down many a fair cheek. When the vessels' foaming prows pressed through the deep and drew near, how pleased I was to see the seaman's active limb, the muscular arm to grasp and hang on the twisted cord; and not less to hear the watchful commander cry, 'Thus, and no nearer,' while the shrill youthful voice echoes the just mandate."

In 1804 Mr. Matthew Shout entered the Commissioners' service. He found the distance between the ends of the North and South Piers at the entrance to be 570 feet; gaping to receive the heavy seas driven by every easterly wind between the north and south points of the compass.

To lessen the width of the entrance, and in some degree to exclude the surge from the south-east, he took up that part of the South Pier which was commenced by Mr. Robson in 1757, and extended it more in a line with the old pier, building it upon wooden carcasses, and leaving it open at the top or upper part above high water mark.

In 1807, December 19th, Mr. William Jessop made a report to the Commissioners, from which we extract the following. He said "So far, what Mr. Shout has done has been manifestly productive of advantage to the harbour, and under the circumstances in which he found it, I do not know that he could have done better." Mr. Jessop then recommends "that the South Pier should be extended as far as the meridian of the present extension of the North Pier, in the direction laid down in the plan, &c. When this shall be done, both the piers may be extended, as shewn in the plan, terminating on a line due north and south from each other by the compass."

"I am of opinion that 250 feet, agreeably to the plan, or even less, will be sufficient."

"I think a considerable improvement may be effected by building a wall on the verge of the flat ground, on the north side of the harbour, from C to D, about the height of the flow of neap tides, so as to suffer the surge from the entrance to break over it at high water; this wall should be founded on a row of sheet piles, and be made water tight, having a pair of gates, thirty feet wide, opening at the west end, with sluices therein, to receive and discharge the water, through which ships and keels may enter when there may be a want of room in the harbour."

"On this wall a gangway may be constructed, by which vessels may be haled to and from the North Pier."

He says "It would be possible to make a floating dock on the flat beach north of the harbour, and this is the only place where it would be at all worth while to attempt it. By a considerable excavation, about 30 acres might be floated."

Mr. Jessop was also of opinion "that very extensive ground might be formed at the back of the South Pier, by projecting a wall or breastwork, at right angles to the pier, from, at, or near the end of the stone pier, which might be extended progressively to any length southward, as it may be wanted. Besides retaining the shingle which would travel down to the harbour mouth, another advantage will result from this operation. So far as this wall may be extended so far will it effectually protect the Moorland, which appears to be rapidly wasting away."

"By this proposed wall, valuable ground will be formed, whereon ballast may be discharged to any extent; towards this purpose, an opening may be made through one of the archways in the South Pier, with a drawbridge over it, to admit vessels into a small dock behind it."

"I had at first an idea that a large scouring basin of 30 or 40 acres might be made on this rocky ground, which, if it could have been done would have had a very powerful effect in deepening the harbour and bar, by discharging its waters by sluices through the archway, near the west end of the South Pier; but on considering that while it would be under execution there would hardly be a possibility of preventing it being filled with shingle before the wall could be closed to shut it out, I was compelled to abandon this project."

"Respecting the extension of the piers, as I could not recommend any mode of construction which would be less liable to hazard and derangement during the execution, than what has been practised by Mr. Shout in the extensions which he has effected, I shall estimate upon that mode of construction."

"I recommend that the freestone facings, instead of being three feet, should be four feet in bed or thickness; with this thickness, a great portion of the backing or filling may be done with the rubble limestone to be got on the shore, or at the quarries immediately above the bridge."

"I cannot recommend any attempt to improve the navigation of the river within the tide way by any *Locks or Dams.*"

Mr. Jessop, in concluding his report, says, "I think I may safely venture to predict, that with such an extension of the piers, the depth of water over the bar will be at least three feet more than it now is, and that it will completely accommodate the trade of the port."

In May, 1817, Mr. John Milton was appointed engineer to the Commissioners.

The piers at the mouth of the river having been originally executed chiefly with timber work, and masonry built thereon, to a certain height became ruinous, and it was found necessary to rebuild the outward or seaward portion of them.

The timber carcasses at the bottom were completely eaten away by the worms; indeed the tops of the piles that had been driven were honeycombed, and refused to carry the superincumbent weight laid upon them, hence the shrinkage of the masonry. Rafts of timber, used for floating oak logs in the dock, have been after a few years immersion, found to be utterly useless, more than half the balks were eaten by the worms, and scarce any of the wood left except the top skin, which occasionally came to the surface. Oak logs, after lying at the bottom of the dock in the mud for some years, when taken out have been completely eaten through and through by the worms from end to end. (Personal observation and experience.)

In the year 1821, Mr. Rennie recommended certain lines to be adopted for the extension of the South and North Piers.

Instead of the frame or carcass work previously adopted, he recommended that blocks of stone, varying from five to seven tons in weight, should be laid at such a depth as to guard as much as possible against any injury which the piers might sustain from the effects of scouring, and also backing the wall so founded with a rubble glacis.

From 1821 to 1824, as I remember the old Pier, it was built upon carcasses partly filled with stones up to about high water mark, and at the top of the carcasses a flooring of deals was laid, on which the public used to walk to the end of the pier, where the tide-light house stood.

It was upon this pier that the thick warp or towline was clutched for a hail up the harbour. A protecting balk was laid along the edge of the pier.

The new or present pier ran more in a southward direction. As the new pier progressed the old one stood to the north or inside of it; thus there were two piers running or radiating from the solid end of the old pier at one time. A third one, built by Robson in 1757, also radiated from, and was to the south of, both the former; the foundations of this latter were then being picked up and utilized in the new works.

The pier wall recommended by Jessop in 1807-08 had been partly built, and ran straight south from the old pier head, almost at right angles with the low shed.

The piers or moles built upon the rocks by Robson in 1767-68 were nearly all gone, though a few stones remained embedded on the rock and jamphered together with iron let into the stones, were still to be seen; the other stones had been utilized for the new pier. A kind of pier was shewn further south (when a boy, searching for crabs and whelks, I remember seeing some stones which were said to have been laid for a pier).

The Stone Heads were an accumulation of stones which had been thrown into the sea at the end or edge of the rocks to break the force of the south-east sea upon the bar or harbour mouth, as well as to act as a protection to the battery, barracks' hospital, and the moor in general, which were fast washing away.

The position on which the barracks' hospital stood was completely washed away.

There used to be a footpath on the banks round the east of the battery, facing the sea. The banks, the footpath, and the east face of the battery itself were all washed away.

Under Mr. Milton's superintendence a length of 230 yards of the South Pier was built in this manner, as laid down by Mr. Rennie in 1821.

The top of the pier was $10\frac{1}{2}$ feet above high water of ordinary spring tides, and it was paved with freestone for a width of 40 feet, divided into two parts—the one raised 2 feet above the other, as a promenade A handsome parapet, raised a step in height, separated the raised platform from the rubble backing. The whole breadth, from the river wall to the foot of the glacis, was about 250 feet.

The total length of this pier, to its eastern extremity, was then 650 yards. It required an extension of 57 yards further to the eastward to complete the project of Mr. Rennie.

Mr. Murray succeeded Mr. Milton. Between the years 1832 and 1843 he took down the seaward part of the North Pier, and executed Mr. Rennie's design on nearly the same lines as laid down by him. This pier has been built in the strongest manner with excellent materials, forming altogether a handsome and substantial piece of masonry. The length of the pier so built on the river's side measures about 600 feet; and its extension and renewal, with the pier head, and the glacis on the north side, cost upwards of £75,000. The foundations were laid by means of the diving-bell, partly upon piles, the heads of which were cut level at a depth of 6 feet below low water (spring tides). In other cases the foundations were laid upon the rock, at a depth varying from 4 to 18 feet below low water. The total length of the pier, from its west to east head, is 1770 feet. Mr. Murray also succeeded in removing to the North Pier head, in 1841, in one entire mass, on railways, the stone lighthouse erected in 1802.*

After the opening of the Durham and Sunderland Railway, in 1836, when colliers began to load from the drops on the Low Quay, many complaints were made by the shipowners of the uneasy state of the lower part of the harbour during stormy weather, caused by the waves hugging the pier and rolling upwards.

In 1843 a large portion of the South Pier had its foundations undermined by the current; and a large portion of the western part of the old pier required extensive repairs, being in a very shattered condition.

Mr. Murray suggested that instead of re-building the pier it would be better to take about 800 feet of it down altogether, and set it back in a circular direction, so as to make a receptacle somewhat similar to that opposite (the Potato Garth), on which the swell or range of the sea might break and be dispersed during storms from the eastward. This work is now completed, and has tended to lessen the rolling motion in the harbour.

---

* Mr. Murray does not seem to have learnt the fact that piles will not endure in our waters. The portion of the North Pier which is built on piles with the heads cut level six feet below low water mark, under Mr. Murray's direction, has fallen into the river twice, and at the present time will take the estimated amount of £3,900 to replace it. The piles themselves have been eaten by the sand worm—completely honeycombed, and refused to carry any longer the mass of masonry built thereon. The lesson had been taught in ruins of the South Piers, but Mr. Murray had evidently not learnt it; he had intended to fill in the chasm in the rocks, but time shows he had not succeeded in the venture.

The remaining or the oldest portion of the old South Pier was entirely removed on the formation of the South Docks.

The Commissioners, who had had various pier schemes by Stevenson, Meik, Coode, and Wake (the present engineer), laid before them, in 1876 referred the question of "Harbour Piers" to Sir John Coode, with the result that, after considering the matter for nearly eight years, in 1884 a commencement was made with the works for Roker Pier. The site of the pier is one upon which all engineers, reporting upon outer piers, have selected, though the directions and lengths for a pier have varied—going back to 1758, the time of Robson.

The pier it was decided to proceed with at Roker was to extend a distance of 2,760 feet in a south-easterly direction into the sea, and having a curve of 2,280 feet radius.

On the 14th September, 1885, the first block was laid by Mr. James Laing, Chairman of the River Wear Commission; previous to this date the sea wall and a portion of the shore end of the pier had been already built by means of concrete deposit, *en masse*, and faced with granite within cofferdams, which were required to remove the sand down to the rocks. Since the first block was laid satisfactory progress has been made. On October 16th, 1890—the end of the season—a total length of 2,183 feet 10 inches had been completed, leaving a length of 576 feet 2 inches yet to be done, which will probably take three or four years to complete.

The pier is being constructed in complete lengths of 42 feet 7 inches, or measuring from the end of the top course to bottom course blocks 53 feet 7 inches, this being the amount of block work that the radial crane will set without being moved.

A subway, 6 feet high and 4 feet wide, is formed in the heart of the pier, as a means of access to the lighthouse in stormy weather, and for carrying the gas and water pipes necessary for lighting the pier and supplying the radial crane with water and gas during the progress of the work.

For a considerable distance out the block work, of a height of 23 feet, was set on the rock, dressed and levelled up with concrete to receive the blocks; but when deeper water was reached the foundations, to a height of 18 inches above low water—ordinary spring tides, were made up of large concrete bags of 116, 75, and 52 tons weight, laid across the site of the foundation; the surfaces of the bags, where necessary, are dressed down to the required level, and where the bagwork is too low it is levelled up with strong concrete.

The pier is built of four courses of blocks, each block averaging 43 tons in weight. All outside blocks have a facing of red granite in courses of 10, 11, and 12 inches deep.

A substantial red granite coping runs the full length of the pier on each side, and this is surmounted with cast-iron standards placed 7 feet apart, with 2 galvanized 1½-inch wrought iron square rails fixed diagonally; lamp-posts, of a similar design to the standards, are placed at intervals. A flight of grey granite steps, with landings, has been constructed on the south side of the pier at a distance of 1,540 feet from the shore end; and it is intended that a similar set of steps and landings shall be put in when further progress with the pier has been made. The top of the pier is finished with a crushed granite concrete pavement, having a rise of 4 inches at the centre of the pier. The width of the structure from coping to coping is 35 feet, and 39 feet 7 inches across the bottom course, the sides of the pier having a batter of 1 inch in 10.

At the present end of the pier there is a depth of water of about 20 feet below low water, ordinary spring tides; and towards the completion of the pier, at the roundheads, a depth will be reached of about 30 feet below low water, ordinary spring tides, or 44 feet 6 inches below high water, ordinary spring tides.

BLOCK SETTING CRANE.

The whole of the blocks in the superstructure are lifted and placed in position by means of a 60-ton hydraulic radial crane, which embraces the advanced development of block setting plant; the special feature of the crane is the application of the hydraulic power with all motions perfectly independent of each other, yet under the control of one man in the valve house for lifting, lowering, and radiating.

The crane, in all its movements, has been found to work very steadily; the speeds of the various motions being as follows:

Rate of lifting with 50 tons load   5 feet per minute.
    „   without 50 tons load...20 „   „
Rate of lowering with load ....20 „   „
Travel of Monkey ....25 „   „

A complete radiation from side to side of pier is made in two minutes. A 43-ton block, when required to be set, is lifted by the crane by means of a sheave block, the hook of which works on a live ring, the block being moved by setting accurately by means of a worm wheel and screw, acted upon by a ratchet, and thus avoiding any twisting of the chains.

The crane rests on a travelling "Goliath," constructed of dressed pitch pine and greenheart timber, strongly keyed, bracketted, and bolted together. The weight of the crane, with Goliath frame complete, is 273 tons, which, with 17 tons keutledge, gives a total of 290 tons.

The calculations, designing and preparation of the working drawings for the crane were done in the offices of the Engineer to the Commissioners, and a large portion of the structure and machinery were made in their shops.

The following figures shew the quantities of material which have been used in the construction of the works since their commencement in the year 1884, up to the completion of last season's work, on October 16th, 1890.

MATERIALS USED.

14,800 tons of Portland cement; 155,054 tons of concrete; 26,655 tons of granite chips; 2,387 tons of granite coping and steps; 11,274 tons of red granite facing blocks; 252 tons Roman cement. Total weight of material, 210,422 tons. These weights include 644 bags laid on the foundation by the barges, and equal to a weight of 51,155 tons.

The radial crane, since starting block setting, September 14th, 1885, has lifted and set in position 1929 blocks, and has lifted a total weight of material, exclusive of tubs, waggons, &c., equal to 117,370 tons.

The following table shews the different lengths of pier that have been completed in each year since the commencement:

	Feet.	in.	Lengths.
In 1884, April to September 14th, 1885	283	9	
„ 1885, September 14th to December 22nd	183	0	...
„ 1886, February 2nd to October 29th	596	2	...
„ 1887, March 25th to October 6th	246	4	
„ 1888, April 14th to September 28th	298	1	
„ 1889, April 19th to September 19th	253	7	
„ 1890, June 5th to October 15th	222	11	..
Total length of pier	2,183	10	

Special blocks have been set in the pier by the Chairman, Mr. James Laing, who laid the foundation block, 14th September, 1885; Mr. H. T. Morton, in 1886; Lord Brabourne, Lord Ravensworth, and Lady Williamson, in 1887; and by the Earl of Durham and Mons. De Lesseps in 1889. The exact position of each block is marked by the name being blocked in the face.

On the 24th June, 1891, the monthly meeting of the Commission was held in the board room, when the chairman of the Works Committee, Mr. Robert Thompson, stated in reply to Col. Eminson, that the total cost of the Roker Pier up to that date had been £157,000, which included the plant, estimated at £30,000 to £32,000.

On June 5th, 1891, an important special meeting of the Works Committee was held, Mr. Robert Thompson presiding. The report of Sir John Coode, on the proposal of the Commissioners to construct a new pier on the south side of the river was submitted. Of the three alternative schemes which have from time to time been before the Commission, he recommended the third, with some alterations, but practically as drawn up by the chief engineer, Mr. H. H. Wake.

The scheme provides for a pier 2,870 feet long, at an estimated cost of £160,000; and Sir John Coode suggested that the best energies of the engineer and his staff should now be devoted to constructing the South Pier for about half its length. It was ultimately resolved to go on with the new pier, and construct about 1,400 feet, at an estimated cost, including the sea wall, block yard, concrete plant and crane of £63,981, beginning at a point about 500 yards south of the present South Pier.

CHAPTER XV.

THE BRIDGE.

Before the opening of the Bridge, travellers in general, and the inhabitants of Sunderland and Bishopwearmouth, were frequently put to great inconvenience. Foot passengers could manage to cross by the ferry to the north side of the river, but carriages, chaises, or other conveyances were under the necessity of crossing the river at Deptford for Southwick, which means that they had to go past the Church, round by Silksworth Row, and to the west of Messrs. Hartley's works for the road to Deptford by a country lane, called in later days Wellington Lane; or if for Newcastle, by the horse ferry at Hylton.

Rowland Burdon, Esq., M.P., who already had procured a turnpike road from Stockton to Sunderland, being returned to Parliament in the year 1790, began to move in the matter for a bridge across the Wear.

On January 26th, 1792, a meeting was held in favour of the scheme for providing a bridge to cross the Wear near to Sunderland.

In the same year, *i.e.* 1792, an Act of Parliament was obtained for the building of a bridge.

At first, a stone bridge was proposed, of 200 feet span and 80 feet to the crown of the arch, but the expense appeared to be beyond all reasonable bounds; besides, on searching for foundations, none were to be found within the limits of the space covered by the tide, which flowed between rocky shores, distant from each other at the narrowest part about 240 feet.

Mr. Burdon's plan was to make an iron bridge, according to his own idea, after having caused an experimental rib to be cast and set up by Messrs. Walker, of Rotherham, under the direction of Mr. Thomas Wilson. He brought forward a proposal to the town of Sunderland and the county, of constructing a bridge on his principles over the Wear, between the Wearmouths, immediately adjoining Sunderland and its harbour. His proposal was adopted, and the iron bridge which now spans the river is the result.

The span of the bridge is 236 feet 8 inches; the arch is the segment of a circle 444 feet in diameter, formed by 6 ribs, each containing 105 blocks of cast iron, each of them five feet in height, four inches in thickness, two feet four-and-a-half inches in length at the top and two feet four inches at the bottom, which butt on each other in the same manner as a stone arch. The ribs are respectively placed at six feet distance, but are connected and braced together by hollow tubes or bridles of cast iron with projecting shoulders. The mode of bracing the ribs was so simple and expeditious that the whole was put together and thrown over the river in ten days, and the scaffolding immediately removed.

The weight of iron used was 260 tons—214 tons cast and 46 tons malleable. The spring of the arch is only thirty-four feet; and the spandrills are fixed by cast iron circles placed upon the ribs and gradually diminishing from the abutments towards the centre of the bridge, supporting the platform for the roadway and footpath, bounded by a neat iron balustrade; above which, in the centre on each side, is the following inscription:—

"Nil Desperandum, Auspice Deo."

(nothing to be despaired of under the auspices of Providence.)

The piers or abutments are piles of almost solid masonry, twenty-four feet in thickness, forty-two feet in breadth at the bottom, and thirty-seven feet at the top. The south pier is founded on the solid rock, and rises from about twenty-two feet above the bed of the river. On the north side the ground was not so favourable, on which account the foundation was obliged to be carried ten feet below the bed of the river.

In 1793, September 24th, the foundation stone was laid, on which occasion the provincial grand lodge of Free Masons in the county of Durham took part. A grand lodge was opened in ample form in the Phœnix Hall by the late William Henry Lambton, Esq., provincial grand master, assisted by about 200 brethren clothed in the badges, jewels, and other insignia of the different orders of masonry, being joined by the Magistrates, Commissioners, and others who were not masons, at the gates of the hall, conducted by one of the stewards of the day; they went to church (whether by Pewterer's Lane or Queen Street and the Back Lonnin, or by the High Street and Church Street, is not recorded,) through an immense crowd of spectators; the Magistrates and Commissioners occupying the body of the church, and the brethren the galleries, according to their several ranks and degrees in masonry. After a sermon by the Rev. Mr. Heskett the procession moved from the church through the town by way of the Low Street, passing what was called the manor house—in which the celebrated Col. John Lilburn was born—through Panns, passing the house in which Mr. Nicholson the shipbuilder lived at that date (who owned the docks opposite the house), and on to the crowded banks of the river, over which they passed at the Panns on a platform or bridge of keels admirably constructed and disposed for that purpose.

At the north-west part of the intended bridge was formed a large area, where the first stone was to be laid, around which the brethren were arranged; and on the cliff above a conspicuous station was railed in for the grand honours, the oration, and other purposes; from this position Mr. Burdon delivered his speech.

The inscription, written by Tipping Brown, M.D., was then read by the Senior Grand Warden, in Latin, and the translation by the Grand Secretary is as follows:—

Translation:

At that time,
When the mad fury of the French citizens,
Dictating acts of extreme depravity,
Disturbed the peace of Europe
with iron war,
ROWLAND BURDON, ESQ., M.P.,
Aiming at worthier purposes,
Hath resolved to join the steep and
Craggy Shores
Of the River Wear
With an iron bridge.
He happily laid the foundation
ON THE 24TH DAY OF SEPTEMBER,
In the Year of human salvation 1793,
And the 33rd of the reign
Of George the Third,
In the presence of
WILLIAM HENRY LAMBTON, ESQ., M.P.,
P.G.M.,
With a respectable circle of the Brethren
Of the Society
Of Free and Accepted Masons,
And of the Magistrates and principal gentlemen of the County of Durham;
Attended by an immense concourse of
People.

Long may the vestiges endure
Of a hope not formed in vain.

The plate was then deposited and the stone laid by Mr. Rowland Burdon, assisted by Mr. Lambton and the other grand officers, according to ancient usages. The grand honours were then given, and at this moment perhaps a more gratifying spectacle was never presented at one view.

The procession returned (we presume, by the way they came,) to the Sea Captain's Lodge, in Mailing's Rig, where the grand lodge was closed. A sumptuous dinner was provided in the Phœnix Hall,* to which above two hundred persons sat down; and the evening was spent with conviviality and harmony worthy of the occasion.—*Garbutt.*

The net cost of the bridge was £33,400; of this sum Mr. Burdon advanced £33,000, the other was raised by subscription. The sums advanced were secured by tolls at five per cent. interest.

The bridge was opened for passengers on the 9th August, 1796, in the presence of His Royal Highness the Duke of Gloucester, after a very splendid masonic ceremony and procession. The number of spectators was computed at 80,000.

In 1858 the bridge was strengthened and widened under the supervision of the late Robert Stephenson. The three iron tubes placed upon the ribs of the arch were put in; the overhanging footpaths formed; the cast-iron circles placed upon the ribs were removed and straight iron supports placed in their stead; the roadway and footpaths levelled up, as now seen; and the bridge re-opened in March, 1859.

---

* The Phœnix Hall was visited in December, 1891. A small portrait of Tipping Brown, M.D. (the author of the inscription deposited in the stone, and said to have been picked up on an old bo kstall in Newcastle), hanging above one of the chimney pieces, seems to be the only memorial that they have of the event. As to above two hundred persons dining in the hall, they certainly could not have been such jolly masons as the historian here represents, or the probabilities are that the second lot occupied the places of those who had fallen or rolled under the tables.

In 1846, November 12th, the foot toll was abolished; and on November 9th, 1885, the tolls on vehicles ceased, and the bridge was declared free—just eighty-nine years after its first opening.

COST OF WEARMOUTH BRIDGE.

Obtaining Act of Parliament		2	
Consulting Architect		4	
Purchase of ground and houses on north side		5	
Ground on the south side		0	
		13	
Stones and Lime	£5,450 11 1		
Timber	1,966 8 8		
Cast and Wrought Iron	6,130 4 4		
Wages to Masons, Joiners, &c.	12,078 9 5		
Floats, Boats and other incidentals	1,712 14 4		
Cost of Materials and Labour		27,408 7 10	
Interest on Capital during building		2,699 18 9	
Purchase of Sunderland Ferry	£6,300 0 0		
Purchase of Panns Ferry	1,600 0 0		
Law expenses thereon	985 0 8		
		8,885 0 5	
Total amount		£41,800 0 0	
Amount paid for Ferries	£7,900 0 0		
Amount paid for Ground	500 0 0		
		8,400 0 0	
		£33,400 0 0	

WEARMOUTH COLLIERY.

The pit was commenced in May, 1826. It is situated on the north bank of the Wear, about half a mile from the bridge. In sinking it, 31 seams of coal were passed through, varying in thickness from 1¼ins. to 6ft. 2½ins., and forming an aggregate of 47ft. 2ins. of coal. Only one of them, however, has been found of workable thickness and merchantable quality. Sir George Elliott, in his evidence before a Committee of the House of Commons, says, "The peculiarities of this pit are the extraordinary depth, viz. 285 fathoms, to the Bensham seam, 15 fathoms lower being sunk for standage or for a reservoir of water.

The ordinary time consumed in going down and coming up the shaft is about from two to three minutes, respectively.

The tub for drawing coals, and also men and boys, holds about 30 cwt. of coals. The weight of the rope itself is nearly five tons.

The average temperature in the pit ranges from 78 to 80 degrees, and in some parts of the mine it occasionally rises to 89 degrees.

The total vend of the colliery in 1842, was 20,854 chaldrons, or 55,263 tons.

In 1890, the total quantity of coals vended was,

In the river	209,616	tons
,, South Dock	2,508	,,
Total	212,124	tons

exclusive of the landsale.

Originally, the pit was sunk by the Pemberton family and others. It is now turned into a limited company, of which Mr. William Stobart is Chairman and Mr. Walker Secretary.

THE DOCKS.

The first report we have of docks or basins is furnished by Ralph Dodd, in his report to the Commissioners, in 1794. The North Pier had then been built, and the sand between the Pier and Roker formed. His idea was to build a wall, running from the North Pier up to the Folly End, and to enclose the Bite, to have two entrances, one at the west for ships and keels, and one at the east end for vessels going to sea. Mr. Dodd says, "I mean here to make you one of the first Docks or Basins of any I know in this kingdom for its convenience, being so near the open sea."

"The first moment I cast my eye here in a survey, it struck me as being adapted for the purpose I now mention, for nature has formed two sides of it already. I never saw a place better adapted, considering the local situation of your harbour. The upper surface, now occupied by the tide at high water, contains 567,000 square feet, which when properly deepened will contain 237 ships, supposing their extreme beam, or to the outside of their bends 27ft., and from the aftermost part of the taffle rail to the foremost part of the stem to be 90 feet, each of these occupying a space of 2,430 feet, with 90 feet remaining. I understand vessels of this scantling are much larger than the generality of those in your trade. If you want to enlarge and improve it, it may be made to contain twice that number." Such was the idea of dock accommodation in the last century, the depth of water required, and the size of vessels frequenting the port; but the engineer omitted in his calculations the expansion of the trade of the port, also the enlargement of the vessels requiring the depth of water over the bar, the lift of wave at the entrance near the sea, and the stell caunch to contend with from the west gates near the Folly End, as planned.

In 1808 Mr. W. Jessop, asked by the Commissioners to report, amongst other things, how far the erection of a bason or wet dock, in any situation, would accommodate the trade and repay the expense of such an undertaking, says: "I can say nothing encouraging. It would be possible to make a floating dock on the flat beach north of the harbour, and this is the only place where it would be at all worth while to attempt it. By a considerable excavation about 30 acres might be floated; but to make it at all useful it should be divided into two basons—one of about three or four acres as a tide bason, into which thirty or forty sail might enter with a rising tide, through a single pair of gates, which would be shut at high water, from whence there might be a passage into the other bason, through which ships might pass at their leisure. As there is yet room in the harbour, above the bridge, for a considerable extension of moorings; and, when the piers are completed, much room might be obtained below the present moorings; I can hardly think that the convenience of a floating dock will be considered as worth the cost of it; for though the wall, which has been proposed for the formation of a scouring bason, would become the foundation of a dock wall, the additional expense for constructing a floating dock would be at least £50,000."

Mr. Jessop also projected a wall or breast work at right angles to the pier, from, at, or near the end of the stone pier, as shewn in the plan at E.G., which might be extended progressively, as might be wanted, to any length southwards, etc. And then he goes on to say: "I had at first an idea that a large scouring basin of thirty or forty acres might be made on this rocky ground, which, if it could have been done, would have had a very powerful effect in deepening the harbour and bar by discharging its water by sluices through the archway near the west end of the South Pier. But on considering that, while it would be under execution, there would hardly be a possibility of preventing its being filled with shingle before the walls could be closed to shut it out, I was compelled to abandon this project."

In 1816—the latter part of the year—a proposal for establishing a Floating or Wet Dock near the mouth of the river Wear was submitted to the Commissioners by Mr. William Bell. It was suggested that it might be carried into effect on the south side of the river, where the flat and bare rock, which extends to the north nearly as far as the extremity of the piles formerly driven down for the formation of a pier, and which runs southward almost on a level with low water, would afford the best foundation that could be for a floating dock wall fronting the sea, which should be carried at a right angle with the end of those piles as far to the south as might be thought necessary, say as far as opposite the south-east corner of the battery; from thence up to that corner, and then by a straight line to join the pier at the engineer's house, which would circumscribe a space for nearly three hundred vessel averaging from ten to twelve keels.—*Garbutt, page 272*.

As the trade of the port increased, the want of room for the accommodation of shipping was almost constantly before the Commissioners, and room could only be had in the shape of wet docks.

We give excerps from the minutes of the proceedings of the Commissioners of the River Wear, to show that this was so.

Excerp No. 1—25th January, 1826.—" Resolved that Sir Cuthbert Sharp, the Chairman; the Honourable Archibald

Cochrane, John Davison, Esq., William Loraine, Esq., and Addison Fenwick, Esq., be, and they are hereby appointed a committee, to bore, excavate, and otherwise obtain such information as may enable them to make a report as to the necessity and advantage of forming a dock or docks on the river Wear."

Excerp No. 2—23rd January, 1828.—"Ordered that the committee for considering and framing such plans as they shall conceive will be most desirable to submit to Parliament for the renewal of the subsisting Acts for the improvement of the river Wear, and port and haven of Sunderland, and for the better accommodation of the shipping frequenting the said river and port, shall consist of nine Commissioners, five of whom shall be a quorum, and that Sir Cuthbert Sharp, the honourable Captain Cochrane, Mr. Addison Fenwick, Mr. William Stobart, jun., Mr. Scott, Mr. William Loraine, Mr. Buddle, Mr. Ogden and Mr. Hunter be, and they are hereby appointed such committee."

Excerp No. 3—11th June, 1828.—"Ordered that Mr. Robert Stephenson, engineer, of Edinburgh, be requested to come to Sunderland, at the expense of the Commissioners, to examine into the localities of the Wear, and make a report for the consideration of the Commissioners as to the places where it will be practicable to form Wet Docks."

Excerp No. 4—8th April, 1829.—"Ordered that the committee already appointed (on the 23rd day of January, 1828—see page 195) be requested to consider Mr. Stephenson's plan for the formation of a dock or docks, and to report thereon at the next meeting of the Commissioners."

Excerp No. 5—2nd December, 1829.—"The committee appointed on the 23rd day of January, 1828, (page 196) having delivered in their final report (the first having been presented and read on the first day of July, 1829) and the same being read and approved of, 'Resolved, that they be requested to continue their labours, and that they do appoint three of their own body to proceed to London to obtain a new Act of Parliament when required by the Board.'"

The two reports mentioned in the last minute are not to be found.

In 1830, Burnett writes :—

"At several different periods the idea has been suggested to the Commissioners of forming a wet dock at Sunderland, and the Commissioners have given the matter some consideration ; but after viewing the subject in all its bearings, the committee report and advise that the present Commissioners may entirely avoid entering upon the subject further as a Board, and the 49th and 59th George III., leaving the matter perfectly open to any body of adventurers who may be inclined to undertake the same, and in which project they might receive the assurance that they would be assisted to the utmost by the Commissioners of the River Wear, but on the direct understanding that their income will only be considered responsible for the purposes of the present or any future Act limited like the present, to the preservation and improvement of the river, port and haven. The committee then say 'We are of opinion that the interests of the two would clash, and that they ought to be kept entirely separate.' Thus, so far as the Commissioners are concerned as a body, the idea of forming a wet dock falls to the ground."—*Burnett, pages 38 and 39.*

So wrote Burnett, but the idea of forming a wet dock had not fallen to the ground, for we find at a meeting of the Commissioners, held on the 14th September, 1830, a special committee was appointed by them, consisting of the Chairman, Mr. A. Fenwick, Mr. Wilkinson, Mr. Davison, Mr. Ogden, Mr. Backhouse, Mr. Scurfield, Mr. Mowbray. Mr. T. Pemberton, Mr. Morton, Mr. Stobart, Mr. Scott and Mr. Tanner, on this very subject. Let us hear their report.

REPORT.

To the Commissioners of the River Wear.

Gentlemen—The Special Committee, appointed on the 14th Sept. last " to obtain and disseminate accurate information on the subject of wet docks, and to report thereon at an early meeting of the Board," have, in pursuance of the above order, proceeded to the examination of such documents as have been submitted to our consideration.

First—By a Committee appointed at a Public Meeting of the Shipowners, Merchants and other inhabitants of Sunderland, the Wearmouth and their vicinities, holden at the Assembly Room on the 5th September.

Secondly—By a Committee appointed at a General Meeting of the Shipowners, holden at the Exchange on the 23rd day of September; and

Thirdly—By a Committee from the General Meeting of Merchants, holden at the Exchange on the 29th September.

The first committee presented us with Resolutions agreed upon at the Assembly Rooms, together with a statement of probable revenue, for the purpose of meeting the expenses of a wet dock, according to the commerce of the port in 1830 ; which statement we transmitted to the shipowners, and to the merchants, not as a document emanating in any way from the committee, but as a statement which might in some measure influence the nature of their deliberations.

The shipowners did not adopt the scale laid down therein so far as regarded their own particular interest, but framed another on a different principle, without stating the general amount to be derived therefrom. This statement, therefore, required an examination in detail, and also to be submitted to the test of the official returns.

The Merchants Committee presented a scale of rates also, but without giving the general amount, and their statement has been examined in a similar way.

Deputations from the said committees, together with a deputation from this committee, applied to the Coalowners of the river Wear, at a meeting of the trade convened for that purpose, on the 4th October, for 2d. per chaldron on the annual vend, in aid, but no answer has yet been received from them.

On the Shipping the duties or rate would appear to be (See appendix)...................................	£8,848	16	4
On the Merchants' dues, according to their schedule......	895	9	5
	£9,744	5	9
And on the vend, if granted, 2d. per chaldron on 523,557 chaldrons	4,362	19	6
Forming a total of	£14,107	5	3

Various other presumed sources of revenue have been pointed out, which are stated in the appendix ; and we may add, on the best authority, that the general trade of the port is constantly and rapidly increasing.

The rates and duties will naturally become payable from the date of the passing of the intended Act ; the revenues of the Commissioners being solely applicable to the improvement and preservation of the River Wear. And the full amount of duty will soon be required, as you have recently given orders for the most extensive preparations for the building of the North Pier, which is reported by Sir John Rennie, and which is perfectly well known to be in a dangerous and insecure state ; and the South Pier is yet unfinished.

The Committee, however, have to consider the question—taking it for granted that the Coalowners agree to give 2d. per chaldron on the vend (without which the Committee do not see how they can recommend the subject to the consideration of the Board), will the amount of revenue stated, together with the probable increase, be sufficient, in the estimation of the Committee, to warrant further proceedings ?

The Committee are anxious to come to an honest and conscientious conclusion. We feel the question to be one of momentous and even gigantic importance ; and although the time of our deliberations has been extremely limited, yet we have applied to the question the best consideration in our power.

A former Committee, in 1829, reported (page 23) that the matter of Docks should be left perfectly open to any body of adventurers who might be inclined to undertake the same, and in which project they might receive the assurance that they would be assisted to the utmost by the Commissioners of the River Wear. They were also of opinion that the interests of the two would clash, and that they ought to be kept entirely separate."

The present Committee, however, trust that by proper care and sound regulations, no conflicting interes's may arise, though we strongly recommend that a similar assurance should be expressed by the Commissioners to any respectable body connected with the interests of the town and neighbourhood, who are inclined to undertake the formation of Wet Docks, that they will receive every accommodation from the Commissioners of the River Wear.

In the hands of individuals, and as a private speculation, the direct interests of the parties would ensure the most zealous and watchful care.

In the hands of the Commissioners, who would desire no pecuniary advantage whatever from it as individuals, but which would naturally add considerably to their labours, zealous and constant attention would only be the result of exalted sense of public duty.

Still, however, if after due and mature consideration it is the wish of all parties that the Commissioners, as an acknowledged and legally constituted body, should undertake the same, the Committee have come to the conclusion that the Board may entertain the subject favourably ; and by the appointment of a Select Committee of your own body, examine further and more deeply into the subject, pursuing their examinations with steady, calm, and unremitting attention ; free, however, from all extrinsic interference, yet open to all friendly communications from whatever quarter they may come, and reporting from time to time their progress to the General Board.

By such an open, candid, and straightforward course the Committee have no doubt that many difficulties, which now appear of the most serious importance, may be smoothed and modified, if not entirely removed ; and that when the subject has been fully considered in all its bearings it will receive the sanction and assent of all parties.

Taking it, therefore, for granted, that the proposition will be entertained by the Board, and that such a Committee may be appointed, it becomes our further duty to report that, on a reference to the Standing Orders of the House of Commons (see appendix), it is absolutely necessary that the plan should be lodged with the Clerk of the Peace before the 30th November ; and various other objects of serious importance must be effected in compliance with the Standing Orders. At present there is no fixed plan. Mr. Stephenson, in his report, has named four different situations which appear to him to be eligible ; but he gives the preference to that on the Sunderland side of the river, opposite the Potato Garth, and immediately east from the Barracks; and on that site he forms his estimate. But his estimate is made, according to his own report, without fully ascertaining the nature of the subsoil by boring or mining, and also without taking into consideration the value of private property to be purchased.

His plan sweeps away the whole of the Commissioners' houses, grounds, workshops, and other buildings; and he further recommends that the whole of the Barrack grounds should be included (and the Barracks have recently been repaired by Government at a heavy expense). He also states that the staiths and other establishments for trade purposes would fall to be connected by branch railways with those already leading to the inland collieries, on which he has furnished no estimate whatever.

On Mr. Stephenson's plan and estimate it would be in vain to go to Parliament at any time, and particularly next session, as they are not formed in compliance with the Standing Orders of the House; and before a petition is presented the assents and dissents of all those whose property is to be affected must be ascertained, etc.

It appears, therefore, to this Committee, that the Commissioners should, in the first place, by careful examination, satisfy themselves that the means proposed are sufficient; they should then consider the most eligible site (which has never been done); and it may be necessary to assist their judgment by the advice of an able and competent engineer, and who should form a plan according to the mode prescribed by the Standing Orders of the House, together with an estimate of the probable expense of the Docks, and, if necessary, of the Railway—if that should be considered a necessary portion of the undertaking. And until these essential preliminaries are completed, it appears to your Committee that nothing effective can be done; for not only must the Commissioners be perfectly satisfied with the feasibility of the plan, of the correctness of the estimates, and the extent of the means proposed, but the public favor must also be conciliated by a clear and convincing statement, which statement shall be above suspicion.

In conclusion, we consider the object of such immense importance that we would recommend the Board to enter upon the consideration of the subject, free from all prejudice; not to enter upon a measure of this magnitude rashly, lest by one false step at the commencement the object should be lost for ever; but to proceed on safe and stable grounds, and with due deliberation.

And the Committee have come to the unanimous conclusion that the question may be advantageously entertained by the Board, in the hope that the more fully it is discussed, and the more maturely it is considered, means may be adopted, and facilities may arise, to bring to a happy conclusion an object so closely connected with the future welfare and prosperity of the Port of Sunderland.

Commission Room,
   October 12th, 1831.

In 1831 Mr. Giles and Mr. Brunel designed docks on the south and north side of the river, near its mouth, but both these schemes were rejected by Parliament.

In 1832 the Commissioners employed Mr. George Rennie and Mr. Walker to give designs for a small dock on each side of the river, capable of extension as the necessities of the port might require. These plans were deposited by the Commissioners in Parliament, but were afterwards abandoned. The original proprietors of the north side dock, wishing to carry out the plan themselves, under the sanction of a charter; and having been served with notice of injunction from the Hetton Coal Co. and others, the idea of a dock on the south side was also abandoned.

In the plan for the South Docks, Mr. Walker† designed Groynes or Jetties from the new works towards the sea, to increase the safety of this place. "The operation of these will be to stop the sand on its passage from north to south, which is the natural direction, and to fill the spaces on the north side of them. The Groynes will, in fact, form, as respects the sand, other North Piers, and their effects, though not equal in extent, will be similar." Mr. Walker, in describing the Docks, refers to his drawings for the

---

†I am aware that Mr. Murray has the reputation of designing the groynes at the South Docks, and also for preparing the plans, etc., for the docks. The extracts above, from Mr. Walker's report to the Commissioners, dated Great George Street, London, 24th November, 1832, I think will settle the matter.

particular arrangement of the works, etc. Then he observes "The depth of the Docks, on both sides, is 16ft. 6ins. at ordinary spring tides, that of the basons, locks, etc., 17ft. .6ins."

"The south dock, you will observe, communicates by a lock with the inner bason, which again has two communications with the tide bason, one by a lock of 130 feet long and 32ft. wide, the other by a single pair of gates 50ft. wide, to admit large steam boats as well as steam tugs. If steam vessels for light goods and passengers should ply from Sunderland, the west sides of the basons would form berths very convenient for communication with the town."

In 1832, November 24th, Mr. George Rennie in his report, observes :—

"A plan has been exhibited to us, which in justice to your resident engineer it is proper to notice. Mr. Murray's plan is to convert part of the existing river, amounting to upwards of 24 acres, into a wet dock, with suitable basons. The advantages he proposes are deserving of attention ; but though we willingly bear him out in several of his positions there appear to be practical difficulties attendant upon it which can hardly compensate for the expense of carrying it into effect."

Meanwhile, the sites of the docks had become a political cry, and party spirit ran high, insomuch as the remarks made by Mr. Walker seemed pertinent when he observes, "If, however, Sunderland allows itself to be divided into parties, and time to be wasted in bickering as to the advantages and disadvantages of the north and south sides, and the exact manner in which shipping or property is to be rated, while your enterprising neighbours at Seaham and Hartepool are in full activity, it requires no power of divination to foresee the consequences. More important interests than even those of Sunderland and Monkwearmouth have been sacrificed in this way." But Mr. Walker's remarks could not still the cry between the political parties of North and South Docks.

It was at this election that Jeremiah Summers (author of the "History and Antiquities of Sunderland,") made his first public speech, from the windows of Bradill's committee rooms, which was above Bulman the draper's shop, and the election cry was for Bradill and the South Docks, whilst the cry of the Whig party was Sir Hedworth Williamson and the North Docks. Politics did not seem at that time to influence the mass of them. Sir Hedworth Williamson's committee room, at the head of Beggar's Bank, in High Street, was wrecked. I saw books and papers thrown out of the windows into the street, the clerks in charge making their escape into the side street; the windows were broken, and so would the baronet's skull had it been there. Of course, this had to be repaid with interest; but, in the meanwhile, Bradill's party took good care to block up their rooms and windows, to guard against a similar fate.

Such was the political spleen exhibited here. It was the same elsewhere, even the precincts of the House of Commons were not free from personal assaults. Two opponents, meeting within the boundaries of the House of Commons, got to work to wrangle, from words came action, and one pulled the other's nose, from which streams of blood flowed freely. The aggressor was duly summoned, and committed to prison for 14 days.

The aggressor was then a shipbuilder, the sufferer a celebrated attorney on the other side.

The proprietors of the North Dock having obtained a charter, set to work on the salt grass, as afore named; and in 1835, February 17th, the foundation stone was laid. In excavating the dock the old north channel was cut through. The soil and marl excavated were deposited over the rocks and cliffs at Roker, which hid the natural beauty of the cliffs, otherwise the cliffs from the holey rock to Dame Dolly's rock, from view.

In 1837, November 1st, the North Dock was opened for traffic by Lady Williamson, and was finished in 1838. There were four coal drops erected—two on the north and two on the east side. In 1860, the year of the first separate returns, there were shipped from the North Dock 90,515 tons of coals; the exports from thence have gradually fallen off, till in the year 1881 there were shipped only 18,435 tons: the North-Eastern Railway Company preferring to ship at the Tyne Docks, though both places belong to them. There were two wood shipbuilding yards on the east side of the dock; and, later, one on the west side, now occupied by Blumer & Robson as an iron shipbuilding yard; the two formed were occupied by Ratcliffe & Spence and Rawson, Watson & Co. This dock, of about six acres, was the only dock on the Wear for thirteen years. Its inconvenience and the uncertainty of getting vessels in and out, on account of the seas, was felt very much by those using it; and only ships of middle size could get in and out even then. (This shows the inutility of the plans formed by R. Dodd and Mr. Jessop for making the Potato Garth into a floating dock with an entrance at the lower part.) A large bonding yard for timber and deals occupied part of the site. Some time after the election of George Hudson the dock was bought by him for and on account of the North-Eastern Railway Company, and on his fall was one of the things brought against him.

In 1842 Mr. Murray brought forward a project for converting the river into a floating dock. Though all the engineers, from Labelle downward, gave their opinion against any scheme for damming up the river, yet, still the Commissioners had so much confidence in his ability and skill that the measure was carried into Parliament by them (*i.e.* the Commissioners); but the opinion of the Admiralty, upon the advice of Mr. Walker, being adverse to the plan, it was abandoned.*

In 1845, Alderman Thompson having resigned, a vacancy occurred in the representation of the Borough, and George Hudson, the "Railway King" as he was then called, was asked to come forward to represent the Borough in Parliament; he consented, and was elected in that year, August 16th, 1845. Shortly after his election, the Sunderland Dock Co. was formed, of which he was chairman and Michael Coxon secretary. Such was the energy displayed by the company and the chairman, that in 1846, May 14th, the Sunderland Dock Bill was passed, the engineers being Robert Stephenson and Mr. Murray. The plan was to build a dock and basons at the north end of the site, in connection with the river, and ultimately to extend them southwards, with an outlet into Hendon Bay.

Meanwhile, the stone groynes were put down in accordance with the report furnished by Mr. Walker to the Commissioners on November 24th, 1832, which fulfilled the object for which they were designed, viz. to form a beach.

In 1848, February 4th, the foundation stone was laid by the Chairman. The contractors were John Craven & Sons; and the marl and rock excavated from the dock was deposited on the east or sea side of the dock wall.

---

* This Mr. Walker, upon whose advice the Admiralty acted, I take to be the same Mr. Walker who, in 1832—ten years previously—in conjunction with Mr. George Rennie, as already noticed, says: "Mr. Murray's plan is to convert part of the existing river, amounting to upwards of twenty-four acres, into a Wet Dock, with suitable basons, etc." Then, in 1832, the advice of these two able engineers was against it.

In 1850, July 10th, the South Dock was opened with great manifestations of rejoicing, by George Hudson, chairman of the company. Shortly after the opening, the directors gave their attention to the enlargement of the dock and the formation of the South Outlet. The contract was let to Messrs. Pawson & Dyson to do the work, and at the ordinary half-yearly general meeting of the shareholders, held on the 23rd day of February, 1852, Mr. Murray's report to the directors, under date February 12th, 1852, says "The works of the sea outlet, contracted for by Messrs. Pawson & Dyson are in the following condition—the enlargement of the dock has been nearly excavated, and part of the surrounding walls built. The coffer-dam of the great dock is also put, etc., etc."

One of the principal features of the South Outlet was the sluice in the North Pier or jetty, formed for the purpose of scouring the entrance channel outside at low tide, to keep the channel clear from silting up with sand and gravel.

This sluice was opened once in the presence of George Hudson, who received a shower of filth and dirt, thrown on him through the airpipes put down through the pier to the sluice.

The water had been kept in the dock at a high level, so that the sluicing power might have full play. I saw the waters rushing and tumbling and tossing from the sluice outside the entrance, and a beautiful sight it was, whilst it lasted; but when they tried to shut the sluice it would not act against the volume of water rushing through; the check gate of the sluice got so far down, and there it stuck; the sluice was a complete failure—it was not used again, though it was said that a sunken coble got sucked into the aperture and prevented it from acting; the pier head had to be blocked up, and gave place to one, named hereafter as the "New Lock."

The opening of the South Outlet would be in the early part of 1856.‡

In July, 1859, the South Dock, after lengthened negotiations, passed into the hands of the Commissioners (irrespective of the report of the Committee in 1829, who reported that the interests of the two would clash), who found that a dock with deeper water and of larger capacity for large vessels was needed to meet the wants of the trade, and they undertook to make it themselves.

In 1864, September 19th, the foundation stone of the Hendon Dock was laid, and the work was pushed on with such vigour that the piers and gates in connection with the Hudson Extension Dock, and the deep gates at the sea entrance, as well as the whole of the works in connection with the scheme, were so far complete that in 1868, June 9th, the Hendon Dock was opened.

In 1876, April 26th, the first spout in the Hendon Dock was opened. The entrance to the South Outlet from the Hudson Docks not being considered safe, it was resolved to close it and built an entrance lock, so that vessels could be locked either in or out before the usual time of opening the gates.

During the time that this transformation was going on, it was ordered that the Hendon Dock Outlet should be used for the purpose of the traffic.

The cills of the gates, together with the bottom of the lock, were to be placed 4 feet 6 inches lower than the old entrance, in order to meet the necessities of the trade, ships of larger size and tonnage being built and using the dock, both for import and export.

---

‡ The "Warrior Queen," new ship, of 988 tons register, 13 years A1 at Lloyd's, sailed from the South Outlet in May, 1856, and struck on one of the stump piles that had not been drawn, and had to put into dock at Calcutta, when it was found that she had split a lump off the keel, which was temporarily repaired by a graving piece let in till her return home.

In 1878, December 21st, the foundation stone of the South Dock Lock was laid, and so steadily did the work progress, that in less than two years, viz.: in 1880, October 20th, the new lock at the South Dock was opened.

The gates at the north end, next the river, having gone out of order, a coffer-dam was put down, when it was found that the gates required renewal; the mason work in the piers was also in a rotten and shaky condition. It was also thought expedient in the renewal to take up the old cills, &c., in short, to make a new entrance gate, both wider and deeper, and more substantial in every respect than the one taken out, the traffic, meanwhile, being carried on by the smaller gate on the east side. When this was accomplished, and the gates opened, the one on the east side being in a bad condition, was closed for traffic, which it still is whilst we write. When this improvement was made, the water was deeper at the entrances of the dock at both ends than it was over the cills to the main dock from the river entrance. It was therefore resolved to make a temporary entrance to the west of the then gate, which was done, and a coffer-dam put down. When the whole of the old masonry was removed, the cills were laid at a lower level and a new gate put in to enable the Commissioners to meet the requirements of the trade.

Meanwhile, the engineer carried on the deepening of the original dock, by blasting in the centre by sections, taking care not to approach too near the quay and jetty walls, which operation was completed by the time the gates at the north end were ready to be opened.

The attention of the Commissioners had long been drawn to the advisability of improving the shipment of coals, and to give equal facilities to the two railway companies supplying the coals for shipment.

The coal drops and berths erected on the quays and jetties by the Sunderland Dock Company had long been discarded; the drops were too low, the berths too short; neither the drops or berths were ever intended for the class of vessels now requiring accommodation. In 1850, on the opening of the dock, the company thought that they had so far provided for the trade, when provision had or was being made for vessels of 1,000 to 1,250 tons, and never could have anticipated such immense strides in shipbuilding as have since taken place; they were providing for the wants of the trade then, and when they made the South Outlet their work was complete, and they looked forward their expected returns, to reimburse them for their speculations.

On the transference of the dock to the Comissioners, in July, 1859, the latter seem to have found out all the shortcomings of the Dock Company. As the trade increased provision had to be made for it, hence the deepening of the dock gates, &c., and now the facilities for the shipment of coals. In the Hendon Dock there was only one drop, and the Londonderry Co. had the monopoly of it. It was circumscribed in its delivery both for height and length. In the Hudson Dock, the works or gearing had been carried almost to mid dock, and yet this was not sufficient. Under these circumstances, their attention was directed to No. 19 drop, as being directly opposite the outlet, upon which the improvements had been made. No. 19 was one of the drops erected by the Dock Company in 1853, with a turntable, and was afterwards converted by the Commissioners into a spout. Possession was obtained of the spout on the 4th March, 1889; the cofferdam was put down, for what to some was then expected to be a difficult and troublesome job; the engineer had his misgivings, and therefore erected powerful pumping machinery, thought to be sufficient to keep the water under in the cofferdam.

In deepening the dock, in order to underset the quay wall, the engineer's troubles began, the water flowed under the cofferdam through a rotten rift in the rock; this we call No. 1 trouble. By deepening he struck the fresh water strata, from which the inhabitants in former days drew their supply, which flowed in large quantities, this was trouble No. 2.

Trouble No. 3 was caused by the water oozing through what was thought to be solid jetty, from the quay of No. 18 drop, through defective mortar and mason work in the backing. To meet these troubles, extra pumping power had to be employed, and kept constantly at work, throwing about 4,224,960,000 gallons, or about 18,816,785 tons of water. The old quay wall or tongue jetty had to be underset for six feet in height, the foundation being thirty-one feet below high water; the extended berth was built of concrete faced with freestone, ashlar, and finished with granite coping.

The gearing is constructed of metal columns, steel lattice girders, with pitch pine timber flooring, and the rail level is about 43 feet above high water.

There are two sets of spouts, varying from 10 to 20 feet above high water mark, at a distance of about 110 feet apart. They are made to radiate from 90 to 130 feet, and are capable of loading about 420 tons per hour. A third auxiliary spout is provided for especially long vessels, or to enable two ordinary colliers to be loaded at the same time. On the 22nd April, 1890, the pumps were removed, and the water let into the new berth, and a start was made with the removal of the cofferdams. The new drop was formally opened on Monday, July 28th, 1890.

Both the North-Eastern and Londonderry Railway Companies have carried out their share of the work to make the approach and standage as perfect as possible.

The cost of these works carried out by the River Wear Commissioners, the North-Eastern Railway Company and Londonderry Company amounts to about £36,000.*

The works have been carried out under the plans and supervision of the engineer to the Commissioners, H. H. Wake, Esq.

THE NEW DROP, BERTH AND STANDAGE ROOM.

	Length of berth. Lin. ft. in.	Depth of Water H.W. O.S. tides. feet.	Average depth of water in dock. feet.	N.E.R. lin. ft.	London-derry. lin. ft.
Original Berth	263 0	24	20	260	1150
New Berth	383 3	30	26	1500	2250

At the luncheon at the "Queen's" Hotel, on July 28th, 1890, in connection with the opening of the new drop at the South Dock, Mr. Laing read the following interesting paper, prepared by Mr. Taylor Potts:—

"There was loaded in the South Dock, on board the *Mary Beyts*, in March, 1890, 5,516 tons of coal, and in the *Queensland*, in July, 1890, 5,381 tons of coal—together, 10,897 tons, the average being 5,459 tons, or thereabouts; both boats drawing 22ft. 7ins. of water when loaded. The cost of the latter boat was £46,800, or thereabouts. In 1820 the average registered tonnage of the collier was about 221 tons; in dead weight she carried about one-third more than the registered tonnage, so that the average carrying capacity would be 295 tons, or nearly 14 keels of coals. It would therefore require 18½ colliers to carry the cargo of one steamboat in 1890, i.e. 5,450 tons representing 257 keels of coals of 21 tons 4 cwts. each. In former times the cost of bringing a keel of coals down the river from the staiths and casting them into the collier was—

	£ s. d.
1 Keelman per tide	0 15 0
5 Casters at 2/- each	0 10 0
5 Casters, one pint of Ale each	0 1 3
Payment for hire of keel, or interest on value and repairs per tide	0 ᵕ ᵕ
	£1 11 3

---

* Made up as follows:—River Wear Commissioners, £32,395 19s. 3d.; North-Eastern Railway Company, £1,964 15s. 4d.; Londonderry, about £1,640.

or nearly 1/6 per ton on 5,450 tons. The amount paid by the fitter would be £408 15s., distributed amongst 257 keels, and 1,285 casters. The 5,450 tons could be cast on board the 18½ colliers in from twelve to fourteen hours. For every keel of coals cast there was consumed six pints of ale, making in all 1,542 pints or 193 gallons, or more than five barrels of 36 gallons each. When loaded, the collier drew from 13 to 14½ or 15 feet of water; vessels of a heavier draught of water could only proceed to sea on spring tides. If there was a sea on, then she had to wait till the next spring, or a favourable opportunity. Each collier would carry 8 hands, or for the whole, 148 hands all told.

The cost of a new collier in 1823 was £11 12s. per ton, therefore 18½ colliers of 221 tons, at £11 12s. per ton, would cost £47,426 tons. Colliers carrying 5,381 tons would cost £46,825.

Thus in 1823 the carrying capacity of wooden colliers for 5,381 tons of coals cost £46,825; in 1890 the carrying capacity for 5,381 tons of coals in the above named screw-boat cost £46,800, or £25 more in the whole for wooden collier vessels than for a steel screw-steamer now. Then a collier drawing 13, 14, or 15 feet of water would sometimes be detained two or four weeks before she could get to sea. Now a steamer drawing 22 feet 7 inches can get to sea two hours before high water."

In 1794, in Dodds' report, he sets the dimensions at 90 feet over all, 27 feet beam as being above the average size of the ships then frequenting the port. And for such vessels, his plan of converting the potato garth into a wet dock, he says it would accommodate 237 vessels and keels, and it could be made to contain twice that number.

Mr. Jessop, in 1808, was against a floating dock; he says "I can hardly think that the convenience of a floating dock would be considered worth the cost, for the additional expense would be at least £50,000."

Mr. Bell, in 1816, proposes a dock that would hold nearly 300 vessels, averaging from ten to twelve keels.

In 1832, Mr. Walker's designs for docks were for the depth of water at ordinary spring tides to be 16 feet 6 inches, that of the basons, locks, &c., 17 feet 6 inches. I wonder what he would have said now, for the depth of water in the dock at ordinary spring tides is 24 to 30 feet, and the average depth 20 to 26 feet, and a steamer drawing 22 feet 6 inches can go to sea two hours before high water.

Or what would the eloquent Mr. Dodd think that in less than 100 years, 90 feet extreme length would be multiplied by 4, and that 25 colliers, as in 1794, would be required to carry one cargo of coals now.

Some years ago we chartered the "Orynthia" to load a cargo of patent fuel at Middlesbro' for the Cape de Verdes, wanting her to go to Sierra Leone to bring home a cargo of African Oak to Sunderland. The vessel being light was towed round to Middlesbro' to load, and went into the dock for that purpose. When taking in her cargo it was found that if she was loaded she could not be got out, the gates being too narrow for her exit, this was caused by the garboard or gate boards being added to the breadth of the vessel when deep in the water, together with the dock cills not being of sufficient depth; she had therefore to be brought out of the dock and moored at the third buoy lower down the river to load up.

At the Hartlepools, Ralph Ward Jackson and the Old Hartlepool Dock and Railway Company were competitors; the former made docks at West Hartlepool, with an inlet and outlet direct from the sea; the latter having the entrance to the old harbour for their outlet. The North-Eastern Railway Company ultimately became possessors or proprietors of both, for large vessels frequenting or likely to frequent their docks; they afterwards felt the deficiency of water in their docks for such vessels, and they resolved to make a larger and a deeper dock for the accommodation of the trade. The dock was made at a large cost, but, unfortunately, the outlet by West Hartlepool was too shallow, and the outlet by the old harbour was too crooked, shallow, and short, so that although they had made a large and deep dock in connection with both the others, yet they had neglected to provide an outlet for the large class of vessels the new dock was intended to accommodate.

The North-Eastern Railway Company's Dock at Jarrow boasts of the largest shipment of coals of any dock in the kingdom; but here the same difficulty occurs—want of water in the dock and over the cills. Large long steamers can hardly find room to turn in the dock, and others have to leave and take in their bunker coals on the river or at the spout opposite.*

The River Tyne Commissioners have made the same mistake—want of water in the dock and over the cills; and have had to erect drops in the river at White Hill Point, to accommodate the larger class of vessels. 'Tis true they have made the "Albert Edward" Dock where there is plenty of room and depth of water, but commercially it is a failure; want of facilities and large expenses debar merchants from patronizing it.

In considering the question of docks we have come to the conclusion that the docks at Sunderland are the most convenient on the east coast for the larger class of vessels now built—for depth of water, safety, and economy in the discharge of large vessels from over-sea, and in shipping cargoes for abroad. A vessel carrying between 5,000 and 6,000 tons of coal can be loaded in 24 hours; and, when loaded, can leave the berth where she has taken in her cargo, and in 10 or 15 minutes after be on the German ocean.

---

* This difficulty, I am told, is being overcome by the erection of new staiths, deepening the dock, and the construction of a new entrance.

LIST OF THE RIVER WEAR COMMISSIONERS,
11TH APRIL, 1892.

John Storey Barwick, George Robert Booth, Charles James Briggs, Robert Scott Briggs, John Oswald Clazey, Collector of Customs (John Ross Buckley), Vincent Charles Stuart Wortley Corbett, James Henry Wood Culliford, John Dickinson, Samuel James Ditchfield, The Right Hon. John George Earl of Durham, John Brett Eminson, Edward Featherstonhaugh, John Firth, Robert Heydon Gayner, Edward Temperley Gourley, William Fairbairn Hall, Ralph Milbanke Hudson, Ralph Milbanke Hudson, the younger; Thomas George Hutton, Richard Sheraton Johnson, Thomas Jones, Arthur Laing, James Laing (Chairman of the Commission), William Lishman, the Most Honourable Charles Stuart, Marquis of Londonderry; William Lough, Henry Thomas Morton, Robert Todd Nicholson, Thomas Nicholson, Matthew William Parrington, Thomas Pinkney, Edwin Richardson, Edward Capper Robson, John Sanderson, John Scott, John George Scurfield, Robert Shadforth, John Young Short, Frank Stobart, William Stobart, Robert Thompson (Whitburn), Robert Thompson (Fulwell), William Thompson, John Todd, Christopher Maling Webster, Sir Hedworth Williamson, Bart., William Sparkes Wilson, Lindsay Wood, William Outterson Wood, Thomas William Pinkney.

OFFICIALS.

Clerk to the Commissioners, John George Morris; General Manager, Charles Henry Dodds; Engineer, Henry Hay Wake, M. Inst. C.E.; Accountant, George Davie Johnson; Traffic Manager, Thomas Atkinson; Dock Master, Peter Wilson.

CHAPTER XVII.

PARLIAMENTARY REPRESENTATION AND OUR FIRST ELECTION.

The Commons' House of Parliament seems to have been summoned or established by Edward I., 1295.

This period, which is the 23rd of his reign, seems to be the real and true epoch of the House of Commons, and the faint dawn of popular government in England —*Hume.*

Edward issued writs to the sheriffs enjoining them to send to Parliament, along with the knights of the shire, two deputies from each borough within their county. Writs were issued to about 120 cities and boroughs, and these provided with sufficient powers from their community to consent in their name to what he and his council should require of them. "As it is a most equitable rule," says he, in his preamble to this writ, " That what concerns all should be approved by all; and common dangers be repelled by united efforts."

A noble principle, which may seem to indicate a liberal mind in the king, and which laid the foundation of a free and equitable government.

After the election of these deputies by the Aldermen and Common Council, they gave sureties for their attendance before the King and Parliament; their charges were respectively borne by the borough which sent them.—*Hume, vol. 2, page 287.*

These writs were not issued to the County Palatine of Durham and Sadberge. The Prince Bishop had his own Court of Barons and Council.

The inhabitants of the palatinate were not represented in the House of Commons for the period of 350 years, *i.e.* from 1295 till 1650, the time of the Commonwealth, when the See was dissolved. It was under the fostering care of the Parliament and Commonwealth that the County Palatine and City of Durham were called upon to send their representatives to the House of Commons. From some cause or other, the borough of Sunderland, which had done so much in favour of the Parliament and Commonwealth, seems to have been overlooked.

At the restoration of Charles II. to the throne and the Bishop to his See, the animosity displayed by the Royalists was so bitter against the county, that an unsuccessful attempt was made to discontinue the practice of summoning members to the house, or to disfranchise both county and city. The representation continued for 180 years, *i e.* till the year 1832, or 537 years after the faint dawn of popular government in England.

On the 7th day of June, 1832, the first Reform Bill was passed, whereby Sunderland became a Parliamentary Borough, with the right or privilege of sending two members to represent the borough and its inhabitants in the Commons' House of Parliament.

Previous to the passing of this bill the parliamentary representation of the borough and its inhabitants was by or through the two members for the county, who were supposed to represent all the different classes and interests therein contained.

The election for the two knights of the shire was by the votes of the independent freeholders of the whole county. The head quarters of the elections were in the county town or City of Durham, the polling being kept open for days and weeks together. The City of Durham also sent its two representatives, whilst Sunderland, with four times the population of the city or county town, was counted at that period as an outlying district.

During the agitations and struggles that had preceded the passing of the Reform Bill, the inhabitants of the borough seemed to have laid aside, for the time being, all their trifling differences, and had acted together, both by petitions and public meetings in favour of the bill. Open-air meetings were held on the town moor and other places, where the old and young democratic orators held forth in speech and action. The principal public meetings were held in the Assembly Hall, Church Street, then the largest hall in the town.

At one of these meetings, in 1831-32, the crush of the people was so great that the meeting was adjourned to the Garth outside. The chairman and speakers occupied the flat space at the top of the broad stone steps leading into the hall; the steps were occupied by the principal supporters of the meeting, and the whole of the Garth in front was filled with people; some of those at the far back, next to Church Street, climbed up on to the stone coping, holding on by the railing, and whilst more were trying to get up the whole of the railing fell with those clinging thereto. Looking from the steps, where I stood, only the heads and faces of the surging mass were seen.

No sooner had the royal assent been given to the bill than the leaders of the agitation, who had been acting together to secure the passing of the bill and the enfranchisement of the borough, separated into parties, each one striving to secure the return of representatives according to their own peculiar political bias. And some of the supposed Radicals, who had been amongst the most clamorous for the Reform Bill, hoisted the Tory colours. Amongst those were the late Joseph John Wright, the most eloquent and enthusiastic speaker at those meetings; and Christopher Thomas Potts, then quite a young man, but generally a prominent figure at the meetings, also sided with the Tories. The latter, being afterwards asked how long it was since he had changed his principles, replied: "Ever since I learned discretion."

There were two seats, and four candidates were brought forward to contest them, viz. :—

Sir William Chaytor, Bart., head of the firm of bankers known as "Chaytor, Franklin, Wilkinson, Chaytor & Co." He professed to be a reformer and a Whig, and was supported by the trading classes.

Captain Barrington, who had the support of the whole Lambton interest, also a professed Whig.

David Barclay, a London merchant, whose supporters were principally to be found amongst the Friends, also a professed Whig.

William Thompson, an Alderman of the City of London, and merchant; supported principally by and amongst the shipowners—Tory candidate.

Committees for each candidate were formed, consisting of as many electors and non-electors as would enroll themselves to assist. Each candidate canvassed personally, accompanied by his numerous committee; whilst he and some of the most influential of his supporters entered the tradesman's shop to solicit his vote a crowd was left outside waiting the result. Two or more of the candidates, with their followers, were to be seen at the same time in the High Street, soliciting the vote and interest of the newly enfranchised burgesses of the borough.

The free and independent electors of that day would have scorned secret voting, or voting by ballot. Each elector felt himself to be a man of some consequence in being waited on by the candidate and his committee ; indeed, he sometimes showed himself to be of ridiculous consequence by the way in which he treated them.

When asked for his vote, he had not made up his mind, would see, would consider, would consult with his wife, hear what she said ; would not promise, no use them waiting, they could call again if they thought it worth their while, but they could please themselves. And when pressed for his decision, he did not want to be bothered with them, he would please himself for whom he voted. Such electors (and there were many) left the candidate quite in a quandary as to how they would ultimately cast their votes.

Through continual canvassing, and the printing and circulating of election bills and squibs, for and against the different candidates, a great deal of interest and excitement was aroused amongst the inhabitants generally.

The date for the nomination of candidates was fixed for December 5th or 6th, 1832.

As the day of election drew near, there was being erected on the north side of the High Street, a little to the west of the Exchange Buildings, and facing the broad part of the street, a long large wooden platform or hustings, sixteen or eighteen feet above the level of the street, and which was divided into five compartments by a partition or rail ; the middle or central portion was set apart for the returning officer and his officials ; the other parts, on the right and left, were apportioned to the candidates and their friends—the name of each candidate being placarded in front of the position to be occupied by him. There was a long narrow wooden box, seemingly tacked on to the front of the hustings, for the accommodation of the reporters.

As the hour of the nomination drew near, the different candidates emerged from their committee rooms, linked arm-in-arm with their proposer and seconder, and followed by their supporters, the band heading the procession, with colours flying. On arriving in front of the position to be occupied by their candidate on the hustings, there they took their station, while the leading colour bearer mounted the hustings and stood with his colour in front, the committee following, sporting the colours of their candidate, which were as follows, viz.:—Chaytor's, white and light blue; Barrington's, pink and buff; Barclay's, buff and blue; Thompson's, dark blue and white.

After some preliminary business had been gone through in the Justices' room, in the Exchange, the different candidates ascended the hustings, followed by their proposers and seconders. On making their appearance in front of the position, their respective supporters cheered and shouted as loud as they could, the band aiding and assisting in the noise; the colours and banners were waving to and fro; whilst the candidates uncovered their heads in the presence of their masters for the time being, kept bowing and smiling to those in front, acknowledging favours, smiles and cheers, also to the fair sex occupying the windows opposite, and in the Exchange and up and down the High Street, which was covered with a mass of human beings from Beggar's Bank to Stob Lane, and every now and then the committee on the hustings would wave their hats and cheer, to keep up the enthusiasm of their adherents in front.

Then the returning officer, Addison Fenwick, Esq., and his retinue appeared in their places, carrying white wands; after standing for a short time, looking right and left to the different candidates, and surveying the unstable mass in front swaying to and fro, taking off his hat, he lifted up his right hand as though commanding silence, when, on the crier moving to the front, all heads on the hustings were uncovered, whilst the proclamation was commenced with the shrill cry of "Oh yez! Oh yez! Oh yez!" which was then read, the reading of the writ followed, and, at the conclusion, the customary God save the King. The returning officer then moved to the front, and enquired whether any burgess present had any person to propose to his fellow burgesses as a fit and proper person to represent the Borough of Sunderland in the Commons' House of Parliament. Whereupon the four candidates who were before the electors were duly proposed and seconded by their respective friends, in speeches setting forth their capabilities, qualifications, and all excellencies which they possessed; and urging on the electors and non-electors to confer the boon sought on their candidate, as being the most fit and proper person amongst the four to represent them and their interests in the Commons' House of Parliament. This necessitated eight speeches, which occupied some time in delivery, whilst the surging, chaffing and hooting of the speakers by the populace rendered it impossible to hear intelligibly what was said by them.

After these each of the candidates came forward in rotation to advocate his personal claims before the electors, thus giving practical evidence of his ability as a public speaker, urging on the electors to support him at the poll, and promising what he would do for the nation at large, and what measures he would support; his motto was "measures, not men," and what benefits the electors and the borough at large might expect through his influence and exertions in the House. Three of the speakers were Whigs, and one was a Tory.

After these twelve speeches in all had been delivered, the returning officer took the vote of the assembly for each candidate by a show of hands. Two candidates were declared by the officer as having the show of hands in their favour, whereupon the representative burgesses of the other candidates demanded a poll, which was appointed to take place on the two following days. The different candidates then marched back to the committee rooms, headed by the bands with colours flying, to make or complete the arrangements for bringing their supporters to the poll on the day of election as fixed, viz. December 8th, 1832.

The voting was open. On arriving at the polling booth, each burgess was asked his name and qualification, and lastly " For whom do you vote ?" Beside the deputy and the clerks, each candidate had his check clerk marking off the names, so that the vote of every burgess was known for whom it was cast. The day following was set apart by the returning officer for the declaration of the poll. Then the several candidates, together with their supporters, with the bands playing and colours flying, hied again to the hustings, when and where the returning officer read out the number of votes that had been cast for each candidate, and declared the two candidates who had the largest number of votes to be the duly elected members for the borough, who, at this the first election since its enfranchisement under the Reform Bill, were declared to be Sir William Chaytor, Bart., and Capt. Barrington. After the cheers, shouts, groans and hisses had somewhat subsided, the senior member, Sir William Chaytor, Bart., returned thanks for the honour conferred upon him by electing him to such a proud position as head of the poll ; and concluded by proposing a vote of thanks to the returning officer for the manner in which the election had been conducted, etc. One of Captain Barrington's supporters also returned thanks on his behalf, and expressed sorrow on account of the captain's inability to be present through severe indisposition, and seconded the vote of thanks.*

---

* Captain Barrington, unfortunately, went insane (supposed to be caused by the intense excitement during the contest of the election), and he never took his seat as M.P.

David Barclay also spoke, thanking those electors who had supported him by their votes, and promising to come forward again to solicit their support at the next vacancy.

Alderman William Thompson also expressed his warm thanks to the numerous friends, shipowners and others, who had interested themselves on his behalf, declaring his determination to contest the borough till he gained the seat.

On account of the voting of the free and independent electors being open, the state of the poll was pretty well known before the official declaration by the returning officer, and preparations had been made by the committees of the successful candidates for the chairing; consequently, before the close of the speeches, there was carried on men's shoulders, down into the midst of the throng, and halted opposite the station of the successful candidate, a large arm-chair gorgeously decorated with silks and satins, and almost covered with rosettes and flying ribbons of the choice colours of the candidate, and in which the successful candidate had to be chaired. Accordingly, at the conclusion of the meeting, the honourable member having descended from the hustings, was lifted into the chair, which was carried by men, shoulder-high, on a kind of hand-barrow, whilst others walked on each side to steady the chair, and prevent the occupant from falling amidst the surges of the people and the rushes of the crowd; relays of bearers were always ready when required. All things being arranged, and the order for starting given, the band struck up "See, the Conquering Hero comes!" Following the band came the committee, then the honourable member (carried aloft above the heads of the people), followed by his supporters; whilst the populace here, there, and all over were huzzaing and shouting. As the procession progressed, the streets, lanes, and alleys seemed pouring out all kinds and conditions of men, women, and "bairns"; some mothers with their infants tugging at the breast, whilst others, of the smaller fry, were hoisted shoulder-high to enable them to see the grand sight as it was passing. The windows on each side of the street were filled with ladies and others, waving the colours of the candidate. When the bearers came opposite a bevy of fair ladies they made a short halt, and whilst the successful candidate bowed, acknowledging their smiles and favours, the multitude cheered and shouted louder still. In passing some of the ends of the streets and lanes hisses and howls would sometimes be heard, when a dash from the supporters would be made to silence or overwhelm their would-be opponents. Thus the processionists moved to the east end of the town, where they turned and retraced their steps, and on to the west part of the High Street, returning at last to the committee room.

As soon as the candidate had vacated his position, a rush by those close to was made for the chair, each one striving to get a portion of the rosettes, ribbons, or satins with which it was decorated; and, ultimately, the chair itself was smashed to pieces—as many people as could carrying off a portion of the remains of the poor chair, which, a few minutes before, had been filled or occupied by the honourable member during his public ovation.

In the evening the people gathered together in the High Street, around and about the hustings, in expectation of something like sight-seeing—when, at the firing of a rocket, all faces seemed lit up, and then began the firing of squibs, crackers, Roman candles, and other things amongst the multitude; wherever the throng was thickest thither were the squibs and crackers directed, discomforting the crowd, midst the shrieks of the women and the laughter of the men; whilst the windows from which a view could be obtained were filled with sight-seers, amongst whom a squib or a Roman candle would be directed. As the evening wore on tar barrel after tar barrel, with one end knocked in, were lighted and sent from the foot of Sans Street rolling down the steep bank amongst the crowd, scattering them right and left, thus packing the footpaths with a dense mass of people, and a few squibs and crackers thrown amongst them made the most stolid to shake. Thus tar barrel after tar barrel rolled down, some of them being guided down Bodlewell Lane into the Low Street, others would fall to pieces whilst still in a blaze, and others rolling amongst them, caused a huge bon-fire at the bottom of the bank, burning itself out amidst the shouts, and to the people's intense excitement of the sight and fun, and so the night wore on until nearly morn, when the sight-seers dispersed, and the hubbub ceased. Thus ended our first election.

Both of the defeated candidates subsequently fulfilled the declaration they had made at the hustings to contest the borough, and both were afterwards elected.

The number of electors on the first list of voters was between 1,000 and 1,100.

Captain Barrington failing to take his seat, a new writ was ordered, and another contest took place in 1833, between Barclay and Thompson, when David Barclay was elected.

In the process of chairing Barclay, a strong rush was made by the crowd, and the hon. member was hurled from his elevated position on to the street; he was, however, picked up and replaced, whilst a more careful guard was kept, so as to prevent another accident.

At the general election, July 1835, Thompson and Barclay were elected, Thompson heading the poll, the number of votes recorded for him being 574, and Sir

William Chaytor, Bart, who headed the poll at the first election, a little more than two years previously, was defeated. So elated were the supporters of Alderman Thompson at the victory, that one of them called his new vessel by the name of 574.

At the general election, July 1837, Alderman Thompson and Andrew White were elected, throwing over David Barclay.

At the general election, July 1841, David Barclay and Alderman Thompson were again colleagues, and were the two members for the borough ten years after their first defeat, *shewing thus early the fickleness of a Sunderland constituency towards Parliamentary representatives.*

CHAPTER XVIII.

BANKS.

In 1847, March 6th, the North of England Joint Stock Bank stopped payment with joint liabilities on suspension of £1,865,000, or thereabouts. Mr. Burdes, the elder, I believe, was managing director, and his son was manager of the branch in Sunderland. Richard Bradley, the draper, who was a shareholder in the bank, had to do with winding-up the business in Sunderland.

In 1847, October 21st, the Union Joint Stock Bank stopped payment; Mr. Chapman, I think, was managing director. This bank was afterwards resuscitated by Messrs. Woods, Parker, Dryden, Powe, Barker and Ord, under the style of Woods & Co., who have continued the business ever since.*

On one occasion John Smith had a party in his office who wanted a settlement of his account. "Man," said John, "I tell you I have no money, but plenty of stock, take something for the amount." "No," said the party, "I want money, give me a cheque for the account." "I've got no money, take goods," said John. "I don't want the goods," said the other, "I want money." "Well," said John, "if I was to give you a cheque, the bankers would not honour it." John at the time knew they would, but

---

*It was amusing to see three of these bankers wending their way to the station once a week. Powe was a little man, wherewithal rather chatty, Dryden, a tall, broad-shouldered big man, and William Ord tall and rather spare; they were generally twenty minutes too soon for the train, which time was spent in the refreshment room, where they waited for its arrival.

he still persisted in saying that they would not, the party insisting on his giving him the cheque. At last John said, "Well, I will give you the cheque, but mind the bankers won't pay it." Ultimately the party received the cheque, John telling him at the time that the bankers would not pay it.

As soon as the party was gone, John said to one of his clerks, "Be quick, take the boat, pay the fare, and tell the bankers not to pay the cheque," naming the amount. The clerk away to the boat, paid the fare, ran up to the bank, and stopped payment of the cheque. Meanwhile the party, with the cheque in his pocket, leisurely crossing by the bridge, presented it at the bank. The banker looked at it, shook his head, but would not honour the cheque. The party went back to the office with the cheque, to know what he was to do with it. "I don't know," said John, "I told you they would not pay it, but you would have it; send and get goods for the amount while they are there; give me the cheque back and we'll destroy it;" which the party did, handing back the cheque, taking the goods, and so settling the account. Talking to Smith afterwards about this matter, he did nothing but laugh, and said "he was an impudent fellow that, but I think I settled his hash for him."

In the year 1851 the Sunderland Joint Stock Bank closed its doors. It was called the Methodist Bank. It was in connection with this bank that the forgeries of Sacker were brought to light in 1847. These forgeries had been going on for a long time, and amounted in the gross to about £50,000 or upwards.

It is supposed that they were done principally in financing for a certain colliery that was then being sunk. On this occasion the name of a Newcastle merchant was used, who did business with the branch of the Bank of England at Newcastle. The acceptance had been duly advised through a bank, but the London bankers having refused payment, it returned into the hands of the Bank of England, who had discounted the bill, and they, instead of passing the bill back to the parties for whom they had discounted it (suppose cause not known), sent it direct to their branch in Newcastle, to present to their customer for payment, which, on being presented to the merchant, he declared to be a forgery. This brought things to a point. A meeting of the shareholders in the colliery was called, when the amount of the forged bills was ascertained, but as Sacker was shewn not to have appropriated any of the moneys so obtained to his own use, but applied them for the purposes of the general fund, which he named, the whole of the forged bills then running were paid by the proprietors of the colliery. Sacker was dismissed, the partnership of Greenwell and Sacker dissolved, and the matter hushed up. Some years after, talking to Mr. Greenwell about this, he said that they had thrown £80,000 down that hole, naming the colliery.

On November 25th, 1857, the Northumberland and Durham District Banking Company stopped payment. The stoppage of this banking company fell heavily on the trading community. The managing director was Jonathan Richardson. In winding-up, the shareholders ultimately paid 19/6 in the pound to the creditors. The bank ought to have been resuscitated under a different management. They were possessed of the largest and best business in the district. Their deposit and running accounts at one period were large and numerous, reaching, it was said, into millions. When the doors were closed it was estimated that £400,000 were deposited with them in the Sunderland branch alone; they only wanted time and caution, and the man to pull them through. Application was made for assistance, but the authorities in Threadneedle Street refused, and the bank went into liquidation.*

On one occasion a shipbuilder—we will call him P.—had an offer for a vessel, which had been standing on the stocks for a little time, from a merchant called L., part cash and the remainder in bills. Mr. P. came down to the office of the timber merchant to consult and advise. P. told the merchant that he thought the offer was a very fair one, only he did not like the party making it; "Well," said the merchant, "if he pays part cash, stipulate that the balance shall be by good and approved bills." "Yes," said Mr. P., "I told him that, when he asked did I dispute his credit? I had better go to his bankers and ask them." "Well," said the merchant, "and have you been and asked the bankers?" he said "Yes." "And what did they say?" "They said as far as they knew I would be all right; that they would discount the bills for me." "Yes," said the merchant, "but discounting the bills for you is not paying

---

* On the 24th April, 1857, just seven months before R. J. Brown was declared bankrupt, the bank, through their public officer, tendered proof of debts to R. J. Brown's estate for £80,000 to £90,000 for the choice of assignees. The public officer to the bank, R. P. Philipson, had waited upon William Hay, who was a large creditor, to ask him to stand and act as assignee—this Mr. Hay refused to do unless the bank would associate with him, the writer; whereupon Mr. Philipson waited upon the writer, and after weighing matters (as he was also a large creditor), agreed to act with Mr. Hay as joint trade assignees (Mr. Baker being the official assignee) in winding-up R. J. Brown's estate. After the appointment of assignees, R. J. Brown thought them hard on him, and during an interview with them, the bankrupt said: "Well, I am down now, but in six months' time the District Bank will be in my position." And it came to pass.

In winding-up the bank, Coleman, one of the liquidators, wished the original proof of debts to stand for dividend, to which the assignees of Brown objected, telling the liquidator that he must give credit for all moneys that they had received from their securities, whether on bills or on realizing the assets held by them; the matter was brought before Mr. Ellison, the then judge in bankruptcy, and the decision of the assignees upheld, and thus the proof of the bank was reduced to about £73,000. So small an amount of collateral securities had been held by the bank against this large amount of accommodation bills discounted for Brown by the directorate.—*See R. J. Brown's bankruptcy.*

them when they become due; go back and ask them if they would discount the bills for you without recourse to you." Mr. P. went back to the bankers, who, he said, told him that to endorse the bills without recourse would make no difference to him; that they would discount the bills in the usual way, and that he was perfectly safe. With this assurance the ship was sold, the cash part paid, and the bills drawn and paid into the bank to the builder's credit.

Now, in order to raise the cash, the merchant had to overdraw his account at the bank, promising the bankers that he would deposit the builder's certificate as security, or otherwise, which was done, and the vessel was ultimately re-sold by the merchant, and the whole of the proceeds paid to his credit at the bank. The bank, on receiving the proceeds, closed the merchant's account, whereupon he failed, and became bankrupt. Mr. P., the shipbuilder, again betakes himself to the timber merchant on hearing the news of the failure of the purchaser of his ship, to know what he was to do; when the merchant asked him: "Are you afraid of your bankers?" "Me!" he said, "what have I to be afraid of? It was too bad for them to say what they did in order to get my ship to pay another man's debt." "Where are the bills?" asked the timber merchant. "In the bank," replied Mr. P., "they discounted the bills." "Yes," said the timber merchant, "and expect you to pay them." "Me pay them!" said Mr. P., "Yes, they discounted them for you, and they expect you to pay them." "When is the first bill due?" asked the timber merchant. So and so, said Mr. P., naming the date. "Then let it come back" said the timber merchant, "it will be time enough to pay it when you are made." The bill therefore came back into the hands of the bankers, who handed it over to their lawyers, and they commenced an action to recover the amount from Mr. P., the drawer of the bill. Meanwhile, Mr. P. had changed his banking account.

The action was tried in London. Mr. Manisty, afterwards Mr. Justice Manisty, was the counsel engaged by the bank solicitor, and, in opening, said he thought the case so plain that it ought never to have gone for trial. There was only one witness for the defence—the timber merchant, who explained the whole of the transaction to the judge and jury. Mr. Manisty, in cross examination of the witness, seemed to have lost his temper, and shewed his teeth when he found that no bullying of the witness would do; the facts were so plain that the ship would not have been sold had the bankers not said the bills were good, and discounted them. Through the character they had given to the buyer, both seller and buyer doing business at the same bank, they got possession of the builder's certificate, and afterwards the whole proceeds of the sale of the vessel, ultimately closing the buyer's account Verdict for the defendants with costs. In this case the bankers were not able to make the drawer of a bill pay the amount after the acceptor had failed.

APPENDIX.

BISHOPWEARMOUTH GREEN.
GRANT DE NOVO.

The following is the text of the conditional grant *de novo* (referred to on page 89) from Bishop Barrington, as Lord of the Manor of Houghton, to Mr. Nicholson, as extracted from the Rolls of the Halmote Court Office at Durham:

"October 9th, 1799, Grant *de novo* to Thomas Nicholson of Bishopwearmouth, in the County of Durham, Esq. Of all that part of the piece or parcel of ground lately the waste of the lord, in Bishopwearmouth aforesaid, called the Green, as is now enclosed or intended to be enclosed by a dwarf wall and iron rails thereon, and intended to be used and planted as a shrubbery or ornamental pleasure ground, with a gravel or other walks round the same; which said piece or parcel of ground is of an oval form or figure, excepting at or towards the south-eastern end thereof, where the same extends and is contiguous to, and immediately adjoins the house belonging to, and in the occupation of, the said Thomas Nicholson, and as the same part of the said parcel of ground is now enclosed. To have to the said Thomas Nicholson and his sequels in right, according to the customs of the court, rendering therefore by the year, to the Lord Bishop of Durham and his successors, Lords of the Manor of Houghton, the rent or sum of 5/-, at the feast of St. Martin the Bishop, in winter and pentecost, by even and equal portions; and doing to the lord and the neighbours the duties and services accustomed by pledges and so forth; and he gives to the lord, for a fine, 5/-, and thereupon he is thereof admitted tenant. Provided, nevertheless, and it is hereby agreed and declared that the said piece of waste ground hereby granted to the said Thomas Nicholson and his sequels in right, as aforesaid, was and is granted to him and them upon condition that he and they do, and shall from time to time, and at all times hereafter, at his and their expense, keep and preserve the same as a shrubbery or ornamental pleasure ground; and, also, that he and they shall not at any time or times hereafter, on any pretence or account whatsoever, make or erect thereon, or any part thereof, any houses, stables, or other erections or building whatsoever, or any wall round or surrounding the same, or any part thereof, excepting pillars of a greater height than 5 feet. And, also, upon condition that if the said Thomas Nicholson, or his sequels in right, shall at any court to be holden for the Manor of Houghton, whereof the said piece of ground is parcel, be duly found by the jury thereof to have used or converted the same to or for any other use or purpose than as above expressed, or to have made or continued any such erections or buildings thereon, or any part thereof as ought not to be made or erected thereon, according to the condition hereinbefore mentioned, then, and in either of the said cases, the grant hereby made shall cease and be no longer of any validity or effect, and the said piece of waste ground hereby granted shall thenceforth be again considered waste or common."

The enclosure and planting of the shrubbery were not completed until the year 1802; but the gates (the one on the north side still remains) were immediately put up and the gravel walk formed. Mr. Thomas Nicholson, during his life, and his family after him, doing to the lord and the neighbours the duties and services accustomed by pledges, and so forth.

They paid the lord his due in the nominal yearly rent levied by the grant, and the neighbours had free ingress and egress to the shrubbery, and promenaded its gravel walk and grass plot at pleasure, as was, and is now their due as a matter of right, without let or hinderance from the Nicholson family down to the year 1824, when they sold their possession to Robert Fenwick, Esq.

On the perambulation of the boundaries of the Burn Fields in the year 1824, by the inhabitants, headed, as in the olden times, by that ancient dignitary of the Mayor of Houghton—the Greeve of Wearmouth, then Mr. Andrew Sanders, who led the perambulators into the south gate, round the gravel walk, thence through the north gate of the shrubbery into the enclosure on its north side, made by Mr. Robert Fenwick in the year 1819, with the consent of a few of the neighbours on the Green, without any grant from the Lord of the Manor.

Thus the Greeve of Wearmouth and the inhabitants exercised a legal right upon this the almost only remaining part of the wastes within this greeveship which had belonged equally to the lord and the neighbours for nearly 180 years after the diversion and enclosure of the moors, commons and wastes in Bishopwearmouth during the commonwealth.